COCAINE AND HEROIN ABUSE RESEARCH

COCAINE AND HEROIN ABUSE RESEARCH

LIDIA A. PIZZOLI
EDITOR

Nova Science Publishers, Inc.
New York

For permission to use material from this book please contact us:
Telephone 631-231-7269; Fax 631-231-8175
Web Site: http://www.novapublishers.com

LIBRARY OF CONGRESS CATALOGING-IN-PUBLICATION DATA
Cocaine and heroin abuse research / Lidia A. Pizzoli (editor).
p. ; cm.
Includes bibliographical references and index.
ISBN 1-60021-076-7
1. Cocaine abuse. 2. Heroin abuse. 3. Cocaine abuse--Research. 4. Heroin abuse--Research. I. Pizzoli, Lidia A.
[DNLM: 1. Cocaine-Related Disorders. 2. Heroin Dependence. WM 280 C659335 2006]
RC568.C6C6273 2006
362.29'8--dc22 2006006504

Published by Nova Science Publishers, Inc. ✢New York

CONTENTS

Preface vii

Chapter 1 The Treatment of Cocaine Abuse: Problems and Perspectives 1
Antonio Preti

Chapter 2 The Sigma$_1$ (σ_1) Protein as a New Target for Anti-Cocaine Therapy 37
Pascal Romieu and Tangui Maurice

Chapter 3 Cardiovascular Complications Related to Acute and Chronic Cocaine Abuse: Necropsy Studies, Pathogenetic Mechanisms and Echocardiographic Findings 61
Gianluca Iacobellis

Chapter 4 Cognitive Dysfunction in Cocaine Abuse: Evidence for Impairments in Impulse Control and Decision-Making 81
Laurie M. Rilling and Bryon Adinoff

Chapter 5 Cocaine-Dependent Patients with Antisocial Personality Disorder 97
Nena Messina, David Farabee and Richard Rawson

Chapter 6 Current Controversies in the Assessment and Treatment of Heroin Addiction 121
Robert J. Craig

Chapter 7 Heroin Addiction in Pregnancy - Ongoing Demands and Actual Therapy Modalities 143
Maki Kashiwagi, Urs Zimmermann-Baer, Margaret Huesler and André Seidenberg

Index 173

PREFACE

Addiction does begin with drug abuse when an individual makes a conscious choice to use drugs, but addiction is not just "a lot of drug use." Recent scientific research provides overwhelming evidence that not only do drugs interfere with normal brain functioning creating powerful feelings of pleasure, but they also have long-term effects on brain metabolism and activity. At some point, changes occur in the brain that can turn drug abuse into addiction, a chronic, relapsing illness. Those addicted to drugs suffer from a compulsive drug craving and usage and cannot quit by themselves. Treatment is necessary to end this compulsive behavior. This book includes within its scope leading-edge research on cocaine and heroin abuse.

Despite huge advances in the neuroscience of substance abuse and dependence in the past twenty years, no approved pharmacological treatment exists for cocaine abuse. Chapter 1 discusses how targeting symptoms might improve treatment effectiveness.

Cocaine is a highly addictive substance that is abused worldwide. The main molecular targets of cocaine in the brain are the neuronal monoamine transporters, *i.e.*, the dopamine (DAT), serotonin (SERT) and norepinephrine (NET) transporters as reported in chapter 2. Moreover, most of the behavioral effects of the drug are mediated mainly through its ability to inhibit the DAT and/or the SERT, thus by its ability to act as an indirect dopamine or serotonin agonist. Many laboratories are currently exploring alternative targets with potential therapeutic efficacy against cocaine addiction. The observation that cocaine binds with a moderate affinity *in vitro* to the σ_1 site and the recent increase of interest for this target derives from such tendency. Indeed, cocaine presents a moderate affinity for the σ_1 receptor, in a concentration range achieved *in vivo*. Moreover, behavioral studies clearly demonstrated that the drug acts as a σ_1 protein agonist through either a direct or indirect interaction, since σ_1 receptor blocking strategies allowed to diminish or abolish cocaine behavioral effects in preclinical studies.

Chapter 3 reviews the necropsy findings and the latest information on the pathogenetic mechanisms and imaging diagnostic techniques of the cardiovascular abnormalities associated with an acute and chronic cocaine abuse. Unusual and rare echocardiographic findings and images from published and unpublished case reports are also described.

Cocaine is one of the most widely abused psychoactive substances in the United States, with an estimated 1.3 million Americans using the drug on a regular (at least monthly) basis. Even occasional cocaine use can result in serious medical complications, such as cardiac damage, vascular ischemia, respiratory failure, and persistent alterations in neural function. In chapter 4 the authors examine the most recent research on impulsivity and decision-making in cocaine use. First, they present a brief overview of the cognitive processes affected by cocaine use. Next, they review the relevant literature detailing the status of inhibitory control and decision-making in cocaine users, as well as their proposed neuroanatomical correlates. Finally, they attempt to integrate these findings with the current view of cocaine addiction and relapse, with an emphasis on the role of impulsivity and decision-making in continued cocaine use despite the elevated risk of negative consequences

Chapter 5 compares the efficacy of two commonly used treatment approaches (cognitive–behavioral treatment and contingency management) for the treatment of cocaine dependence among methadone-maintained patients with and without antisocial personality disorder (ASPD). This disorder is strongly associated with substance abuse and recent study findings provide a strong argument against the perception that substance abusers with ASPD are unresponsive to drug treatment.

Chapter 6 addresses controversial topics in the assessment and treatment of heroin addiction. Included in the discussion are issues of dose and outcome, difficulties with toxicology screens, the role of co-occurring Axis I and Axis II disorders, the introduction (and extinction) of newer medications to treat heroin dependence, difficulties of measuring treatment outcome, models of heroin dependence, the role of user personality, and the question of heroin maintenance treatment.

More than 35 years after its introduction into the therapy of pregnant heroin addicts methadone maintenance continues to be the standard therapy of opiate addiction in pregnancy. However, there is ongoing need for clinical research to further improve the management of craving during pregnancy as well as the prevention and therapy of neonatal abstinence syndrome. Chapter 7 reviews different approaches in improving these problems.

In: Cocaine and Heroin Abuse Research
Editor: Lidia A. Pizzoli, pp. 1-35 ISBN 1-60021-076-7

Chapter 1

THE TREATMENT OF COCAINE ABUSE: PROBLEMS AND PERSPECTIVES

Antonio Preti*
University of Cagliari, Italy

ABSTRACT

Despite huge advances in the neuroscience of substance abuse and dependence in the past twenty years, no approved pharmacological treatment exists for cocaine abuse.

The systematic reviews of treatments with available medications have found no evidence supporting the use of antidepressants, carbamazepine, or dopamine agonists in the pharmacotherapy of cocaine abuse. Dopamine receptor antagonists (neuroleptics) proved somehow effective in reducing cue-induced craving; however these medications are poorly tolerated, and record a significantly high dropout rate. Finally, high-dose methadone and buprenorphine were reported to promote cocaine abstinence in cocaine- and opioid-dependent patients, but their long-term effectiveness is still unknown.

Targeting symptoms might improve treatment effectiveness. Cocaine is thought to produce its addictive effect by four mechanisms basically: cocaine-induced euphoria; hedonic dysregulation; disruption of pre-frontal functioning; and cue-induced craving.

On the basis of the known neurochemistry of cocaine some target compounds have been studied, the most promising being BP897, a D3 partial agonist, and vanoxerine, a highly selective inhibitor of dopamine uptake. Results on humans, however, are pending. Recently modafinil, a glutamate-enhancing medication that inhibits GABA release too, proved effective in favouring cocaine abstinence in cocaine abusing people. Some open-label studies also reported the effectiveness of g-vinyl GABA, an irreversible inhibitor of GABA-transaminase, and of tiogabine, a GABA reuptake inhibitor, both compounds preventing relapse and thus increasing cocaine abstinence.

An alternative approach rests on the use of vaccines. Studies on rats showed that cocaine antibodies block cocaine from reaching the brain and prevent the reinstatement of cocaine

* Address for correspondence: Dr Antonio Preti: Centro Medico Genneruxi via Costantinopoli 42, I-09129 Cagliari – ITALY; e-mail: apreti@tin.it

self-administration. Ethical issues, however, are raised by the recourse to immunotherapy, particularly when proposed under legal coercion.
Psychosocial treatments are a useful companion in the pharmacotherapy of cocaine abuse, with group therapy and contingency management therapies capable to improve motivation and social functioning, particularly in patients abusing alcohol too.

Keywords: Cocaine, Treatment, Substance abuse, Investigational compound

INTRODUCTION

Cocaine abuse is a serious health problem; its impact on society entails a heightened burden of illness, crime, domestic violence, lower productivity, inability to work and death (Gawin & Kleber, 1986; Hanzlick & Gowitt, 1991; Marzuk, Tardiff, & Leon, 1992; Marzuk, Tardiff, Leon, et al, 1998; Stein, 1999). The costs deriving from this health-hazarding behaviour depend directly upon the strong reviving properties of cocaine, which can cause dependence in the abuser through its stimulating and rewarding effects.

In addition to personal consequences, which include a higher prevalence of cardiovascular accidents (stroke and myocardial infarction), pulmonary diseases, trauma and violent death (by both homicide and suicide), cocaine use affects the life of all the people exposed to the environments where it is abused through a wider spread of infectious diseases (HIV, hepatitis B and C, tuberculosis) and increased exposure to violence (Stein, 1999). On the whole the financial costs due to untreated substance abuse are estimated, in the USA only, at about $400 billion per year, with untreated cocaine abuse contributing to the burden substantially (Schneider Institute for Health Policy, 2001).

Because of these reasons cocaine abuse has become a focus of medical, social and political concerns worldwide, encouraging research on the mechanisms of cocaine action and on the development of effective pharmacotherapies for the treatment and the prevention of cocaine abuse (Carroll, Howell, & Kuhar, 1999; Kreek, 1997; Mello, & Negus, 1996).

PSYCHOPHARMACOLOGY OF COCAINE

Cocaine is a powerful stimulant of the nervous system that increases alertness, energy and motor activity, and induces feelings of well-being and euphoria, as well as enhancing personal sensations of competence and sexual ability. Activation of the sympathetic nervous system occurs concomitantly with the behavioural stimulatory effects of cocaine, with tachycardia, hypertension and an enhanced risk of myocardial infarct and cerebrovascular haemorrhages in case of cocaine overdosing. At higher doses, anxiety, paranoia and restlessness can result from the over-stimulation of monoaminergic receptors.

Cocaine, indeed, is thought to produce its effects by blocking the monoamine system of re-uptake, with equipollent affinities for dopamine, serotonin, and norepinephrine transporters (Ritz, Cone, & Kuhar, 1990). Because of antagonism at the re-uptake site, more monoaminergic neurotransmitters become available for both pre- and post-synaptic receptors. As subjective effects fade away dysphoria, tiredness, depression, and irritability replace the stimulating action of cocaine, prompting subsequent drug re-use to regain the previously experienced positive sensations.

There is considerable evidence that most of cocaine reinforcing effects are mediated by its blocking the dopamine reuptake at the presynaptic terminals (Kuhar, Ritz, & Boja, 1991; Ritz, Lamb, Goldberg, & Kuhar, 1987). The resulting increase in dopamine at its receptors is thought to produce most cocaine effects (Carboni, Imperato, Perezzani, & Di Chiara, 1989; Koob, Caine, Parsons, Markou, & Weiss, 1997; Pontieri, Tanda, & Di Chiara,1995; Roberts, Corcoran, & Fibiger, 1977; Wise & Bozarth, 1987). In fact dopamine uptake inhibitors and direct-acting dopamine agonists can maintain drug self-administration in laboratory animals; dopamine uptake inhibitors and, partially, direct-acting dopamine agonists also substitute for cocaine; conversely dopamine antagonists can attenuate specific behavioural effects of cocaine including its reinforcing, locomotor activity, and discriminative stimulus effects (Carroll, Howell, & Kuhar, 1999; Kuhar, Ritz, & Boja, 1991).

In humans, increases in brain dopamine and D2 receptor occupancy associate to the reinforcing effects of cocaine, as well as of other psychostimulants (Volkow, Wang, Fowler, et al., 1999). However the occupancy of both D1 and D2 receptors is thought to be implicated in the reinforcing properties of cocaine, and in animal studies D1 and D2-like receptor antagonists attenuated cocaine self-administration (Caine, & Kook, 1994) whereas D1 and D2-like receptor agonists maintain it (Platt, Rowlett, & Spealman, 2001).

To date the mechanisms through which cocaine induces all its effects and produces the brain adaptations leading to dependence are not well understood yet. The molecular carrier of dopamine that is responsible for dopamine up-take, and thus for the termination of dopamine effects at the synapse, was isolated and cloned (Giros, El-Mestikawy, Godinot, et al., 1992; Kilty, Lorang, & Amara, 1991; Shimada, Kitayama, Lin, et al., 1991), allowing a better determination of the binding properties and activities of many ligands that are thought to exert their effects by interacting with this transporter (Preti, 2000a).

However dopamine might not be the sole mediator of the reinforcing properties of cocaine, since dopamine transporter knock-out mice, lacking the gene expressing the dopamine re-uptake carrier, were found to keep self-administering cocaine (Rocha, et al., 1998).

Mechanisms of Tolerance, Withdrawal and Adaptation to Long-Term Use

Cocaine can be taken intranasally, it can be smoked or injected intravenously. This drug has a relatively short half-life and its symptoms and signs of intoxication, and the pleasurable effects as well, usually decrease within 60-120 minutes (Table 1). The short duration of its effects is likely to contribute to the addictive power of cocaine, together with its ability to induce a rapidly mounting sensation of euphoria. The rate at which cocaine enters the brain seems associated with the "high" sensations (Volkow, et al., 1999).

Little tolerance to the effects of cocaine was reported and, generally, cocaine withdrawal syndrome is not so severe as classical opioid withdrawal. However, tolerance to cocaine sexual stimulation develops rapidly, sometimes resulting in impotence or sexual frigidity (Gold, 1992).

Table 1: Pharmacokinetic of cocaine according to the route of administration

Route	Onset of action	Duration of the effects
Oral (by licking)	1 hour	Several hours
Intranasal	3-5 minutes	45-60 minutes
Intravenous	1-2 minutes	10-20 minutes
Inhalation (by smoking)	30 seconds	5-10 minutes

Withdrawal symptoms manifest themselves as the inverse of cocaine effects, and include decreased energy, limited ability to experience pleasure, and reduced interest in the environment (Gold, 1992). Cocaine abusers, and crack consumers particularly, feel anxious, depressed and sometimes paranoid as the "high" sensations subside. Such a rapid shift may trigger a sudden strong desire for reuse. These feelings, classified under the "craving" label, form a distinct part of the withdrawal syndrome in cocaine users.

Despite low levels of tolerance and the limited extent of the withdrawal syndrome, even "recreational" users (once or twice a week; weekend users) report severe problems stemming from their drug use. Most of those who developed long-term or heavy usage of the substance are unable to "say no" to cocaine when available. Clearly the addictive power of cocaine goes well beyond its tolerance and withdrawal effects. The route of administration influences the ability to quit use: cocaine smokers are less likely to complete a treatment program than intranasal users, and intravenous users are even less able to achieve abstinence. Also doses influence the ability to reach and maintain abstinence, with higher doses and/or higher purity of the substance increasing the chance of reuse.

Chronic use of cocaine also associates to observable and measurable neuropsychological adaptations. Cognitive deficits were reported in long-term users, which mainly concerned executive functions such as decision-making and judgement (Rogers & Robbins, 2001). These deficits could also interfere with rehabilitation programmes (Rogers & Robbins, 2001). Impaired performance in motor-system functioning tests and slower reaction times were also reported in chronic cocaine abusers.

Persistent neurological and psychiatric impairments seem a feature of long-term cocaine abuse. Neurological and psychiatric symptoms could be as well the result of pre-existing abnormalities, revealed by chronic usage, as are the result of neuronal degeneration stemming from multifocal cerebral ischaemia, cerebral haemorrhages and/or infarction, and cerebral atrophy following cocaine use and/or health complications of substance abuse. Cocaine is an epileptogenic agent, too: with repeated administration, the risk of clonic convulsion increases (Merriam, Medalia, & Levine, 1988).

Neurobiological adaptations to prolonged use are also accounted for in some psychiatric disorders occurring in chronic abusers. The "crash" syndrome reported by some consumers when the psychostimulant effects of the compound cease, an extreme exhaustion that follows a binge immediately, may exhibit major depressive-like features with an enhanced risk of suicide (Gawin & Kleber, 1986).

Following a prolonged binge, symptoms of sleeplessness, irritability, paranoia, and acute toxic psychosis may develop (Vereby & Gold, 1988). Chronic cocaine usage can also produce a depletion of dopamine supply; since dopamine inhibits the secretion of prolactin, hyperprolactinemia could result leading to sexual dysfunctions in both males and females.

Many neurobiological changes are described in animal studies as a consequence of acute and chronic cocaine use, principally in the dopaminergic circuits (Woolverton, & Johnson, 1992). Dopaminergic mechanisms are known to mediate the incentive motivational properties of perceptual stimuli, and to contribute to the attributional salience of incentive stimuli (Schultz, Dayan, & Montague, 1997). Sensitisation, i.e. the incremental augmentation of motor and behavioural effects with a repeated administration of the drug, is the main finding resulting from the enhanced dopamine release induced by cocaine blocking the dopamine re-uptake carrier (Panikkar, 1999; Robinson & Berridge, 1993). Among other consequences, sensitisation is thought to mediate the higher likelihood of relapse in people sensitised to the psychotic effects of the compound (Panikkar, 1999).

A major change following cocaine long-term use is the so-called hedonic dysregulation, which shows as apathy, irritability, depression and suicidality. Such negative mood states are likely to instate and reinforce cocaine craving, because they are alleviated by cocaine use (Dackis & O'Brien, 2002). Hedonic dysregulation results from a cycle of addiction alternating negative and positive reinforcements due to withdrawal and euphoria enhancement respectively, that are consequent to cocaine reuse (Kalivas & McFarland, 2003). Disruption of the integrity of the mesolimbic dopaminergic pathway is thought to contribute to hedonic dysregulation significantly (Dackis & O'Brien, 2002).

Another target of cocaine effects, the prefrontal cortex, seems to mediate many aspects of addiction (Goldstein & Volkow, 2002). In particular, an activator of G protein signalling (AGS3) is persistently up-regulated in the prefrontal cortex after cessation of chronic cocaine treatment (Bowers, McFarland, Lake, et al., 2004).

TREATMENT OF COCAINE ABUSE

Despite huge advances in the neuroscience of substance abuse and dependence in the past twenty years, no approved pharmacological treatment was found for cocaine abuse (Dackis, 2004; Shearer, & Gowing, 2004; Lima, Soares, Reisser, & Farrell, 2002).

On the basis of the known psychopharmacology of cocaine, some existing psychotropic compounds were tested for treatment effectiveness. Substitution therapy with dopamine agonists was experimented by analogy with methadone substitution therapy for heroin dependent patients. Antidepressants were used because of the high occurrence of symptoms of depression among chronic cocaine users. On the other hand the anti-epileptic drug carbamazepine, also effective as a mood stabilizer in a subgroup of patients with bipolar disorders, and neuroleptics, effective as antipsychotic agents, were tested for they ability to overcome mood swing (carbamazepine) or to antagonize dopamine stimulation (neuroleptics).

Several systematic reviews of the treatment with available medications found no evidence supporting the use of antidepressants, carbamazepine, or dopamine agonists in the pharmacotherapy of cocaine abuse (Table 2).

Antidepressants were tested on the assumption that, by increasing monoamine levels, they may alleviate cocaine abstinence symptomatology, and relieve dysphoria with associated craving by a general antidepressant action. Compared to other drugs, desipramine performed better in promoting abstinence (six trials), but it showed just a non-significant trend (Levin & Lehman, 1991; Lima, Reisser, Soares, & Farrell, 2003). One single trial saw imipramine performing better than placebo in terms of clinical response according to the patient's self-report. The results of some trials also suggest that patients on fluoxetine are less likely to dropout (Batki, Washburn, Deluchi, & Jones, 1996; Covi, Hess, Kreiter, & Haertzen, 1995). On the whole no evidence was found indicating the clinical efficacy of antidepressants compared to placebo in the treatment of cocaine abuse. Antidepressant medications, however, exert modest beneficial effects on patients with both depression and substance use disorders, though the rates of sustained abstinence are low in this population (Nunes, & Levin, 2004).

Table 2: Systematic reviews of known available pharmacological treatments of cocaine abuse

Author/year	Participants	Intervention	Outcome	Results
Lima, et al., 2003	18 studies, with 1177 people randomised	Antidepressants	Positive urine sample for cocaine metabolites	No evidence supporting the clinical effectiveness of antidepressants
Lima, et al., 2002	5 studies, with 455 people randomised	Carbamazepine	Positive urine sample for cocaine metabolites	No evidence supporting the clinical effectiveness of carbamazepine
Soares, et al., 2003	17 studies, with 1224 people randomised	Dopamine agonists	Positive urine sample for cocaine metabolites, retention in treatment	No evidence supporting the clinical effectiveness of dopamine agonists

The effectiveness of carbamazepine in the treatment of cocaine abuse was suggested by positive open label trials on 35 patients, such result being replicated in a cross-over randomized controlled study on 32 subjects (Halikas, Crosby, Pearson, & Graves, 1997). After pooling data from 5 randomized controlled trials, however, Lima and co-workers (2002) found no evidence of the efficacy of carbamazepine, with high dropout rates for both people taking the active compound (61%) and placebo (69%).

Among dopamine agonists, amantadine, bromocriptine, and pergolide were evaluated against positive urine sample for cocaine metabolites and retention in treatment. Again, no evidence was found on the clinical efficacy of these compounds, and a high rate of dropouts was observed in this population (Soares, Lima, Reisser, & Farrell., 2003). However the administration of methylphenidate to a small group of patients (12 individuals) with attention-deficit hyperactivity disorder led to a significant improvement in both primary psychopathology and cocaine use (Levin, Evans, & Kleber, 1998).

Dopamine receptor antagonists (neuroleptics) proved somehow effective in reducing cue-induced craving; however these medications are poorly tolerated, and record a significantly high dropout rate (Mello & Negus, 1996). Moreover neuroleptics are contraindicated because of acute reactions, since these compounds lower the seizure threshold. On the other hand, persistent symptoms of psychosis following cessation of cocaine use prompt a trial with antipsychotic medication. In these cases atypical anti-psychotics were marked as effective in reducing craving and relapse in patients dually diagnosed with schizophrenia and cocaine abuse (Smelson, Losonczy, Davis, et al., 2002). However the use of atypical neuroleptic drugs such as olanzapine in people lacking the relevant psychotic symptoms may be hazardous, since olanzapine may reduce treatment retention with no significant improvement in abstinence or craving (Kampman, K.M., Pettinati, H., Lynch, et al., 2003).

PERSPECTIVES ON TREATMENT OF COCAINE ABUSE

Treatment retention and compliance with prescriptions are two critical factors in the recovery from substance abuse (Meyer, 1992). Impulsivity was found to be a significant predictor of cocaine use and treatment retention, suggesting the need to target this personality dimension in cocaine pharmacotherapy (Moeller, Dougherty, Barratt, et al., 2001; Patkar, Murray, Mannelli, et al., 2004). Motivation for behaviour change is another key element in the treatment of people abusing psychoactive substances (Margolin, Avants, Rounsaville, et al., 1997). Testing a pharmacologic agent in a motivationally inappropriate sample might not provide a good estimate of the agent's effectiveness.

Clinical observations are an invaluable source of information on cocaine pharmacotherapy, also because the animal models that yielded valuable contributions to research sometimes offer a questionable utility on a clinical ground (Carter, & Tiffany, 1999; Modesto-Lowe, & Kranzler, 1999; Siegel, 1999). Indeed, trials based on preclinical findings often yielded poor results in patient samples (Mello & Negus, 1996). Moreover the paradigms that are effective in animals, which cannot refuse to take the drug administered by the experimenter, fail when tested in a clinical sample, composed of people with the power to refuse to follow the clinician's advice. Dopamine antagonists, for example, are expected to be effective in reducing the reinforcing effects of cocaine, and in fact chronic treatment with low doses of flupenthixol was reported to decrease both cocaine craving and cocaine use in cocaine smokers (Gawin, Allen, & Humblestone, 1989). However due to unacceptable adverse side effects, pure dopamine antagonists are unlikely to become the ideal treatment of cocaine abuse unless this co-exists with a psychotic disorder, and compliance to treatment with a dopamine antagonist is expected to be poor.

PATTERNS OF USE AND DUALLY DIAGNOSED POPULATION

Patterns of use influence sensitivity to treatment: a fraction of those abusing cocaine also abuse one or more other psychoactive substances (Table 3). Some abuse alcohol or sedatives to overcome the hyper-arousal induced by cocaine; others discover cocaine when they are already addicted to another psychotropic compound, opioids frequently (Leri, Bruneau, & Stewart, 2003). Another fraction of poly-drug abusing people suffers from a mental disorder, and cocaine is used together with legally prescribed drugs and other illegally available compounds to overcome some of the symptoms of the disorder or the unwanted side effects of medications (Khantzian, 1985).

Multiple substance use seems to be the predominant pattern of cocaine use. In a recent multi-centre cross-sectional study carried out in Europe, about 96% of all participants had used at least another substance in addition to cocaine in the previous 30 days (Prinzleve, Haasen, Zurhold, et al., 2004).

Cocaine abuse complicates the course of heroin dependence, leading to poorer response to methadone substitution therapy and lower treatment retention. Methadone doses were increased in some trials to improve both retention and efficacy, but other studies recorded negative results (Kreek, 1997; Margolin, Avants, Rounsaville, et al., 1997). However a recent meta-analysis, including 11 randomized controlled trials with 2279 randomised people and 10 controlled prospective studies with 3715 followed-up people, found a significantly higher chance of urine-based cocaine abstinence at higher doses of methadone (60 to 100 mg/die) in heroin dependent patients also abusing cocaine, with a Reduced Risk=1.81 (c.i. 1.15 – 2.85) (Faggiano, Vigna-Taglianti, Versino, & Lemma, 2004).

Table 3: Typologies of cocaine-abusing people

Type of use	- occasional - recurrent, on the basis of availability - week-end user - remitting-relapsing user - chronic user
Pattern of drug use	- cocaine only - cocaine and alcohol - cocaine, alcohol, and sedatives - heroin and cocaine - poly-drug user
Co-morbidity	- no co-morbidity - physical co-morbidity - psychiatric co-morbidity - physical and psychiatric co-morbidity
Dually diagnosed	- mental disorder preceding cocaine abuse - mental disorder co-occurring with cocaine abuse - mental disorder subsequent to cocaine abuse
Legal complications	- absent - present

Also buprenorphine proved an effective intervention in the maintenance treatment of heroin dependence, as effective as methadone at adequate dosages (Mattick, Kimber, Breen, & Davoli, 2003). Buprenorphine was reported to promote cocaine abstinence in cocaine- and opioid-dependent patients, but its long-term effectiveness is still unknown (Montoya, Gorelick, Preston, et al., 2004).

Alcohol and cocaine use was found to be highly correlated in a subpopulation of patients. Disulfiram, prescribed with active psychosocial therapy, was found to lead to higher retention rates and longer abstinence periods from both alcohol and cocaine (Carroll, Nich, Ball, et al., 1998; Carroll, Fenton, Ball, et al., 2004). However heroin-dependent patients also abusing cocaine and alcohol were less likely to obtain positive support from disulfiram (George, Chawarski, Pakes, et al., 2000; Patrakis, Carroll, Nich, et al., 2000).

Mixed results were found for naltrexone, another adjunctive therapeutic bullet in the treatment of alcohol abuse and dependence. Prescription of naltrexone (50 mg/die) together with active psychosocial therapy (relapse prevention or drug counselling) proved no more effective than placebo in reducing cocaine or alcohol use in cocaine-alcohol dependent patients (Schmitz, Stotts, Sayre, et al., 2004).

End Point and Outcome Measures

Establishing adequate and sensitive measures to ascertain the efficacy of a therapy in the treatment of cocaine abuse is mandatory because of the heterogeneity of samples and the high dropout rate in this population. Appropriate diagnostic criteria to standardise cocaine abuse in terms of type (single- or poly-drug abuse), severity and co-morbidity (co-occurring mental and/or personality disorders), together with a profile of the patient according to the five major axes in DSM-IV are a useful procedure to define samples. Gold standard studies are prospective, parallel-group, double-blind, randomised controlled clinical trials; however due to the high costs of cocaine abuse, investigational safety trials can also offer important elements for evaluation, despite small sample size and the frequent lack of an appropriate control group.

Effective treatments are thought to achieve one or more goals out of five major objectives:

1. reducing drug use or inducing abstinence;
2. relieving the symptoms of withdrawal;
3. preventing relapse and restoring functioning;
4. reducing high-risk behaviours;
5. reducing morbidity and mortality due to substance abuse.

On the basis of these end-point criteria, several outcome measures were established to evaluate the efficacy of currently available as well as of novel compounds in the treatment of cocaine abuse (Table 4).

Due to the high drop-out rates among people seeking treatment for cocaine abuse, treatment retention and acceptability are as relevant as any other outcome measure based on abstinence or reduction of use. Ideally the best treatment should be acceptable to the patients, retain them in treatment, engender measurable levels of cocaine abstinence and be adaptable to the different typologies of cocaine abuse.

It is unlikely that a single pharmaceutical compound may achieve all these effects, or even any intermediate stage towards their fulfilment without a concurrent appropriate integrative psychosocial programme (Bobes & McCann, 2000; Nathan, Bresnick, & Batki, 1998). The treatment of cocaine abuse requires the activation of a complex programme including detailed diagnostic assessment, evaluation of patients needs, and the settlement of active psychosocial interventions aimed at reinforcing treatment retention and therapy compliance. On the other hand, relying on psychosocial or behavioural procedures only is likewise unlikely to achieve full efficacy nor even any substantial result as far as complete cocaine abstinence is concerned, due to the high craving potential of the substance.

Table 4: Measures of outcome in the study of the efficacy of cocaine abuse treatment

Main outcome	Type of measure
Efficacy	- urine samples positive for metabolites - self-reported use - self-reported relapse - frequency of drug intake - changes in craving for the drug - severity of dependence (using scales such as the Addiction Severity Index, Symptoms Checklist 90)
Acceptability and retention	- total number of dropouts at the end of the trial - side effects - number of subjects who dropped out because of lack of efficacy
General outcomes	- death - medical problems - legal problems - social and family relations - employment and support

Table 5: Major pathways to addiction in cocaine abuse

Mechanism	Neurotransmitter(s)	Area or circuitry
Cocaine-induced euphoria	Dopamine Glutamate	Nucleus accumbens
Hedonic dysregulation	Dopamine Glutamate GABA [?]	Mesolimbic pathways Orbitofrontal cortex Ventral tegmental area
Disruption of pre-frontal functioning	Glutamate	Prefrontal cortex Anterior cingulated Orbitofrontal cortex
Cue-induced craving	Glutamate Dopamine Norepinephrine CRF	Anterior cingulated Nucleus accumbens Basolateral amygdala Orbitofrontal cortex Bed of the stria terminalis

Pharmacotherapy, therefore, preserves its primacy in the treatment of cocaine abuse, although currently available therapeutics have shown scanty effectiveness or are effective on limited groups of patients, such as methylphenidate for patients with attention-deficit hyperactivity disorder.

Targeting symptoms might improve treatment effectiveness. Cocaine is thought to produce its addictive effect by four mechanisms basically: cocaine-induced euphoria; hedonic dysregulation; disruption of pre-frontal functioning; and cue-induced craving.

These cocaine effects involve different neurochemical pathways and cerebral areas (Table 5). Neurotransmitters dopamine and glutamate are mainly involved in the addictive effects of cocaine, as they act on a wide and interconnected network of circuits including the nucleus accumbens, the ventral tegmental area, the mesolimbic pathways, the orbitofrontal cortex, the anterior cingulated, the basolateral amygdala, and the bed of the stria terminalis (a synthesis in Dackis, 2004).

Despite some shortcomings, pre-clinical models remain invaluable tools in the development of effective therapeutic compounds. Efficacy, indeed, should be firstly demonstrated by the models predicting a clinical outcome. Though no indisputable animal model exists for cocaine treatment efficacy, pre-clinical studies point to some requisites a desired medication should posses: high potency and selectivity to limit unwanted side effects, the main reason for discontinuation of treatment together with lack of efficacy; an active action when administered according the most appropriate route, with oral administration preferred to any other method. A long-lasting action, to allow for reasonable dosing schedule, and slow penetration in the brain to avoid any 'high' sensation, are the two major pharmacokinetic requirements (Carroll, Howell, & Kuhar, 1999).

Screening and Testing Novel Compounds in the Treatment of Cocaine Abuse

The scanty efficacy of currently available psychotropic drugs in the treatment of cocaine abuse urges novel compounds to be screened and tested for efficacy. Drug screening for novel compounds to be tested as putative anti-cocaine agents consists in a sequence including selection by neurochemical assays, to ascertain the pertinence of the compound to the neurobiological networks implied in cocaine actions; then exploration in behavioural models testing the influence of the novel substance on cocaine drug discrimination and self-administration (Table 6).

The dopamine hypothesis of cocaine abuse is generally at the basis of neurochemical and behavioural assays for the screening of new effective therapeutic compounds for cocaine treatment. This hypothesis holds that cocaine produces most of its effects by blocking dopamine reuptake at the presynaptic side of the inter-neuron synapse (Kuhar, Ritz, & Boja, 1991). Cocaine interaction with the dopamine transporter would block the inward carrying action on the neurotransmitter, thus causing more dopamine molecules to be available for the activation of postsynaptic receptors (Figure 1).

Dopamine, however, is not the whole story in cocaine abuse, and a wide range of neurotransmitters was proved to contribute to the development of cocaine addictive properties

(Carroll, Howell, & Kuhar, 1999; Dackis, 2004; Dackis, & O'Brien, 2003; Gorelick, Gardner, & Xi, 2004; Vetulani, 2001).

Table 6: Preclinical pharmacological models for drug screening and testing

Neurobiological assays	Behavioural assays
Receptor binding	Locomotor activity
Receptor autoradiography	Conditioned place preference
Immuno-cytochemistry	Drug discrimination
In situ hybridization	Drug self-administration
Microdialysis	Schedule-controlled responding
Voltametry	Intracranial self-stimulation
Gene cloning	
Antisense technology	
Knock-out procedures	

On the basis of the known neurochemistry of cocaine, the following target compounds have been studied: dopamine uptake inhibitors, dopamine receptor partial agonists, serotonergic drugs, glutamatergic agents, GABA receptor agonists, GABA-transaminase inhibitor, opioid sigma ligands, calcium channel blockers, CRF antagonist (Table 7).

DOPAMINERGIC AGENTS

The research following the dopamine paradigm of cocaine action focused on three major mechanisms: antagonism and extinction of cocaine-trained self-administration; prevention of drug-seeking reinstatement; reduction of cue-induced and stress-triggered craving (Carroll, Howell, & Kuhar, 1999; Platt, Rowlett, & Spealman, 2002).

Maintenance medications, able to replace the subjective effects engendered by cocaine, are thought to alleviate cocaine craving and to contribute to patient compliance and treatment retention. Dopamine uptake inhibitors and direct dopamine receptor agonists are being explored as candidate maintenance medications.

Both dopamine selective and non-selective uptake inhibitors were tested for their potential usefulness in the treatment of cocaine abuse. The phenyl-substitute piperazine derivative GBR12909, also known as vanoxerine, was studied most extensively for its promising properties (Preti, 2000a; Stafford, Rice, Lewis, & Glowa, 2000; Wong, Cantilena, Elkashef, et al., 1999). Vanoxerine binds with a high affinity at the dopamine transporter site, with affinity in the nanomolar range, and inhibits dopamine reuptake with high selectivity compared to the other monoamine uptake sites (Andersen, 1989). Vanoxerine was shown to decrease cocaine-maintained response without decreasing food-maintained responding in cocaine and food self-administration studies in rhesus monkeys (Glowa, Wojnicki, Matecka, et al., 1995a; 1995b). Vanoxerine, indeed, is able to occupy the dopamine transporter site persistently, to attenuate

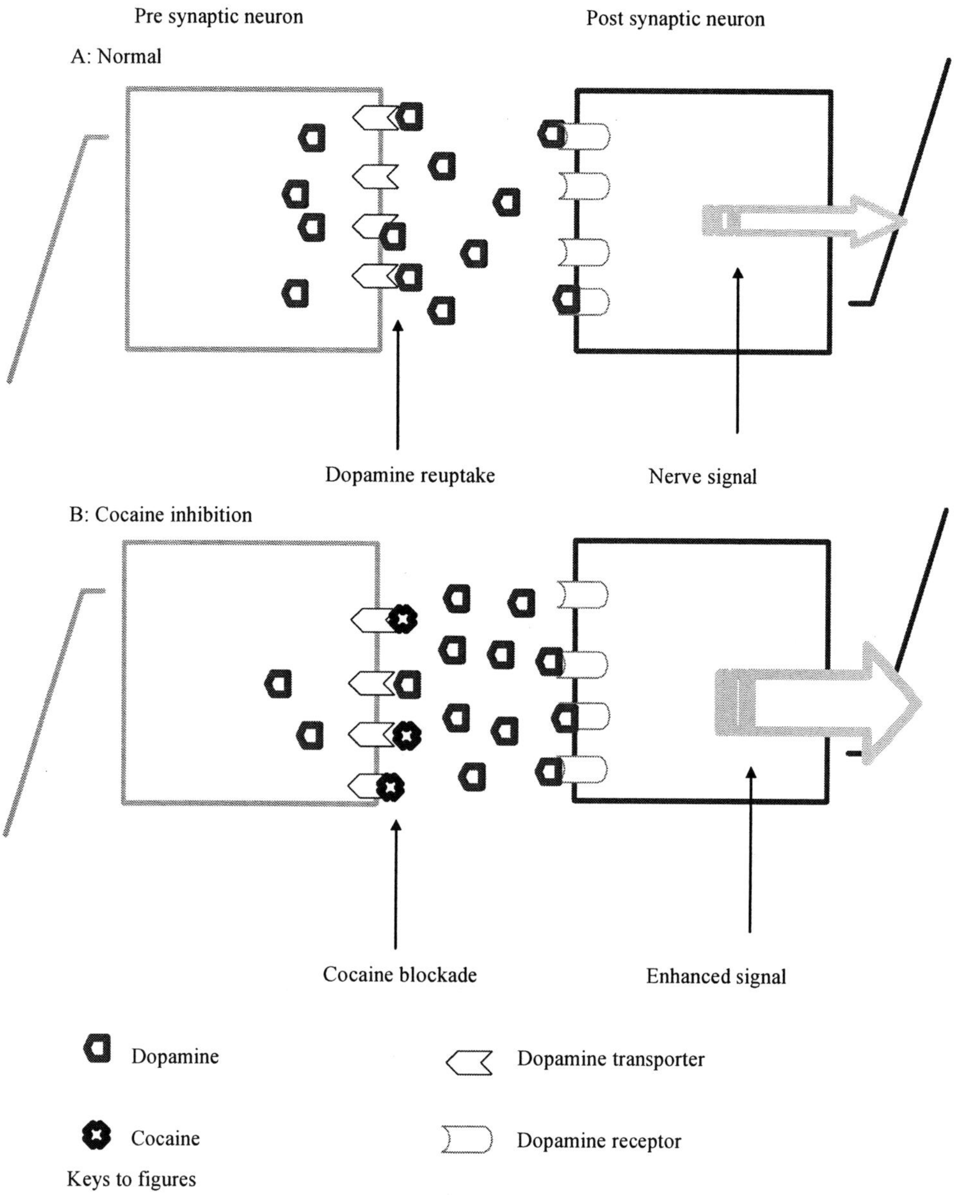

A): Stimulation of neuron releases dopamine from the presynaptic terminal into the synapse, where it binds to dopamine receptors and results in postsynaptic nerve signal; termination of dopamine action occurs by reuptake of dopamine by a specific transporter. B): Cocaine blocks the reuptake of dopamine by binding to the dopamine transporter, resulting in a dopamine excess at the synapse, thereby causing an enhanced postsynaptic nerve signal.

Figure 1: The dopamine hypothesis of cocaine abuse

cocaine-induced increases in extracellular dopamine, and to decrease cocaine self-administration without interfering with other goal-directed behaviours (Rothman, Mele, Reid, et al., 1991; Villemagne, Rothman, Yokoi, et al., 1999). Thanks to its slow onset, long-lasting action, lower in-vivo efficacy as a motor stimulant as compared to cocaine, and with a non-stimulant profile of action in normal human beings following oral administration, vanoxerine could be an ideal candidate for the treatment of cocaine abuse (Matecka, Rothman, Radesca, et al., 1996).

Table 7: Classes of compounds studied as potential medications of cocaine abuse

Target	Class of agent	Type of compound
Dopamine	Uptake inhibitors	Selective: Vanoxerine Non-selective: PTT, Mazindol Dopamine sparing: 4-Cl-BZT
	Dopamine agonists	D2-like agonists: Bromocriptine, Quinpirole D3-selective: 7-OH-DPAT D1-like agonists: Adrogolide
	Dopamine antagonists	Non-selective D2-like antagonists: Flupenthixol Selective D3 antagonists: Nafadotride D1-like antagonists: SCH39166
	Partial agonists	D2-like partial agonists: SDZ208-911 Selective D3 partial agonists: BP897 D1-like partial agonists: SKF38393, SKF83959
	Indirect agonists	Monoamine oxidase B inhibitor: Selegiline
Serotonin	Uptake inhibitors	Selective: Fluoxetine
	Serotonin agonists	Non selective (also 5-HT2 antagonist): Quipazine
	Serotonin antagonists	Selective 5-HT3 antagonists: Ondansentron
Glutamate	NMDA antagonists	Noncompetitive antagonists: MK801, Ibogaine
	Glutamaergics	Glutamate enhancing agents: Modafinil
GABA	Uptake inhibitors	Selective: Tiagabine
	Transaminase inhibitors	Irreversible: G-vinyl-GABA (Vigabatrin)
	Gabaergic	GABA enhancing agents: Gabapentin Mixed action: Topiramate
	GABA agonists	Selective GABA-B agonists: Baclofen
Calcium channel	Blockers	L-type calcium channel blockers: Nimodipine
Opioids	Antagonists	Non selective antagonists: Naltrexone Sigma antagonists: BMY14807, DuP734
CRF	Antagonists	Putatively selective CRF1 antagonists:

Vanoxerine could work by virtue of its cocaine-like effects, preventing craving for cocaine and attenuating cocaine withdrawal symptoms, on the one hand; exerting a "blocking" effect on superimposed cocaine by virtue of its high affinity and slow dissociating binding mixed with low intrinsic activity as a stimulant, on the other. Results in animals are promising, and phase I studies on healthy volunteers predict a good safety and tolerability profile for vanoxerine (Preti, 2000a). Definitive results, however, are pending. Moreover some unwanted effect of the compound was reported: vanoxerine was found to induce a reinstatement of extinguished cocaine-seeking behaviour in animal models of relapse (De Vries, Schoffelmeer, Binnekade, & Vanderschuren, 1999), and to enhance the behavioural stimulant and discriminative stimulus effects of cocaine (Holtzman, 2001). Such effects, however, are dose-mediated: low doses of vanoxerine seem unable to elicit drug-seeking behaviours (Schenk, 2002).

The substitution of direct dopamine agonists for cocaine-enhanced dopamine action produced less straightforward results, with D1-like dopamine agonists able to reduce both cocaine self-administration and cocaine and/or cue-induced reinstatement in animal models, but at the price of adverse side effects (Platt, Rowlett, & Spealman, 2002).

The enhancement of dopamine action through indirect agonists is another direction of research that attempts at normalizing cocaine-induced dysregulation of dopaminergic pathways rather than replacing the addictive substance. Long-term cocaine use, indeed, reduces extracellular dopamine levels in the nucleus accumbens, but acute cocaine administration is able to produce a markedly enhanced dopamine signal due to a sudden hyper-stimulation of post synaptic receptors under low baseline levels (Zhang, Schlussman, Ho, et al., 2003). Such effect is likely to participate to the sensitisation observed after chronic cocaine use, and might also contribute to cue-induced craving. The administration of selegiline (20 mg/day), which inhibits monoamine oxidase B - a dopamine metabolic enzyme - and results in heightened baseline dopamine levels, was found to substantially reduce the euphoric effects of intravenous cocaine in 12 chronic consumers (Houtsmuller, Notes, Newton, et al., 2004). A randomized, 16-week placebo controlled study found that amantidine, another dopamine enhancing agent, significantly favoured abstinence in cocaine abusers (100 mg twice a day; Shoptaw, Kintaudi, Charuvastra, et al, 2002). The success reported in some trials with disulfiram (250 mg/day) in patients abusing both cocaine and alcohol was also attributed to the dopamine enhancing properties of the compound, which can inhibit dopamine-beta hydroxylase, an enzyme involved in the catabolism of the neurotransmitter (Carroll, Fenton, Ball, et al., 2004). An agonist approach, however, is believed to be potentially problematic because of effects on cardiovascular functions and temperature regulation (Klein, 1998).

Antagonizing cocaine effects by blocking its action at the dopamine reuptake site, or suppressing its enhancement of dopaminergic neurotransmission, is another strategy in the screening of putatively therapeutic compounds. Some evidence suggests that the binding profile of dopamine does not overlap with the binding profile of cocaine fully: theoretically it could be possible to design a compound able to block cocaine binding without interfering with dopamine transport, the so-called dopamine-sparing cocaine antagonist (Uhl, Lin, Metzger, & Dar, 1998). Compounds with a "binding/inhibition" ratio greater than 1 would be suitable for specific cocaine antagonism. Some putatively dopamine-sparing cocaine antagonists were proposed, but none has undergone extensive testing (Platt, Rowlett, & Spealman, 2002).

The use of nonselective dopamine receptor antagonists has produced some positive results in a selected sample of cocaine-abusing patients (Gawin, Allen, & Humblestone, 1989). However undesirable side effects and the possibility that direct dopamine antagonism could be overcome by higher doses of cocaine make their large-scale use unlikely. Nevertheless some D1-like selective antagonists, such as SCH39166, proved able to reduce the euphoric and stimulant effects of i.v. administered cocaine significantly, although under chronic conditions SCH39166 was unable to decrease cocaine subjective effects (Nann-Vernotica, Donny, Bigelow, & Walsh, 2001). So far no putatively cocaine antagonist was found to posses an effect profile favourable enough to justify clinical trials in patients (Platt, Rowlett, & Spealman, 2002).

In between substitution therapy and cocaine antagonism there are some compounds provided with a partial dopamine agonist profile of action. A partial dopamine agonist is able to mimic some effects of cocaine without producing the relevant toxic effects, due to the full blockade of dopamine receptors: partial agonists could act as synaptic "buffers" by reducing the dopaminergic activity when this is excessive and by promoting it when it is too low. Therefore in the presence of cocaine, a partial dopamine agonist should function as a cocaine antagonist; in the absence of cocaine, the partial dopamine agonist should act as a weak agonist primarily.

In this class the most promising compound is BP897, a ligand selective at the D3 receptor (Pilla, Parachon, Sautel, et al., 1999; Preti, 2000b). In animal models BP897 was shown to inhibit the cocaine-seeking behaviour that depends on the presentation of drug-associated cues, without having any intrinsic reinforcing properties (Cervo, Carnovali, Stark, & Mennini, 2003; Pilla, Parachon, Sautel, et al., 1999). The potential usefulness of BP897 in the treatment of drug-seeking behaviour is further supported by its effects on drug conditioning models (Garcia-Ladona & Cox, 2003). The effects elicited by BP897 on cocaine-associated cues seem selective for the behaviour controlled by cocaine, since BP897 did not alter the behaviour maintained by other drugs such as heroin, or by non-drug reinforcers such as sucrose (Pilla, Hutcheson, Adib-Samil, et al., 2001). BP897 has entered phase II clinical studies recently. Detailed pharmacokinetic and toxicological data, however, have not been published yet.

Compounds Acting on Glutamate and GABA Circuits

Various types of NMDA receptor antagonists, competitive, noncompetitive, and glycine site antagonists, have the potential to counteract relapse and drug-seeking behaviour in drug-dependent animals (Popik & Skolnick, 1996; Vetulani, 2001). NMDA receptor antagonists also inhibit dopamine receptor sensitisation, a feature of cocaine addiction, mainly by preventing its development rather than its expression (Vetulani, 2001).

Memantine, a non-competitive NMDA antagonist approved for use in acute and chronic neurodegenerative diseases, inhibits cocaine self-administration and suppresses cocaine-conditioned motor response in a dose-dependent manner, though without blocking cocaine cue-induced craving (Bespalov, Dravolina, Zvartau, et al., 2000; Hyytia, Backstrom, & Liljequist, 1999). However in humans memantine enhances the subjective feeling of pleasure induced by cocaine (Collins, Ward, McDowell, et al., 1998).

Another substance acting on the glutamate NMDA receptor, ibogaine, was reported to abolish heroin and cocaine craving in addicted poly-users (Vetulani, 2001). The ibogaine compound, as commonly used by inhabitants in Gabon, is subject to abuse and it exerts some NMDA receptor antagonism, but it also enhances glutamate effects by inhibiting its uptake by glial cells and enhancing its release from cortical synaptsomes (Popik, Layer, & Skolnick, 1996). One might wonder whether it is safe to replace cocaine with a potentially addictive compound, which was also reported to induce neurotoxic effects (O'Hearn & Molliver, 1993), with the risk of treating a bad disorder with a remedy that is worse than the disease. At the beginning of his career, indeed, Sigmund Freud (1884; 1984) proposed cocaine as a remedy for morphine and alcohol dependency. The effects were so devastating, that these early pharmacological writings were excluded from the *Standard Edition* of his complete works.

Glutamate, nevertheless, is a most likely target in the treatment of cocaine abuse. The dopaminergic bundle arising from the ventral tegmental area creates glutamatergic synaptic contacts in the nucleus accumbens, a major site of cocaine action. Cocaine increases glutamate levels in the nucleus accumbens sharply (Dackis & O'Brien, 2002); conversely, mice lacking glutamatergic mGluR5 receptors are unable to self-administer cocaine (Chiamulera, Epping-Jordan, Zocchi, et al., 2001).

It is known that chronic cocaine exposure lowers glutamate levels in the nucleus accumbens, but it sensitises the release of glutamate after acute administration (Dackis, 2004). Such an enhanced glutamate release from low baseline levels could partially explain the stronger rewarding effects of acute cocaine administration after some time of cocaine abstinence, resulting in cocaine reinstatement (Kalivas, McFarland, Bowers, et al., 2003). It is the same mechanism thought to be involved in dopamine signal potentiation after chronic cocaine use, where a markedly enhanced dopamine signal occurs despite reduced extracellular dopamine levels in the nucleus accumbens, due to a sudden hyper-stimulation of post synaptic receptors under low baseline levels (Zhang, Schlussman, Ho, et al., 2003). Given this scenario, some authors proposed that normalizing baseline levels in the dopamine and/or glutamate circuitry could contribute to blunt cocaine euphoria (Dackis, 2004).

Recently some small sample trials found that modafinil, a glutamate enhancing agent approved for the treatment of narcolepsy, reduces the euphoric effect of intravenous cocaine (Dackis, Lynch, Yu, et al., 2003; Dackis, 2004). Modafinil was well tolerated, thus leading to valid treatment retention. The authors of these studies proposed that modafinil would promote cocaine abstinence by reversing cocaine-induced dopamine dysregulation through its ability to restore glutamate normal baseline levels in the nucleus accumbens (Dackis, 2004).

More recently a report on a double-blind, placebo-controlled trial of modafinil (400 mg, single dose in the morning) in 62 cocaine dependent patients free of significant medical and psychiatric conditions found significantly more negative urine samples over the 8-week trial when compared to placebo, and a higher chance of achieving prolonged cocaine abstinence in the sample, with no serious adverse events and a high retention rate (no dropout) (Dackis, Kampman, Lynch, et al., 2004).

Modafinil exerts its action by enhancing glutamate effects and by inhibiting GABA release too (Ferraro, Tanganelli, O'Connor, et al., 1996). Cocaine dependence alone can decrease GABA levels in humans (Ke, Streeter, Nassar, et al., 2004); conversely, GABAergic agents were proved able to modulate the neurochemical and behavioural effects of cocaine (Brebner, Childress, & Roberts, 2002; Cousins, Roberts, & de Wit, 2002). GABA-B are particularly effective in promoting abstinence and reducing the use of cocaine, as well as that of heroin, alcohol and nicotine (Brebner, Childress, & Roberts, 2002; Cousins, Roberts, & de Wit, 2002).

Baclofen, a selective GABA-B agonist licensed as an antispasmodic for patients with spinal cord injuries or multiple sclerosis, is the most promising compound of this class, and the unique available for experimentation in humans. Baclofen attenuates cocaine- and heroin-seeking behaviour in rodents (Di Ciano & Everitt, 2003). Baclofen also inhibits self-administration of cocaine in animals dose-dependently, at doses that do not influence responding for food (Brebner, Froestl, Andrews, et al., 1999; Roberts, Andrews, & Vickers 1996). The agents that selectively bind to the GABA-B receptors with antagonist properties attenuate baclofen effects on cocaine self-administration, further confirming the specificity of baclofen action on the GABA-B receptor (Brebner, Froestl, & Roberts, 2002).

Baclofen might act by modulating dopamine neurotransmission in the mesolimbic pathways: injecting baclofen in the ventral tegmental area, indeed, decreases extracellular dopamine in the nucleus accumbens and in the medial prefrontal cortex (Yoshida, Yokoo, Tanaka, et al., 1994). Anecdotic reports indicate that the main effect of baclofen is to deprive cocaine of its peculiar 'taste' (the 'high' sensation), and this effect was also reported in the case of nicotine smoking (reported in Brebner, Childress, & Roberts, 2002). Unlike the similar cocaine blunting produced by neuroleptic drugs, so far no progressive escalation in cocaine use was reported following baclofen administration in cocaine-dependent subjects.

Both open-label studies and controlled trials showed the effectiveness of baclofen (20 mg, three times a day) in reducing cocaine usage (Brebner, Childress, & Roberts, 2002). Higher dosage, in the range of 20 mg four times a day, seems able to blunt the reinforcing properties of cocaine. A randomized, double-blind, placebo-controlled trial in 70 cocaine-dependent patients (16 weeks, 20 mg baclofen, three times/day) showed statistically significant reductions in cocaine use among baclofen-assigned subjects over those receiving the placebo, as indicated by urine drug screening results (Shoptaw, Yang, Rotheram-Fuller, et al., 2003). No significant adverse effects were reported and in general baclofen seems to be well tolerated, despite its muscle relaxant and sedative properties.

It has been proposed that baclofen may help against cue-induced craving (Di Ciano & Everitt, 2003) preventing relapse into use after abstinence, but the placebo-controlled trial showed no statistically significant advantage in terms of cocaine craving for the active compound over the placebo (Shoptaw, Yang, Rotheram-Fuller, et al., 2003). The short-lived action of baclofen (3-4 hours) is the major limitation for its use in large scale samples, since the motivation to take the medication is likely to wax and wane in the course of the day, particularly for such an instable population as that of cocaine abusers. Slow release preparations, or depot combinations, are likely to circumvent this limitation. Moreover the sedative and muscle relaxant effects of baclofen could be enhanced by alcohol and/or commonly prescribed sedatives, frequently co-abused with cocaine by a fraction of abusers. Careful evaluation of the pattern of abuse could aid in avoiding unhelpful drug interactions.

Other GABA enhancing agents have been tested as putatively anti-cocaine agents, many having already been approved as anticonvulsant therapeutics. An 8-week, open-label trial of 1,200 mg/day of gabapentin, a GABA agonist, found it effective in decreasing cocaine use without significant side effects or adverse events (Myrick, Henderson, Brady, & Malcolm, 2001). However in a 48-day double-blind, crossover design study gabapentin (600 to 1200 mg/day) was found to decrease some subjective effects of cocaine, though without affecting cocaine self-administration significantly (Hart, Ward, Collins, et al., 2004).

Gamma-vinyl-GABA (vigabatrin), an irreversible inhibitor of GABA-transaminase, another approved antiepileptic drug, showed a favourable profile in preclinical studies, suppressing elevation of the nucleus accumbens extracellular dopamine levels induced by the administration of addictive substances (Brodie, Figueroa, E., & Dewey, 2003; Gerasimov, Ashby, Gardner, et al., 1999). An open-label study showed some improvement in cocaine abusers (Brodie, Figueroa, E., & Dewey, 2003), but gamma-vinyl-GABA bears a high risk of undesirable side effects (drop in visual acuity due to irreversible concentric visual field constriction; gingival overgrowth), limiting its use as an anti-addictive agent (Vetulani, 2001). In a recent 9-week open-label trial, however, gamma-vinyl-GABA did not produce significant alterations in visual acuity in 30 polydrug abusers, favouring cocaine abstinence in the subgroup (18/30) who completed the study (Brodie, Figueroa, Laska, & Dewey, 2005).

In a ten-week randomized, placebo-controlled study in 45 cocaine-dependent methadone-treated patients tiagabide, another approved anticonvulsant drug (12-24 mg/day), was found able to moderately decrease (around 30%) both self-reported and urine-measured cocaine use at the higher dose (24 mg), with very few adverse effects (Gonzalez, Sevarino, Sofuoglu, et al., 2003). Even higher doses (24 mg) of tiagabide, however, did not alter the acute effects of oral cocaine (150 mg) in individuals who were used to cocaine (Lile, Stoops, Glaser, et al., 2004).

Topiramate, another licensed antiepileptic drug, is a more complex compound among those acting on the GABA circuitry. Topiramate, indeed, is a GABA-promoting agent that antagonizes the AMPA receptors too, thus interfering with the glutamatergic system (Gryder & Rogawski, 2003). In a 13-week, double-blind, placebo-controlled pilot trial in 40 cocaine abusing subjects topiramate, gradually titrated up to a dose of 200 mg/day, favoured the achievement and maintenance of abstinence from cocaine over placebo (Kampman, Pettinati, Lynch, et al., 2004). Adverse effects to topiramate, however, were reported (Bootsma, Coolen, Aldenkamp, et al., 2004), and the efficacy of the compound in long-term use by cocaine-addicted subjects has still to be demonstrated.

Finally the antiepileptic drug valproate, approved for the treatment of migraine headaches, epilepsy and bipolar affective disorder, was tested for the treatment of substance abuse disorders in individuals with co-occurring bipolar disorder and yielded positive results (Myrick & Brady, 2003). Valproate, as other antiepileptic agents, proved useful in the treatment of affective and anxiety disorders (Davis, Ryan, Adinoff, & Petty, 2000), which often complicate the course of substance abuse, including cocaine abuse. Unlike other psychotropic therapeutics it is unlikely to develop an additive interaction with alcohol, often co-abused with cocaine, and is devoid of any abuse potential. It seems particularly promising in relapse prevention and in the treatment of impulsivity and irritability, two personality dimensions that increase the risk of cocaine abuse reinstatement (Moeller, Dougherty, Barratt, et al., 2001). An 8-week open-label trial of valproate in cocaine dependent patients found a substantial reduction in cocaine use, measured by urine drug screens (from 64% to 28% at week 8), with a good retention in treatment (Myrick, Henderson, Brady, & Measom, 2001). Another open-label trial in 55 cocaine abusing subjects found promising results for valproate serum levels higher than 50 mg/ml (Halikas, Center, Pearson, et al., 2001).

Valproate possesses a limited liability to cause a benign decrease in platelet count, thus requiring careful monitoring of platelet count in treated patients, and some cases of hepatotoxicity have been reported in children treated for seizure disorder. Adults, however, seem less subject to this adverse effect of the treatment and a study on comorbid bipolar disorder and alcoholism found valproate to be safe and well tolerated (Myrick & Brady, 2003).

Other Compounds Under Evaluation for the Treatment of Cocaine Abuse

On the whole, data from clinical studies seem to suggest that GABA-promoting agents might promote abstinence from cocaine by alleviating cue-induced craving associated to the hyper-activity of glutamatergic neurons in prefrontal regions, thus preventing relapse into use (Dackis, 2004). Activation of GABAergic systems in the prefrontal cortex, indeed, can decrease glutamatergic activity.

The role of drug-related cues in substance abuse is relevant to the development of dependence. Indeed, some researchers think that all addictive substances share the property of activating dopaminergic circuits in a specific limbic area involved in the storage of memory, and linked to cues possessing survival value (Di Chiara, 1999). By directly activating the dopaminergic circuits involved in associative learning, addictive drugs escape adaptive modulation of dopamine transmission, though inducing tolerance to their effects after long-term use (and sometimes also producing sensitisation). As a consequence, the stimuli paired to drug reward become able to control behaviour, eliciting desire for the drug (craving) and inducing relapse into use. A role for environmental and also for internal (psychological and physiological) cues in drug abuse has long been acknowledged in the history of the medicine of addiction (O'Brien, Childress, McLellan, & Ehrman, 1992; Siegel, 1999). This paradigm yielded valuable contributions to research (Carter, & Tiffany, 1999), but clinical utility was questioned and the consistency of results on cocaine dependence has been variable and inconstant (Modesto-Lowe, & Kranzler, 1999).

The brain circuits implicated in cue-induced craving overlap with those involved in stress-induced craving, stress being a powerful promoter of relapse into substance abuse. The hypothalamic-pituitary-adrenocortical (HPA) axis is the main system involved in stress response, via a corticotropin-releasing factor (CRF) regulatory mechanism (Stratakis, & Chrousos, 1995). A significant activation of the CRF-HPA axis and of the noradrenergic/sympatho-adreno-medullary (SAM) system response occurs during stress-induced and drug cue-induced cocaine craving states in cocaine dependent individuals (Sinha, Talih, Malison, et al., 2003).

Considerable evidence supports the notion that the CRF brain systems are critically involved in behavioural and physiological manifestations of drug withdrawal and in relapse into drug-taking behaviour induced by environmental stressors (Sarnyai, 1998; Sarnyai, Shaham, & Heinrichs, 2001). Preclinical data provide a rationale for the development of CRF-based pharmacotherapy for the treatment of substance abuse in humans. It is likely, indeed, that CRF antagonists may produce significant therapeutic effects in those disorders where the CRF contributes to the onset or to the maintaining of symptoms. At present some types of non-peptidergic CRF antagonists, able to cross the blood-brain barrier, are being developed for the treatment of mental disorders characterized by a CRF-HPA axis dysregulation (Kehne, & De Lombaert, 2002; Preti, 2001). A water-soluble pyrrolopyrimidine CRF antagonist, R121919, that binds to human CRH(1) receptors with high affinity and is well absorbed in humans, was found - in 24 patients with a major depressive episode - to significantly reduce depression and anxiety scores in both patient and clinician ratings at oral doses between 5-40 and 40-80 mg/die (Zobel, Nickel, Kunzel, et al., 2000).

But preliminary investigations on CRF antagonists in animal models of cocaine seeking-behaviour were disappointing (Lee, Tiefenbacher, Platt, & Spealman, 2003).

The calcium ion plays a crucial role in neuron discharge. Calcium crosses the neuronal membrane via two types of membrane channel: Voltage-dependent channels and Ligand-dependent ones. Among voltage-sensitive channels, L-type calcium channels play a relevant role in regulating adaptive changes in the central nervous system. In animals, infusion with ionophores – that facilitate calcium entry into neuronal cells – enhances the rewarding properties of morphine (Kuzmin, Patkina, & Zvartau, 1994).

Conversely the blockade of L-type calcium channels results in the blunting of the rewarding properties of morphine, cocaine, and amphetamine (Biala & Langwinski, 1996; Kuzmin, Zvartau, Gessa, et al. 1992). The combination of isradipine, an L-type calcium channel blocker, and naltrexone, an opiate receptor blocker, sensibly reduced the rewarding effects of the joint administration of cocaine and alcohol, a 'cocktail' frequently occurring in a subclass of cocaine abusers (Cramer, Gardell, Boedeker, et al., 1998).

Nifedipine, another calcium channel blocker, was reported to decrease subjective cocaine-induced effects in humans (Muntaner, Kumor, Nagoshi, & Jaffe, 1991). However when administered to 2 opiate dependent patients to treat opiate withdrawal precipitated by naltrexone, calcium channel antagonist nifedipine was found to cause confusion, casting some doubts on its use in substance abuse treatment (Silverstone, Attenburrow, & Robson, 1992). On the other hand opposite evidence suggests that nifedipine could alleviate cognitive disturbance in heroin, cocaine, alcohol and marihuana poly-users (Herning, Guo, & Lange, 1995). The verdict on calcium channel blockers, therefore, remains open to further reconsiderations.

Also the verdict on the use of naltrexone in cocaine abusers is still open. Acutely, naltrexone did not antagonize cocaine euphoria in humans, nor did maintenance therapy at full doses (200 mg/day) produce measurable effects on cocaine use (Sufuoglu, Singha, Kosten, et al., 2003; Walsh, Sullivan, Preston, et al., 1996). Despite negative results, some studies reported that abstinent cocaine-dependent patients showed less relapse into cocaine use over time when receiving naltrexone in combination with relapse-prevention therapy, a finding that underpins the need for the combination of pharmacotherapy with appropriate psychosocial intervention (Schmitz, Stotts, Rhoades, & Grabowski, 2001).

Work is in progress also in the field of serotonin-selective reuptake inhibitors (SSRIs) since these are, among antidepressants, the best tolerated and accepted by patients, and trials with fluoxetine showed that patients on this medication are less likely to dropout from treatment (Lima, Soares, Reisser, & Farrell, 2002). The class of SSRIs keeps growing with new compounds, the latter being likely to find their way in trials concerning patients with co-occurring major depression, or who abuse alcohol too, or as a potential treatment of impulsivity. Positive results were reported also for venlafaxine, a mixed norepinephrine and serotonin inhibitor, which produced a small but consistent reduction in cocaine euphoria (225 mg/day; Foltin, Ward, Collins, et al., 2003).

TREATMENT ALTERING THE PHARMACOKINETIC OF COCAINE

Altering the pharmacokinetic of cocaine is another strategy pursued in the search for a treatment able to antagonize cocaine abuse. Both the promotion of cocaine catabolism, by enhancing the activity of the enzymes that can metabolise the compound, and the prevention of its entry in the central nervous system, by blocking its crossing the blood-brain barrier by means of anti-cocaine antibodies, were attempted with variable results (Vetulani, 2001).

Patients with low blood levels of butyrylcholinesterase (BchE) bear an enhanced risk of acute cocaine poisoning, and the natural variability of BchE activity is likely to contribute to the diversified sensitivity to cocaine (Mattes, Belendiuk, Lynch, et al., 1998). The artificial increase of BchE levels in animals was found to decrease the psychostimulatory action of cocaine, concurrently to a change in cocaine metabolism (Carmona, Schindler, Shoaib, et al., 1998). A higher-functioning mutant of human BchE was achieved by genetic engineering, but results are pending (Vetulani, 2001; Xie, Altimirano, Bartels, et al., 1999).

The use of cocaine-selective antibodies was attempted in order to block the compound peripherally and to prevent its crossing of the blood-brain barrier. Immunotherapy, with antibodies used to neutralize the drug, was developed for phencyclidine, nicotine and, precisely, cocaine. Anti-cocaine antibodies are expected to form heavy complexes with the substance unable to cross the blood-brain barrier, thus keeping it in the periphery where it is metabolised and excreted. Immunotherapy is thought to serve as a supplement to the programs aimed at preventing relapse and acute intoxication (Vetulani, 2001).

The production of selective antibodies against cocaine, however, is not an easy task: small molecules, like the ones of cocaine, generally do not alarm the immune system. However coupling cocaine to a protein carrier resulted in strong stimulation of the immune system in the animal. Such a mechanism, for analogy with common vaccination, is promoted as a 'vaccine'. Initial experiments in mice showed that such a 'vaccine' for cocaine prevented the entry of the substance in the central nervous system effectively, with long-lasting effects and a significant reduction in animals' cocaine self-administration (Fox, 1997; Fox, Kantak, Edwards, et al., 1996). The initial success prompted the development of more selective vaccines (Carrera, Ashley, Wirsching, et al., 2001), leading to a specific programme of experimentation in humans (Kosten, Rosen, Bond, et al., 2002).

The perspective of inducing immunization against cocaine use, also without the consent of the subject (compulsory treatment following a court judgement), has raised an intense and still alive debate on the ethical implications of immunotherapy for substance abuse (Cohen, 1997; World Health Organization, 2004). The currently shared vision is that, if the trials prove the safety and tolerability of anti-cocaine vaccines in humans, immunotherapy could be used in adults who voluntarily decide to commit themselves to such a programme after being carefully informed of any risk (World Health Organization, 2004). However, the possibility that long-lasting antibodies against cocaine are detected in the blood of treated patients even after many years raises the issue of the risk of violating privacy and discrimination laws. Preserving privacy and confidentiality should, therefore, become mandatory for any program based on vaccination and/or immunotherapy.

The Need For An All-Embracing Approach

The most effective drug cannot be fully effective without the patient's following prescriptions: compliance with therapy and treatment retention are two major supports to treatment effectiveness. The need for long-term treatment should also be adequately addressed in the case of patients suffering from a chronic, remitting-relapsing disorder such as cocaine abuse and dependence.

An accurate diagnosis and ascertainment of disorder severity is a pre-requisite to define adequate treatments: not all cocaine abusing patients are identical. Cocaine dependence severity, for example, was found to predict the outcome in patients with both cocaine and alcohol dependence (Kampman, Pettinati, Volpicelli, et al., 2004).

Multiple morbidities, including social instability, co-occurring psychiatric illness, infectious diseases and other organic complications of addiction require proper care and interventions. For dually diagnosed patients aggressive treatment of the co-occurring mental disorder is mandatory, even though its effectiveness is unlikely to produce cocaine abstinence per se. Similarly, the use of substitution therapy with methadone is appropriate in patients abusing both opioids and cocaine to the aim of improving compliance and retention, two major and often unachieved goals in the pharmacotherapy of cocaine abuse.

Psychosocial treatments are a useful companion in the pharmacotherapy of cocaine abuse, with group therapy and contingency management therapies being able to improve motivation and social functioning, particularly in patients abusing alcohol as well (Bobes & McCann, 2000). Programs aimed at improving retention in treatment, increasing compliance, providing services that address the patient's comorbid psychosocial problems, and encouraging involvement in self-help groups have been found to correlate with a higher chance of a positive outcome (Carroll, 2000; Crits-Christoph, Siqueland, Blaine, et al., 1999; Weiss, Griffin, Gallop, et al., 2000). Also the community reinforcement approach with abstinence-contingent incentives was found effective at achieving cocaine abstinence (Roozen, Boulogne, van Tulder, et al., 2004).

Other approaches including cognitive-behavioural therapy, 12 Steps, and 28 day Minnesota Model have been suggested to improve the outcome of cocaine treatment (Carroll, Rounsaville, & Gawin, 1991; Marlatt, & Gordon, 1985; Wells, Peterson, Gainey, et al., 1994), but there is lack of a systematic overview of psychosocial and rehabilitation treatments. A large meta-analysis is under way at the Cochrane inter-collaborative *Drugs and Alcohol Group* (Soares, Lima, & Farrell, 2004), and results are awaited to improve knowledge on the psychosocial treatment of cocaine abuse and dependence.

Conclusion

The rapidly increasing knowledge of the mechanisms underlying cocaine abuse, as well as the foreseeable tremendous advances in the understanding of the neurobiology of substance abuse and its related disorders to come in the following years thanks to the continuing improvement in neuroscience-related technology, will have a likely positive impact on the settlement of evidence-based treatments. The deeper our knowledge of the neurochemistry of cocaine effects, the higher our chance to screen potentially therapeutic compounds.

Improving the clinical description of patients' characteristics will further enhance clinicians' ability to select sub-samples that are likely to respond to specific medications or treatment protocols. A more precise definition of sensitive outcome measures will favour the individuation of critical passages in the therapeutic process: side effects and adverse events influence compliance with therapy and treatment retention, as well as the pharmacological effectiveness of the compound under investigation.

Open-label trials and small-sample safety studies may contribute to research into effective treatments: supporting and financing the systematic review of small-scale investigations (meta-analysis) will allow saving on funds for larger randomized, placebo-controlled trials, which are generally more expensive and time-consuming.

Substance abuse and dependence impose high direct and indirect costs on society: the spreading of cocaine abuse in wealthy Western countries is expected to increase in the next years. Investments are therefore required and appropriate on the part of both public health authorities and private companies involved in drug development and research.

ACKNOWLEDGEMENT

The Author wishes to thank Miss Vittoria Rubino for her help in the revision of the English translation.

REFERENCES

Andersen, P.H. (1989). The dopamine uptake inhibitor GBR 12909: selectivity and molecular mechanism of action. *European Journal of Pharmacology*, 166, 493-504

Batki, S.L., Washburn, A.M., Deluchi, K., & Jones, R.T. (1996). A controlled trial of fluoxetine in crack cocaine dependence. *Drug & Alcohol Dependence*, 41, 137-142

Bespalov, A.Y., Dravolina, O.A., Zvartau, E.E., Beardsley, P.M., & Balster, R.L. (2000). Effects of NMDA receptor antagonists on cocaine-conditioned motor activity in rats. *European Journal of Pharmacology*, 390, 303-311

Biala, G., & Langwinski, R. (1996). Effects of calcium channel antagonists on the reinforcing properties of morphine, ethanol and cocaine as measured by place conditioning. *Journal of Physiology & Pharmacology*, 47, 497-502

Bobes, J., & McCann, U.D. (2000). Developments in the treatment of drug dependence. *Current Opinion in Psychiatry*, 13, 333-338

Bootsma, H.P., Coolen, F., Aldenkamp, A.P., Arends, J., Diepman, L., Hulsman, J., Lambrechts, D., Leenen, L., Majoie, M., Schellekens, A., & de Krom, M. (2004). Topiramate in clinical practice: long-term experience in patients with refractory epilepsy referred to a tertiary epilepsy center. *Epilepsy & Behavior*, 5, 380-387

Bowers, M.S., McFarland, K., Lake, R.W., Peterson, Y.K., Lapish, C.C., Gregory, M.L., Lanier, S.M., & Kalivas, P.W. (2004). Activator of G protein signalling 3: a gatekeeper of cocaine sensitization and drug seeking. *Neuron*, 42, 269-281

Brebner, K., Childress, A.R., & Roberts, D.C. (2002). A potential role for GABA(B) agonists in the treatment of psychostimulant addiction. *Alcohol & Alcoholism*, 37, 478-484

Brebner, K., Froestl, W., Andrews, M., Phelan, R., & Roberts, D.C.S. (1999). The GABA(B) agonist CGP44532 decreases cocaine self-administration in rats: demonstration using a progressive ratio and a discrete trials procedure. *Neuropharmacology*, 38, 1797-1804

Brebner, K., Froestl, W., & Roberts, D.C.S. (2002). The GABAB antagonist CGP56433A attenuates the effect of baclofen on cocaine but not heroin self-administration in the rat. *Psychopharmacology*, 160, 49-55

Brodie, J.D., Figueroa, E., & Dewey, S.L. (2003). Treating cocaine addiction: from preclinical to clinical trial experience with gamma-vinyl GABA. *Synapse*, 50, 261-265

Brodie, J.D., Figueroa, E., Laska, E.M., & Dewey, S.L. (2005). Safety and efficacy of gamma-vinyl GABA (GVG) for the treatment of methamphetamine and/or cocaine addiction. *Synapse*, 55, 122-125

Caine, S.B., & Koob, G.F. (1994). Effects of dopamine D-1 and D-2 antagonists on cocaine self-administration under different schedules of reinforcement in the rat. *Journal of Pharmacology & Experimental Therapeutics*, 270, 209-218

Carboni, E., Imperato, A., Perezzani, L., & Di Chiara, G. (1989). Amphetamine, cocaine, phencyclidine, and nomifensine increase extracellular dopamine concentrations preferentially in the nucleus accumbens of freely moving rats. *Neuroscience*, 28, 653-661

Carmona, G.N., Schindler, C.W., Shoaib, M., Jufer, R., Cone, E.J., Goldberg, S.R., Greig, N.H., Yu, Q.S., & Gorelick, D.A. (1998). Attenuation of cocaine-induced locomotr activity by butyrylcholisterinase. *Experimental & Clinical Psychopharmacology*, 6, 274-279

Carrera, M.R.A., Ashley, J.A., Wirsching, P., Koob, G.F., & Janda, K.D. (2001). A second-generation vaccine protects against the psychoactive effects of cocaine. *Proc. Natl. Acad. Sci. USA*, 98, 1988-1992

Carroll, K.M. (2000). Implications of recent research for program quality in cocaine dependence treatment. *Substance Use & Misuse*, 35, 2011-2030

Carroll, K.M., Fenton, L.R., Ball, S.A., Nich, C., Frankforter, T.L., Shi, J., & Rounsaville, B.J. (2004). Efficacy of disulfiram and cognitive behavior therapy in cocaine-dependent outpatients: a randomized placebo-controlled trial. *Archives of General Psychiatry*, 61, 264-272

Carroll, F.I., Howell, L.L., & Kuhar, M.J. (1999). Pharmacotherapies for treatment of cocaine abuse: preclinical aspects. *Journal of Medicinal Chemistry*, 42, 2721-2736

Carroll, K.M., Nich, C., Ball, S.A., McCance, E., & Rounsaville, B.J. (1998). Treatment of cocaine and alcohol dependence with psychotherapy and disulfiram. *Addiction*, 93, 713-728

Carroll, K.M., Rounsaville, B.J., & Gawin, F.H. (1991). A comparative trial of psychotherapies for ambulatory cocaine abusers: relapse prevention and interpersonal psychotherapy. *American Journal of Drug & Alcohol Abuse*, 17, 229-47

Carter, B.L., & Tiffany, S.T. (1999). Meta-analysis of cue-reactivity in addiction research. *Addiction*, 94, 327-340

Cervo, L., Carnovali, F., Stark, J.A., & Mennini, T. (2003). Cocaine-seeking behavior in response to drug-associated stimuli in rats: involvement of D3 and D2 dopamine receptors. *Neuropsychopharmacology*, 28, 1150-1159

Chiamulera, C., Epping-Jordan, M.P., Zocchi, A., Marcon, C., Cottiny, C., Tacconi, S., Corsi, M., Orzi, F., & Conquet, F. (2001). Reinforcing and locomotor stimulant effects of cocaine are absent in mGluR5 null mutant mice. *Nature Neuroscience*, 4, 873-874

Chuhma, N., Zhang, H., Masson, J., Zhuang, X., Sulzer, D., Hen, R., & Rayport, S. (2004). Dopamine neurons mediate a fast excitatory signal via their glutamatergic synapses. *Journal of Neuroscience*, 24, 972-981

Cohen, P.J. (1997). Immunization for prevention and treatment of cocaine abuse: legal and ethical implications. *Drug & Alcohol Dependence*, 48, 167-174

Collins, E.D., Ward, A.S., McDowell, D.M., Foltin, R.W., & Fischman, M.W. (1998). The effects of memantine on the subjective, reinforcing and cardiovascular effects of cocaine in humans. *Behavioural Pharmacology*, 9, 587-598

Cousins MS, Roberts DC, & de Wit H. (2002). GABA(B) receptor agonists for the treatment of drug addiction: a review of recent findings. *Drug & Alcohol Dependence*, 65, 209-220

Covi, L., Hess, J.M., Kreiter, N.A., & Haertzen, C.A. (1995). Effects of combined fluoxetine and counselling in the outpatient treatment of cocaine abusers. *American Journal of Drug & Alcohol Abuse*, 21, 327-344

Cramer, C.M., Gardell, L.R., Boedeker, K.L., Harris, J.R., Hubbell, C.L., & Reid, L.D. (1998). Isradipine combined with naltrexone persistently reduces the reward-relevant effects of cocaine and alcohol. *Pharmacology, Biochemistry & Behavior*, 60, 345-356

Crits-Christoph, P., Siqueland, L., Blaine, J., Frank, A., Luborsky, L., Onken, L.S., Muenz, L.R., Thase, M.E., Weiss, R.D., Gastfriend, D.R., Woody, G.E., Barber, J.P., Butler, S.F., Daley, D., Salloum, I., Bishop, S., Najavits, L.M., Lis, J., Mercer, D., Griffin, M.L., Moras, K., & Beck, A.T. (1999). Psychosocial treatments for cocaine dependence: National Institute on Drug Abuse Collaborative Cocaine Treatment Study. *Archives of General Psychiatry*, 56, 493-502

Dackis, C.A. (2004). Recent advances in the pharmacotherapy of cocaine dependence. *Current Psychiatry Reports*, 6, 232-331

Dackis, C.A., & O'Brien, C.P. (2002). Cocaine dependence: the challenge for pharmacotherapy. *Current Opinion in Psychiatry*, 15, 261-268

Dackis, C.A., & O'Brien, C.P. (2003). Glutamatergic agents for cocaine dependence.. *Annals of the New York Academy of Sciences*, 1003, 328-345

Dackis, C.A., Kampman, K.M., Lynch, K.G., Pettinati, H.M., & O'Brien, C.P. (2004). A Double-Blind, Placebo-Controlled Trial of Modafinil for Cocaine Dependence. *Neuropsychopharmacology*, Epub ahead of print, doi:10.1038/sj.npp.1300600

Dackis, C.A., Lynch, K.G., Yu, E., Samaha, F.F., Kampman, K.M., Cornish, J.W., Rowan, A., Poole, S., White, L., & O'Brien, C.P. (2003). Modafinil and cocaine: a double-blind, placebo-controlled drug interaction study. *Drug & Alcohol Dependence*, 70, 29-37

Davis, L.L., Ryan, W., Adinoff, B., & Petty, F. (2000). Comprehensive review of psychiatric use of valproate. *Journal of Clinical Psychopharmacology*, 20 (Suppl. 1), 1S-17S

De Vries, T.J., Schoffelmeer, A.N., Binnekade, R., & Vanderschuren, L.J. (1999). Dopaminergic mechanisms mediating the incentive to seek cocaine and heroin following long-term withdrawal of IV drug self-administration. *Psychopharmacology*, 143, 254-260

Di Chiara, G. (1999). Drug addiction as dopamine-dependent associative learning disorder. *European Journal of Pharmacology*, 375, 13-30

Di Ciano, P., & Everitt, B.J. (2003). The GABA(B) receptor agonist baclofen attenuates cocaine- and heroin-seeking behavior by rats. *Neuropsychopharmacology*, 28, 510-518

Faggiano, F., Vigna-Taglianti, F., Versino, E., & Lemma, P. (2004). Methadone maintenance at different dosages for opiod dependence. *Cochrane Database of Systematic Reviews*, 3, CD002208

Ferraro, L., Tanganelli, S., O'Connor, W.T., Antonelli, T., Rambert, F., & Fuxe, K. (1996). The vigilance promoting drug modafinil increases dopamine release in the rat nucleus accumbens via the involvement of a local GABAergic mechanism. *European Journal of Pharmacology*, 306, 33-39

Foltin, R.W., Ward, A.S., Collins, E.D., Haney, M., Hart, C.L,, & Fischman, M.W. (2003). The effects of venlafaxine on the subjective, reinforcing and cardiovascular effects of cocaine in opioid-dependent and non opioid-dependent humans. *Experimental & Clinical Psychopharmacology*, 11, 123-130

Fox, B.S. (1997). Development of a therapeutic vaccine for the treatment of cocaine addiction. *Drug & Alcohol Dependence*, 48, 153-158

Fox, B.S., Kantak, K.M., Edwards, M.A., Black, K.M., Bollinger, B.K., Botka, A.J., French, T.L., Thompson, T.L., Schad, V.C., Greenstein, J.L., Gefter, M.L., Exley, M.A., Swain, P.A., & Briner, TJ. (1996). Efficacy of a therapeutic vaccine in rodent models. *Nature Medicine*, 2, 1129-1132

Freud, S. (1884). Über Koka. *Wiener Zentralblatt fur die gesamte Therapie*, 2, 289-314

Freud, S. (1984). Über Coca (classics revisited). *Journal of Substance Abuse Treatment*, 1, 206-217

Garcia-Ladona, F.J., & Cox, B.F. (2003). BP 897, a selective dopamine D3 receptor ligand with therapeutic potential for the treatment of cocaine-addiction. *CNS Drug Reviews*, 9, 141-158

Gawin, F.H., & Kleber, H.D. (1986). Abstinence symptomatology and psychiatric diagnosis in cocaine abusers. *Archives of General Psychiatry*, 43, 107-113

Gawin, F.H., Allen, D., & Humblestone, B. (1989). Outpatient regulation of "crack" cocaine smoking with flupenthixol decanoate. *Archives of General Psychiatry*, 46, 322-325

George, T.P., Chawarski, M.C., Pakes, J., Carroll, K.M., Kosten, T.R., & Schottenfeld, R.S. (2000). Disulfiram versus placebo for cocaine dependence in buprenorphine-maintained subjects: a preliminary trial. *Biological Psychiatry*, 47, 1080-1086

Gerasimov, M.R., Ashby, C.R. Jr., Gardner, E.L., Mills, M.J., Brodie, J.D., & Dewey, S.L. (1999). Gamma-vinyl GABA inhibits methamphetamine, heroin, or ethanol-induced increases in nucleus accumbens dopamine. *Synapse*, 34, 11-19

Giros, B., el-Mestikawy, S., Godinot, N., Zheng, K., Han, H., Yang-Feng, T., & Caron, M.G. (1992). Cloning, pharmacological characterization, and chromosome assignment of the human dopamine transporter. *Molecular Pharmacology*, 42: 383-390

Glowa, J.R., Wojnicki, F.H.E., Matecka, D., Bacher, J., Mansbach, R.S., Balster, R.L., & Rice, K.C. (1995a). Effects of dopamine reuptake inhibitors on food and cocaine maintained responding. I: dependence on unit dose of cocaine. *Experimental & Clinical Psychopharmacology*, 3, 219-231

Glowa, J.R., Wojnicki, F.H.E., Matecka, D., Rice, K.C., & Rothman, R.B. (1995b). Effects of dopamine reuptake inhibitors on food and cocaine maintained responding II: comparison with other drugs and repeated administration. *Experimental & Clinical Psychopharmacology*, 3, 232-239

Gold, M.K. (1992). Cocaine (and crack): clinical aspects. In: Lowinson, J.H., Ruiz, P., Millman, R.B., & Langrod, J.G., Eds, *Substance abuse. A comprehensive textbook.* Baltimore, Williams & Wilkins, Pp. 205-221

Gold, M.K., & Vereby, K. (1984). The psychopharmacology of cocaine. *Psychiatric Annals*, 140, 714-723

Goldstein, R.Z., & Volkow, N.D. (2002). Drug addiction and its underlying neurobiological basis: Neuroimaging evidence for the involvement of the Frontal Cortex. *American Journal of Psychiatry*, 159, 1642-1652

Gonzalez, G., Sevarino, K., Sofuoglu, M., Poling, J., Oliveto, A., Gonsai, K., George, T.P., & Kosten, T.R. (2003). Tiagabine increases cocaine-free urines in cocaine-dependent methadone-treated patients: results of a randomized pilot study. *Addiction*, 98, 1625-1632

Gorelick, D.A., Gardner, E.L., & Xi, Z.X. (2004). Agents in development for the management of cocaine abuse. *Drugs*, 64, 1547-1573

Gryder, D.S., & Rogawski, M.A. (2003). Selective antagonism of GluR5 kainate-receptor-mediated synaptic current by topiramate in rat basolateral amygdala neurons. *Journal of Neuroscience*, 23, 7069-70-7

Halikas, J.A., Center, B.A., Pearson, V.L., Carlson, G.A., & Crea, F. (2001). A pilot open clinical study of depakote in the treatment of cocaine abuse. *Human Psychopharmacology*, 3, 257-264

Halikas, J.A., Crosby, R.D., Pearson, V.L., & Graves, N.M. (1997). A randomised double-blind study of carbamazepine in the treatment of cocaine abuse. *Clinical Pharmacology & Therapeutics*, 62, 89-105

Hanzlick, R., & Gowitt, G.T. (1991). Cocaine metabolite detection in homicide victims. *JAMA*, 265, 760-761

Hart, C.L., Ward, A.S., Collins, E.D., Haney, M., & Foltin, R.W. (2004). Gabapentin maintenance decreases smoked cocaine-related subjective effects, but not self-administration by humans. *Drug & Alcohol Dependence*, 73, 279-287

Herning, R.I., Guo, X., & Lange, W.R. (1995). Nimodipine improves information processing in substance abusers. *Annals of the New York Academy of Sciences*, 765, 152-159

Holtzman, S.G. (2001). Differential interaction of GBR12909, a dopamine uptake inhibitor, with cocaine and methamphetamine in rats discriminating cocaine. *Psychopharmacology*, 155, 180-186

Houtsmuller, E.J., Notes, L.D., Newton, T., van Sluis, N., Chiang, N., Elkashef, A., & Bigelow, G.E. (2004). Transdermal selegiline and intravenous cocaine: safety and interactions. *Psychopharmacology*, 172, 31-40

Hyytia, P., Backstrom, P., & Liljequist, S. (1999). Site-specific NMDA receptor antagonists produce differential effects on cocaine self-administration in rats. *European Journal of Pharmacology*, 378, 9-16

Kalivas, P.W., & McFarland, K. (2003). Brain circuitry and the reinstatement of cocaine-seeking behavior. *Psychopharmacology*, 168, 44-56

Kalivas, P.W., McFarland, K., Bowers, S., Szumlinski, K., Xi, Z.X., & Baker, D. (2003). Glutamate transmission and addiction to cocaine. *Annals of the New York Academy of Sciences*, 1003, 169-175

Kampman, K.M., Pettinati, H., Lynch, K.G., Dackis, C., Sparkman, T., Weigley, C., & O'Brien, C.P. (2004). A pilot trial of topiramate for the treatment of cocaine dependence. *Drug & Alcohol Dependence*, 75, 233-240

Kampman, K.M., Pettinati, H., Lynch, K.G., Sparkman, T., & O'Brien. C.P. (2003). A pilot trial of olanzapine for the treatment of cocaine dependence. *Drug & Alcohol Dependence*, 70, 265-273

Kampman, K.M., Pettinati, H.M., Volpicelli, J.R., Oslin, D.M., Lipkin, C., Sparkman, T., & O'Brien, C.P. (2004). Cocaine dependence severity predicts outcome in outpatient detoxification from cocaine and alcohol. *American Journal of Addiction*,13, 74-82

Ke, Y., Streeter, C.C., Nassar, L.E., Sarid-Segal, O., Hennen, J., Yurgelun-Todd, D.A., Awad, L.A., Rendall, M.J., Gruber, S.A., Nason, A., Mudrick, M.J., Blank, S.R., Meyer, A.A., Knapp, C., Ciraulo, D.A., & Renshaw, P.F. (2004). Frontal lobe GABA levels in cocaine dependence: a two-dimensional, J-resolved magnetic resonance spectroscopy study. *Psychiatry Research*, 130, 283-293

Kehne, J., & De Lombaert, S. (2002). Non-peptidic CRF1 receptor antagonists for the treatment of anxiety, depression and stress disorders. *Current drug targets. CNS and neurological disorders*, 1, 467-493

Khantzian, E.J. (1985) The self-medication hypothesis of addictive disorders: focus on heroin and cocaine dependence. *American Journal of Psychiatry*, 142, 1259-1264

Kilty, J.E., Lorang, D., & Amara, S.G. (1991). Cloning and expression of a cocaine-sensitive rat dopamine transporter. *Science*, 254, 578-579

Klein, M. (1998). Research issues related to development of medications for treatment of cocaine addiction. *Annals of the New York Academy of Sciences*, 844, 75-91

Koob, G.F., Caine, S.B., Parsons, L., Markou, A., & Weiss, F. (1997). Opponent process model and psychostimulant addiction. *Pharmacology, Biochemistry & Behavior,* 57, 513-521

Kosten, T.R., Rosen, M., Bond, J., Settles, M., Roberts, J.S., Shields, J., Jack, L., & Fox, B. (2002). Human therapeutic cocaine vaccine: safety and immunogenicity. *Vaccine*, 20, 1196-1204

Kreek, M.J. (1997). Opiate and cocaine addictions: challenge for pharmacotherapies. *Pharmacology, Biochemistry & Behavior*, 57, 551-569

Kuhar, M.J., Ritz, M.C., & Boja, J.W. (1991). The dopamine hypothesis of the reinforcing properties of cocaine. *Trends in Neurosciences,* 14, 299-302

Kuzmin, A.V., Patkina, N.A., & Zvartau, E.E. (1994). Analgesic and reinforcing effects of morphine in mice. Influence of Bay K-8644 and nimodipine. *Brain Research*, 652, 1-8

Kuzmin, A., Zvartau, E., Gessa, G.L., Martellotta, M.C., & Fratta, W. (1992). Calcium antagonists israpidine and nimodipine suppress cocaine and morphine intravenous self-administration in drug-naïve mice. *Pharmacology, Biochemistry & Behavior*, 41, 497-500

Lee, B., Tiefenbacher, S., Platt, D.M., & Spealman, R.D. (2003). Role of the hypothalamic-pituitary-adrenal axis in reinstatement of cocaine-seeking behavior in squirrel monkeys. *Psychopharmacology*, 168, 177-183

Leri, F., Bruneau, J., & Stewart, J. (2003). Understanding polydrug use: review of heroin and cocaine co-use. *Addiction*, 98, 7-22

Levin, F.R., Evans, S.M., & Kleber, H.D. (1998). Prevalence of adult attention-deficit hyperactivity disorder among cocaine abusers seeking treatment. *Drug & Alcohol Dependence*, 52, 15-25

Levin, R.L., & Lehman, A.E. (1991). Meta-analysis of desipramine as an adjunct in the treatment of cocaine addiction. *Journal of Clinical Psychopharmacology*, 11, 374-378

Lile, J.A., Stoops, W.W., Glaser, P.E., Hays, L.R., & Rush, C.R. (2004). Acute administration of the GABA reuptake inhibitor tiagabine does not alter the effects of oral cocaine in humans. *Drug & Alcohol Dependence*, 76, 81-91

Lima, A.R., Lima, M.S., Soares, B.G., & Farrell, M. (2002). Carbamazepine for cocaine dependence. *Cochrane Database of Systematic Reviews*, 2, CD002023

Lima, M.S., Reisser, A.A., Soares, B.G., & Farrell, M. (2003). Antidepressants for cocaine dependence. *Cochrane Database of Systematic Reviews*, 2, CD002950.

Lima, M.S., Soares, B.G., Reisser, A.A., & Farrell, M. (2002). Pharmacological treatment of cocaine dependence: a systematic review. *Addiction*, 97, 931-949

Margolin, A., Avants, S.K., Rounsaville, B., Kosten, T.R., & Schottenfeld, R.S. (1997). Motivational factors in cocaine pharmacotherapy trials with methadone-maintained patients: problems and paradoxes. *Journal of Psychoactive Drugs*, 29, 205-212

Marlatt, G.A., & Gordon, J.R. (1985). *Relapse Prevention*. New York: Guilford Press

Marzuk, P.M., Tardiff, K., & Leon, A.C. (1992). Prevalence of cocaine use among resident of New York City who committed suicide during a one-year period. *American Journal of Psychiatry*, 149, 371-375

Marzuk, P.M., Tardiff, K., Leon, A.C., Hirsch, C.S., Portera, L., Iqbal, M.I., Nock, M.K., & Hartwell, N. (1998). Ambient temperature and mortality from unintentional cocaine overdose. *JAMA*, 279, 1795-1800

Matecka, D., Rothman, R.B., Radesca, L., de Costa, B.R., Dersch, C.M., Partilla, J.S., Pert, A., Glowa, J.R., Wojnicki, F.H.E., & Rice, K.C. (1996). Development of novel, potent, and selective dopamine reuptake inhibitors through alteration of the piprazine ring of 1-(2-(diphenylmethoxy)ethyl)- and 1 - (2-(bis(4-fluorophenyl)methoxy)ethyl)-4-(3-phenylpropyl) piperazines (GBR 12935 and GBR 12909). *Journal of Medicinal Chemistry*, 39, 4704-4716

Mattes, C.E., Belendiuk, G.W., Lynch, T.J., Brady, R.O., & Dretchen, K.L. (1998). Butyrylcholinesterase: an enzyme antidote for cocaine intoxication. *Addiction Biology*, 3, 171-188

Mattick, R.P., Kimber, J., Breen, C., & Davoli, M. (2003). Buprenorphine maintenance versus placebo or methadone maintenance for opioid dependence. *Cochrane Database of Systematic Reviews*, 2, CD002207.

Mello, N.K., & Negus, S.S. (1996). Preclinical evaluation of pharmacotherapies for treatment of cocaine and opioid abuse using self-administration procedures. *Neuropsychopharmacology*, 14, 375-424

Mendelson, J.H., & Mello, N.K. (1996). Management of cocaine abuse and dependence. *New England Journal of Medicine*, 334, 965-972

Merriam, A.E., Medalia, A., & Levine, B. (1988). Partial complex status epilepticus associated with cocaine abuse. *Biological Psychiatry*, 23, 515-518

Meyer, R.E. (1992). New pharmacotherapies for cocaine dependence ... revisited. *Archives of General Psychiatry*, 49, 900-904

Modesto-Lowe, V., & Kranzler, H.R. (1999). Using cue reactivity to evaluate medication for treatment of cocaine dependence: a critical review. *Addiction*, 94, 1639-1651

Moeller, F.G., Dougherty, D.M., Barratt, E.S., Schmitz, J.M., Swann, A.C., & Grabowski, J. (2001). The impact of impulsivity on cocaine use and retention in treatment. *Journal of Substance Abuse Treatment*, 21, 193-198

Montoya, I.D., Gorelick, D.A., Preston, K.L., Schroeder, J.R., Umbricht, A., Cheskin, L.J., Lange, W.R., Contoreggi, C., Johnson, R.E., & Fudala, P.J. (2004). Randomized trial of buprenorphine for treatment of concurrent opiate and cocaine dependence. *Clinical Pharmacology & Therapeutics*, 75, 34-48

Muntaner, C., Kumor, K.M., Nagoshi, C., & Jaffe, J.H. (1991). Effects of nifedipine pre-treatment on subjective and cardiovascular responses to intravenous cocaine in humans. *Psychopharmacology*, 105, 37-41

Myrick, H., & Brady, K.T. (2003). The use of divalproex in the treatment of affective disorders. *Psychopharmacology Bulletin*, 37 (Suppl. 2), 89-97

Myrick, H., Henderson, S., Brady, K.T., & Malcolm, R. (2001). Gabapentin in the treatment of cocaine dependence: a case series. *Journal of Clinical Psychiatry*, 62, 19-23

Myrick, H., Henderson, S., Brady, K.T., & Measom, M. (2001). Divalproex in the treatment of cocaine dependence. *Journal of Psychoactive Drugs*, 33, 283-287

Nann-Vernotica, E., Donny, E.C., Bigelow, G.E., & Walsh, S.L. (2001). Repeated administration of the D1/5 antagonist ecopipam fails to attenuate the subjective effects of cocaine. *Psychopharmacology*, 155, 338-347

Nathan, K.I, Bresnick, W.H., & Batki, S.L. (1998). Cocaine abuse and dependence. Approaches to management. *CNS Drugs*, 10, 43-59

Nunes EV, & Levin FR. (2004). Treatment of depression in patients with alcohol or other drug dependence: a meta-analysis. *JAMA*, 291,1887-1896

O'Brien, C., Childress, A.R., McLellan, A.T., & Ehrman, R. (1992). Classical conditioning in drug-dependent humans. *Annals of the New York Academy of Sciences*, 654, 400-415

O'Hearn, E., & Molliver, M.E. (1993). Degeneration of Purkinje cells in parasaggital zones of the cerebellar vermis after treatment with ibogaine or harmaline. *Neuroscience*, 55, 303-310

Panikkar, G.P. (1999). Cocaine addiction: neurobiology and related current research in pharmacotherapy. *Substance Abuse*, 20, 149-166

Patkar, A.A., Murray, H.W., Mannelli, P., Gottheil, E., Weinstein, S.P., & Vergare, M.J. (2004). Pre-treatment measures of impulsivity, aggression and sensation seeking are associated with treatment outcome for African-American cocaine-dependent patients. *Journal of Addictive Diseases*, 23, 109-122

Patrakis, I.L., Carroll, K.M., Nich, C., Gordon, L.T., McCance-Katz, E.F., Frankforter, T., & Rousanville, B.J. (2000). Disulfiram treatment for cocaine dependence in methadone-maintained opioid addicts. *Addiction*, 95, 219-228

Pilla, M., Hutcheson, D.M., Adib-Samil, P., Potton, E., & Everitt, B.J. (2001). Seeking responses for cocaine, heroin and natural reinforcers are differentially modulated by dopamine D3 receptors. *Society for Neuroscience*, Abstract 647.16

Pilla, M., Parachon, S., Sautel, F., Garrido, F., Mann, A., Wermuth, C.G., Schwartz, J., Everitt, B.J., & Sokoloff, P. (1999). Selective inhibition of cocaine-seeking behaviour by a partial dopamine D3 receptor agonist. *Nature*, 400, 371-375

Platt, D.M., Rowlett, J.K, & Spealman, R.D. (2001). Discriminative stimulus effects of intravenous heroin and its mechanisms in rhesus monkey: opioid and dopaminergic mechanisms. *Journal of Pharmacology & Experimental Therapeutics*, 299, 760-767

Platt. D.M., Rowlett, J.K, & Spealman, R.D. (2002). Behavioral effects of cocaine and dopaminergic strategies for preclinical medication development. *Psychopharmacology*, 163, 265-282

Pontieri, F.E., Tanda, G., & Di Chiara, G. (1995). Intravenous cocaine, morphine and amphetamine preferentially increase extracellular dopamine in the "shell" as compared with the "core" of the rat nucleus accumbens. *Proc. Natl. Acad. Sci. USA*, 92, 12304-12308

Popik, P., Layer, R.T., & Skolnick, P. (1996). 100 years of ibogaine: neurochemical and pharmacological actions of a putative anti-addictive drug. *Pharmacological Reviews,* 53, 791-798

Popik, P., & Skolnick, P. (1996). The NMDA antagonist memantine blocks the expression and maintenance of morphine dependence. *Pharmacology, Biochemistry & Behavior*, 53, 791-798

Preti, A. (2000a). Vanoxerine. *Current Opinion in Investigational Drugs*, 1, 241-251

Preti, A. (2000b). BP-897. current *Current Opinion in Investigational Drugs*, 1, 110-115

Preti, A. (2001). CRF antagonist. *Current Opinion in Investigational Drugs*, 2, 274-279

Prinzleve, M., Haasen, C., Zurhold, H., Matali, J.L., Bruguera, E., Gerevich, J., Bacskai, E., Ryder, N., Butler, S., Manning, V., Gossop, M., Pezous, A.M., Verster, A., Camposeragna, A., Andersson, P., Olsson, B., Primorac, A., Fischer, G., Guttinger, F., Rehm, J., & Krausz, M. (2004). Cocaine use in Europe – a multi-centre study: patterns of use in different groups. *European Addiction Research*, 10, 147-155

Ritz, M.C., Cone, E.J., & Kuhar, M.J. (1990). Cocaine inhibition of ligand binding at dopamine, norepinephrine and serotonin transporters: a structure-activity study. *Life Sciences*, 46, 635-645

Ritz, M.C., Lamb, R.J., Goldberg, S.R., & Kuhar, M.J. (1987). Cocaine receptors on dopamine transporters are related to self-administration of cocaine. *Science*, 237, 1219-1223

Roberts, D.C.S., Andrews, M.M., & Vickers, G.J. (1996). Baclofen attenuates the reinforcing effects of cocaine in rats. *Neuropsychopharmacology*, 15, 417-423

Roberts, D.C.S., Corcoran, M.E., & Fibiger, H.C. (1977). On the role of ascending catecholaminergic systems in intravenous self-administration of cocaine. *Pharmacology, Biochemistry & Behavior*, 6, 615-620

Robinson, T.E., & Berridge, K.C. (1993). The neural basis of drug craving: an incentive-sensitization theory of addiction. *Brain Research & Brain Research Reviews*, 18, 247-291

Rocha, B.A., Fumagalli, F., Gainetdinov, R.R., Jones, S.R., Ator, R., Giros, B., Miller, G.W., & Caron, M.G. (1998). Cocaine self-administration in dopamine-transporter knokout mice. *Nature Neuroscience*, 1, 132-137

Rogers, R.D., & Robbins, T.W. (2001). Investigating the neurocognitive deficits associated with chronic drug misuse. *Current Opinion in Neurobiology*, 11, 250-257

Roozen, H.G., Boulogne, J.J., van Tulder, M.W., van den Brink, W., De Jong, C.A., & Kerkhof, A.J. (2004). A systematic review of the effectiveness of the community reinforcement approach in alcohol, cocaine and opioid addiction. *Drug & Alcohol Dependence*, 74, 1-13

Rothman, R.B., Mele, A., Reid, A.A., Akunne, H.C., Greig, N., Thurkauf, A., de Costa, B.R., Rice, K.C., & Pert, A. (1991). GBR 12909 antagonizes the ability of cocaine to elevate extracellular levels of dopamine. *Pharmacology, Biochemistry & Behavior*, 40, 387-397

Sarnyai, Z. (1998). Neurobiology of stress and cocaine addiction. Studies on corticotropin-releasing factor in rats, monkeys, and humans. *Annals of the New York Academy of Sciences*, 851, 371-387

Sarnyai, Z., Shaham, Y., & Heinrichs, S.C. (2001). The role of corticotropin-releasing factor in drug addiction. *Pharmacological Reviews*, 53, 209-243

Schenk, S. (2002). Effects of GBR 12909, WIN 35,428 and indatraline on cocaine self-administration and cocaine seeking in rats. *Psychopharmacology*, 160, 263-270

Schmitz, J., Stotts, A., Sayre, S., DeLaune, K., & Grabowski, J. (2004). Treatment of Cocaine-Alcohol Dependence with Naltrexone and Relapse Prevention Therapy. *American Journal of Addiction*, 13, 333-341

Schmitz, J.M., Stotts, A.L., Rhoades, H.M., & Grabowski, J. (2001), Naltrexone and relapse prevention treatment for cocaine-dependent patients. *Addictive Behaviors*, 26,167-180

Schneider Institute for Health Policy. Brandeis University. (2001). *Substance abuse: The Nation's Number One Health Problem*. Princeton, NJ: Robert Wood Johnson Foundation

Schultz, W., Dayan, P., & Montague, P.R. (1997). A neural substrate of prediction and reward. *Science*, 275, 1593-1599

Shoptaw, S., Kintaudi, P.C., Charuvastra, C., & Ling, W. (2002). A screening trial of amantidine as a medication for cocaine dependence. *Drug & Alcohol Dependence*, 66, 217-224

Shoptaw, S., Yang, X., Rotheram-Fuller, E.J., Hsieh, Y.C., Kintaudi, P.C., Charuvastra, V.C., & Ling, W. (2003). Randomized placebo-controlled trial of baclofen for cocaine dependence: preliminary effects for individuals with chronic patterns of cocaine use. *Journal of Clinical Psychiatry*, 64, 1440-1148

Silverstone, PH, Attenburrow, MJ, & Robson, P. (1992). The calcium channel antagonist nifedipine causes confusion when used to treat opiate withdrawal in morphine-dependent patients. *International Clinical Psychopharmacology*, 7, 87-90

Soares, B.G.O., Lima, M.S., & Farrell, M. (2004). Psychosocial treatments for psychostimulants dependence. *Cochrane Database of Systematic Reviews.* 4, [under process]

Stafford, D., Rice, K.C., Lewis, D.B., & Glowa, J.R. (2000), Response requirements and unit dose modify the effects of GBR 12909 on cocaine-maintained behavior. *Experimental & Clininical Psychopharmacology, 8*, 539-548

Shearer, J., & Gowing, L. (2004). Pharmacotherapies for problematic psychostimulant use: a review of current research. *Drug & Alcohol Reviews*, 23, 203-211

Shimada, S., Kitayama, S., Lin, C.L., Patel, A., Nanthakumar, E., Gregor, P., Kuhar, M., & Uhl, G. (1991). Cloning and expression of a cocaine-sensitive dopamine transporter complementary DNA. *Science*, 254, 576-577

Siegel, S. (1999). Drug anticipation and drug addiction. *Addiction*, 94, 1113-1124

Sinha, R., Talih, M., Malison, R., Cooney, N., Anderson, G.M., & Kreek, M.J. (2003). Hypothalamic-pituitary-adrenal axis and sympatho-adreno-medullary responses during stress-induced and drug cue-induced cocaine craving states. *Psychopharmacology*, 170, 62-72

Smelson, D.A., Losonczy, M.F., Davis, C.W., Kaune, M., Williams, J., & Ziedonis, D. (2002). Risperidone decreases craving and relapses in individuals with schizophrenia and cocaine dependence. *Canadian Journal of Psychiatry*, 47, 671-675

Soares, B.G., Lima, M.S., Reisser, A.A., & Farrell, M. (2003). Dopamine agonists for cocaine dependence. *Cochrane Database of Systematic Reviews*, 2, CD003352

Sofuoglu, M., Singha, A., Kosten, T.R., McCance-Katz, F.E., Petrakis, I., & Oliveto, A. (2003). Effects of naltrexone and isradipine, alone or in combination, on cocaine responses in humans. *Pharmacology, Biochemistry, & Behavior*, 75, 801-808

Stein, M.D. (1999). Medical consequences of substance abuse. *Psychiatric Clinics of North America*, 22, 351-370

Stratakis, C.A., & Chrousos, G.P. (1995). Neuroendocrinology and pathophysiology of the stress system. *Annals of the New York Academy of Sciences*, 771, 1-18

Uhl, G.R., Lin, Z., Metzger, T., & Dar, D.E. (1998). Dopamine transporter mutations, small molecules, and approaches to cocaine antagonist/dopamine transport disinhibitor development. *Methods in Enzymology*, 296, 456-465

Vetulani, J. (2001). Drug addiction. Part III. Pharmacotherapy of addiction. *Polish Journal of Pharmacology*, 53, 415-434

Villemagne, V.L., Rothman, R.B., Yokoi, F., Rice, K.C., Matecka, D., Dannals, R.F., & Wong, D.F. (1999). Doses of GBR 12909 that suppress cocaine self-administration in non-human primates substantially occupy dopamine transporters as measured by (11C)WIN 35428 PET scans. *Synapse*, 32:,44-50

Volkow, N.D., Wang, G.J., Fowler, J.S., Logan, J., Gatley, S.J., Wong, C., Hitzemann, R., & Pappas, N.R. (1999). Reinforcing effects of psychostimulants in humans are associated with increases in brain dopamine and occupancy of D2 receptors. *Journal of Pharmacology & Experimental Therapeutics,* 291, 409-415

Walsh, S.L., Sullivan, J.T., Preston, K.L., Garner, J.E., & Bigelow, G.E. (1996). Effects of naltrexone on response to intravenous cocaine, hydromorphone and their combination in humans. *Journal of Pharmacology & Experimental Therapeutics*, 279, 524-538

Weiss, R.D., Griffin, M.L., Gallop, R., Onken, L.S., Gastfriend, D.R., Daley, D., Crits-Christoph, P., Bishop, S., & Barber, J.P. (2000). Self-help group attendance and participation among cocaine dependent patients. *Drug & Alcohol Dependence*, 60, 169-177

Wells, E.A., Peterson, P.L., Gainey, R.R., Hawkins, J.D., & Catalano, R.F. (1994). Outpatient treatment for cocaine abuse: a controlled comparison of relapse prevention and twelve-step approaches. *American Journal of Drug and Alcohol Abuse*, 20, 1-17

Wise, R.A., & Bozarth, M.A. (1987). A psychomotor stimulant theory of addiction. *Psychological Reviews*, 94, 469-492

Wong, D.F., Cantilena, L., Elkashef, A., Yokoi, F., Dogan, S., Stephane, M., Gjedde, A., Rothman, R.B., Mojsiak, J., & Vocci, F. (1999). In vivo human dopamine transporter occupancy of a potential cocaine treatment agent, GBR 12909. *Society for Neuroscience*, Abstract 522.7

Woolverton, W.L., & Johnson, K.M. (1992). Neurobiology of cocaine abuse. *Trends in Pharmacological Sciences*, 13, 193-200

World Health Organization. (2004). Ethical issues in neuroscience research on substance dependence treatment and prevention. In: World Health Organization, *Neuroscience of psychoactive substance use and dependence*. (pp. 209-240). Geneve: World Health Organization

Yoshida, M., Yokoo, H., Tanaka, T., Emoto, H., & Tanaka, M. (1994). Opposite changes in the mesolimbic dopamine metabolism in the nerve terminal and cell body sites induced by locally infused baclofen in the rat. *Brain Research*, 636, 111-114

Xie, W., Altimirano, C.V., Bartels, C.F., Speirs, R.J., Cashman, J.R., & Lockridge, O. (1999). An improved cocaine hydrolase: The A328Y mutant of human butyrylcholinesterase is 4-fold more efficient. *Molecular Pharmacology*, 55, 83-91

Zhang, Y., Schlussman, S.D., Ho, A., & Kreek, M.J. (2003). Effect of chronic 'binge cocaine' on basal levels and cocaine-induced increases of dopamine in the caudate putamen and nucleus accumbens of C57BL/6J and 129/J mice. *Synapse*, 50, 191-199

Zobel, A.W., Nickel, T., Kunzel, H.E., Ackl, N., Sonntag, A., Ising, M., & Holsboer, F. (2000). Effects of the high-affinity corticotropin-releasing hormone receptor 1 antagonist R121919 in major depression: the first 20 patients treated. *Journal of Psychiatric Research*, 34, 171-181

In: Cocaine and Heroin Abuse Research
Editor: Lidia A. Pizzoli, pp. 37-60
ISBN 1-60021-076-7

Chapter 2

THE SIGMA$_1$ (σ_1) PROTEIN AS A NEW TARGET FOR ANTI-COCAINE THERAPY

Pascal Romieu and Tangui Maurice*
Université de Montpellier, France

ABSTRACT

Cocaine is a highly addictive substance that is abused worldwide. The main molecular targets of cocaine in the brain are the neuronal monoamine transporters, *i.e.*, the dopamine (DAT), serotonin (SERT) and norepinephrine (NET) transporters. Moreover, most of the behavioral effects of the drug are mediated mainly through its ability to inhibit the DAT and/or the SERT, thus by its ability to act as an indirect dopamine or serotonin agonist. Many laboratories are currently exploring alternative targets with potential therapeutic efficacy against cocaine addiction. The observation that cocaine binds with a moderate affinity *in vitro* to the σ_1 site and the recent increase of interest for this target derives from such tendency. Indeed, cocaine presents a moderate affinity for the σ_1 receptor, in a concentration range achieved *in vivo*. Moreover, behavioral studies clearly demonstrated that the drug acts as a σ_1 protein agonist through either a direct or indirect interaction, since σ_1 receptor blocking strategies allowed to diminish or abolish cocaine behavioral effects in preclinical studies.

1. INTRODUCTION

Cocaine is a highly addictive substance that is abused worldwide [Warner, 1993; Higgins, 1997]. The main molecular targets of cocaine in the brain are the neuronal monoamine transporters, *i.e.*, the dopamine (DAT), serotonin (SERT) and norepinephrine (NET)

* Correspondance to: Dr T. Maurice, CNRS FRE 2693, Université de Montpellier II, cc 090, place Eugène Bataillon, 34095 Montpellier cedex 5, France (T.M.). Tel.: +33 4 67 14 36 23, Fax: +33 4 67 14 33 86, Email: maurice@univ-montp2.fr

transporters. Moreover, most of the behavioral effects of the drug are mediated mainly through its ability to inhibit the DAT and/or the SERT, thus by its ability to act as an indirect dopamine or serotonin agonist [Kuhar, 1992; Ritz *et al.*, 1987; Woolverton, 1992]. Many laboratories are currently exploring alternative targets with potential therapeutic efficacy against cocaine addiction. The observation that cocaine binds with a moderate affinity *in vitro* to the σ_1 site [Sharkey *et al.*, 1988] and the recent increase of interest for this target derives from such tendency. Indeed, cocaine presents a moderate affinity for the σ_1 receptor, in a concentration range achieved *in vivo*. Moreover, behavioral studies clearly demonstrated that the drug acts as a σ_1 protein agonist through either a direct or indirect interaction, since σ_1 receptor blocking strategies allowed to diminish or abolish cocaine behavioral effects in preclinical studies.

2. Nature and Pharmacology of the σ1 Protein

2.1. History, Structure and Localisation of the Protein

Historically, the σ protein was initially described as a subtype of opiate receptors [Martin, 1976], mediating the unique psychotomimetic effects of the prototypic ligand *N*-allylnormetazocine, (±)-SKF-10,047, in the chronic spinal dog. However, the observation that certain behaviors elicited by *N*-allylnormetazocine were resistant to opiate receptor antagonists, such as naloxone or naltrexone [Vaupel, 1983], led to the complete distinction between the σ 'non-opiate' protein and classical μ-, σ-, and σ-opiate receptors [Quirion, 1987]. The σ sites were then confounded with the high affinity phencyclidine (PCP) binding sites, located within the ionophore of the NMDA receptor macromolecular complex, because of shared affinities of several compounds, including PCP and SKF-10,047, for both σ and PCP sites [Quirion, 1987]. The confusion was cleared up by the availability of new drugs appearing very selective for each site. It is now established that the σ sites represent a unique binding site in the brain and peripheral organs, distinct from any other known proteins. The pharmacological identification of the σprotein was, during more than a decade, characterized mainly by its ability to bind several chemically unrelated drugs with high affinity, including psychotomimetic benzomorphans, cocaine and amphetamine, some neuroleptics, antipsychotics, anticonvulsants, cytochrome P450 inhibitors, monoamine oxidase inhibitors, peptides from the neuropeptide Y (NPY) and calcitonin gene-related peptide (CGRP) families, and some steroids [for reviews, Maurice *et al.*, 1997, 1999, 2001]. Various radioligands have been prepared that allowed to precise the σ pharmacology and, particularly allowed the distinction of distinction of two classes of σ sites, termed σ_1 and σ_2 [Quirion, 1992]. The σ_1 sites present a high affinity and stereoselectivity for the dextrogyre isomers of benzomorphans, whereas σ_2 sites have lower affinity and show the reverse stereoselectivity [Hellewell *et al.*, 1994]. It has also been shown that several drugs, such as haloperidol, reduced haloperidol, σ-(4-fluorophenyl)-4-(5-fluoro-2-pyrimidinyl)-1-piperazinebutanol (BMY-14802), rimcazole, *N,N*-dipropyl-2-(4-methoxy-3-(2-phenylethoxy)phenyl)ethylamine (NE-100) or N-[2-(3,4-dichlorophenyl)ethyl]-N-methyl-2-(dimethylamino)ethylamine

(BD1047) act as antagonists in several physiological and behavioral tests relevant to the σ_1 pharmacology [Taylor & Dekleva, 1987; Okuyama *et al.*, 1994; McCracken *et al.*, 1999].

In the mid-90s, the σ_1 protein has been cloned and sequenced, initially from guinea-pig liver [Hanner *et al.*, 1996] and then from human placental cell line, T leukemia Ichikawa cell line and brain [Kekuda *et al.*, 1996; Jbilo *et al.*, 1997; Prasad *et al.*, 1998], from mouse kidney and brain [Seth *et al.*, 1997; Pan *et al.*, 1998] and from rat brain [Seth *et al.*, 1998]. The amino-acid sequences of the different purified proteins are highly homologous, but share no homology to any known mammalian proteins, confirming that an identical σ_1 receptor is expressed in peripheral tissues and brain and that the σ_1 protein is a distinct entity from any other known receptors.

The σ_1 receptor distribution in the brain has been extensively studied using radiographic procedures such as *in vitro* or *in vivo* binding, autoradiography or positron emission tomography. In rodents, high levels of σ_1 sites were detected in the hippocampal pyramidal cell layers, hypothalamus, pontine and cranial nerve nuclei and cerebellum [Su, 1982; Gundlach *et al.*, 1986; Largent *et al.*, 1986; Contreras *et al.*, 1986; McLean *et al.*, 1988; Graybiel *et al.*, 1989]. However, the different radioligands used in these studies showed different affinity and selectivity for the σ_1 sites.

The immunohistochemical distribution of the σ_1 protein was also recently achieved in mouse and rat tissues. The σ_1 immunostaining was observed throughout the rostro-caudal regions of the rat central nervous system, and it appeared to be associated with ependymocytes bordering the ventricular areas, with neurons located within the parenchyma and oligodendrocytes [Alonso *et al.*, 2000; Palacios *et al.*, 2003]. The highest levels of immunostaining can be observed in the granular layer of the olfactory bulb, various hypothalamic nuclei, the dendate gyrus of the hippocampus, and motor nuclei of the hindbrain. Moderate levels of immunostaining are associated with the pyramidal cell layers of the hippocampus, the superficial layers of the cerebral cortex, the lateral septum, the nucleus centralis of the amygdala, the central gray. Only faint immunostaining was associated with neurons located in the caudate putamen and the cerebellum.

Subcellular fractionation and electron microscope studies indicated that σ_1 protein is mostly associated with neuronal perikarya and dendrites, where it is mainly associated with membranes including both the limiting plasma membrane and the membrane organelles such as mitochondria, some cisternae of the endoplasmic reticulum and vesicles present in the vicinity of the Golgi apparatus or dispersed within the dendritic profiles. At the level of synaptic contacts, intense immunostaining was associated with postsynaptic structures including the postsynaptic thickening and some polymorphous vesicles [Alonso, 2000; Phan, 2000].

2.2. Intracellular Consequences of the σ_1 Receptor Activation: Calcium Mobilisation and Association with Lipid Microdomains

Evidence that activation of the σ_1 protein has a direct effect on intracellular calcium ($[Ca^{2+}]_i$) mobilizations was initially reported by Ela *et al.* [Ela *et al.*, 1994], who described that exposure of cardiomyocytes in culture to σ_1 receptor agonists exerted specific changes in contractility, $[Ca^{2+}]_i$ transients and beating rates. The time-course of changes in the contractility and $[Ca^{2+}]_i$ transients showed a complex but reproducible pattern, with an initial decrease, followed by an important increase, and a final decrease. The increase in $[Ca^{2+}]_i$ and following decrease appeared to be mediated by corresponding changes in Ca^{2+} influx [Ela *et al.*, 1994]. These authors suggested that the time course of the σ_1 agonist effect involved a primary action on Ca^{2+} channels or an action of Ca^{2+} fluxes via modulation of K^+ channels.

The role of the σ_1 protein activation in the regulation of Ca^{2+} mobilization was extensively studied in NG-108 cells by Hayashi and Su [Hayashi *et al.*, 2000]. The σ_1 agonists (+)-pentazocine and PRE-084 were found to potentiate the bradykinin-induced increase in $[Ca^{2+}]_i$ in a bell-shaped manner. After depletion of the endoplasmic reticulum Ca^{2+} stores, the depolarization-induced increase in $[Ca^{2+}]_i$ was potentiated by PRE-084 but inhibited by (+)-pentazocine. Co-immunoprecipitation studies showed that the σ_1 protein is part of a macromolecular complex on the cytoskeleton involving the inositol trisphosphate ($InsP_3$) receptor and an ankyrin B anchor protein. Its activation in NG-108 cells resulted in a dissociaton of the ankyrin from $InsP_3$ receptor, which correlated with the efficacy of each ligand in potentiating the Ca^{2+} efflux induced by bradykinin [Hayashi *et al.*, 2000]. This mode of action was coherent with the subcellular localization of the σ_1 protein observed in electronic microscopy studies, suggesting that the σ_1 protein may play a particular role of sensor/modulator for the neuronal intracellular Ca^{2+} mobilizations. Such effect, occuring in post-synaptic neurons, downstream to the neurotransmission events, may explain — or strengthened the validity of — the apparent wide-range and non-selective neuromodulatory effects induced by selective σ_1 receptor ligands.

At the subcellular level, the localization and dynamics of the σ_1 protein has been examined in NG-108 cells by the same authors [Hayashi & Su, 2001, 2003a,b]. The σ_1 protein has been found to be associated with cholesterol-enriched microdomains on the endoplasmic reticulum membrane functioning as neutral lipid storage sites, from which neutral lipids bud out to form cytosolic lipid droplets [Hayashi & Su, 2002]. Activation of σ_1 protein by a selective agonist provoked a significant decrease of σ_1 protein expression in cholesterol enriched microdomains and a diffused distribution over the entire endoplasmic reticulum reticular network in NG-108 cells, toward peripheries of cells, suggesting that σ_1 protein dynamic translocation might affect lipid transport and distribution in neuronal cells [Hayashi & Su, 2003a]. Moreover, using rat primary hippocampal cultures, the same authors showed that σ_1 proteins form lipid rafts (at endoplasmic reticulum) lipid droplet-like structures in the entire myelin sheet of mature oligodendrocytes [Hayashi & Su, 2004]. Overexpression of σ_1 protein in CG-4 cells enhanced differentiation, whereas reducing σ_1 protein in lipid rafts by transfection of functionally dominant-negative σ_1 protein or siRNA probes inihibited differentiation. Therefore, the σ_1 proteins targeting lipid microdomains are important for oligodendrocytes differentiation and may play a role in the pathogenesis of demyelinating diseases [Hayashi & Su, 2004].

These recent data concerning the cellular dynamics of the σ_1 protein confer a particular role to the protein. It appears more likely related to intracellular trafficking and signaling integration than to a classical neuromodulatory receptor, as historically viewed. Drugs modifying its activation, that could be still considered as agonists, by comparison with drugs impeding its activation and considered as antagonists, will thus induce effective and sometimes long-lasting changes in neurotransmission efficacy. In turn, they show effective neuromodulatory actions on neurotransmitter systems, with marked behavioral consequences.

2.3. The Neuromodulatory Role of σ_1 Ligands

Activation of the σ_1 protein by selective agonists results in modulation of intracellular Ca^{2+} mobilization and/or extracellular Ca^{2+} influx. As a consequence, and although the causal relationship has still to be fully established, the main result of the σ_1 protein activation is an effective neuromodulation affecting the responses induced by several kinds of neurotransmitters. Among the most detailed studies, σ_1 receptor ligands were shown to modulate glutamate responses through the NMDA receptor [Monnet *et al.*, 1990], acetylcholine responses through nicotinic receptor [Paul *et al.*, 1993], dopaminergic [Gonzalez-Alvear & Werling, 1994, 1995], serotoninergic [Bermack & Debonnel, 2005] and opiate systems [Chien & Pasternak, 1994].

The modulation exerted by σ_1 agonists on physiologic responses induced by application of NMDA, particularly in the hippocampus, is now considered as a prototypic pharmacological response induced by σ_1 ligands. They modulate different responses to NMDA, in a stimulatory or inhibitory manner, whereas σ_1 antagonists are devoid of effect alone, but block the agonist-induced modulation. Some differences appear, however, depending on the brain structure or the physiologic response involved. Low doses of σ_1 agonists enhanced for instance, dose-dependently but in a bell-shaped manner: (i) the NMDA-induced [^{3}H]norepinephrine release from rat hippocampal slices; (ii) the [^{3}H]dopamine release from rat striatum slices *in vitro*; and (iii) the excitatory response of CA3 pyramidal neurons in the rat hippocampus *in vivo* or in slice preparations from pyramidal cells of rat prefrontal cortex [Monnet *et al.*, 1990, Gonzalez-Alvear, 1994]. A preliminary report indicated that σ_1 agonists, including DTG, (+)-pentazocine, and igmesine modulated LTP components, i.e., both the magnitude and slope of population spikes and field excitatory postsynaptic potentials, in the rat hippocampus [Monnet *et al.*, 2002]. This observation strengthens the hypothesis of a putative effect of σ_1 agonists on NMDA receptor-mediated learning and memory processes.

2.4. The Neuro(Active)Steroids Interaction with the σ_1 Protein

A particularly interesting point concerning the σ_1 protein is that it represents one of the moleculer targets by which some neuroactive steroids act to exert their rapid nongenomic effects in the brain [Su *et al.*, 1988; Maurice *et al.*, 1999, 2001]. These steroids, including pregnenolone, dehydroepiandrosterone (DHEA), their sulfate esters, progesterone and its reduced metabolites pregnanolone and allopregnanolone, are synthesized in periphery or in the brain by glial cells and neurons, the latter being termed neurosteroids since castration/adrenalectomy did not affect cerebral contents. They modulate the brain activity through both genomic and non-genomic rapid neuromodulatory actions, affecting several neurotransmitters and second messenger systems [Baulieu, 1981: Paul & Purdy, 1992]. *In vitro* and *in vivo* pharmacological tests, as well as behavioral studies, demonstrated that pregnenolone, DHEA and their sulfate esters act as σ_1 agonists, whereas progesterone acts as a potent antagonist [Monnet *et al.*, 1995; Bergeron *et al.*, 1996; Maurice *et al.*, 1997; Maurice & Privat 1997]. The importance of the σ_1 protein in the rapid neuromodulatory response induced by neurosteroids was particularly demonstrated in behavioral studies, since: (i) the anti-amnesic effect of DHEA sulfate against dizocilpine-induced learning deficits was abolished in mice treated repeatedly with an antisense probe down-regulating the σ_1 protein expression; and (ii) endocrine manipulations of endogenous progesterone levels, by surrenalectomy/castration and inhibition of 3σ-hydroxysteroid deshydrogenase or 5σ-reductase enzyme, directly affected the anti-amnesic efficacy of a σ_1 agonist [Phan *et al.*, 1999; Maurice *et al.*, 2001]. These steroids also interact with excitatory and inhibitory neurotransmitter receptors. Pregnenolone and DHEA sulfate are positive mlodulators of the inhibitory $GABA_A$ receptor and positive modulators of NMDA receptors. Progesterone and its reduced metabolites, particularly allopregnanolone that does not interact with the σ_1 protein, are effective positive modulators of the $GABA_A$ receptor and negative modulators of NMDA receptors [Schumacher & McEwen 1989; Maurice *et al.*, 2001].

Neurohormones directly affect cocaine addictive processes. The abused drug is known to affect the hypothalamo-pituitary adrenal axis (HPA), leading to increased levels of corticotropin-releasing hormone (CRH) [Sarnyai *et al.*, 1992], adrenocorticotropin hormone (ACTH) and glucocorticoids [Moldow & Fishman, 1987]. Moreover, glucocorticoids play a particular role in vulnerability to cocaine intake and drug effects, in terms of stress-induced regulation of dopaminergic neurons [Marinelli & Piazza, 2002]. Much less is known on the role of neurosteroids, but the observation that they do interact with the σ_1 protein may be of importance.

3. Involvement of the σ_1 Protein in Cocaine's Effects: Preclinical Studies

3.1. Binding Studies

Most of studies aiming to determine the *in vitro* affinity of cocaine for σ_1 sites used membranes preparation from several rodent tissues and different radiotracers, such as [^{3}H]haloperidol or [^{3}H](+)-SKF-10,047. Affinity values ranged from 1.7 to 6.7 σM [Maurice *et al.*, 2002]. The dextrogyre isomer of cocaine presented a lower affinity, in the 16 to 26 σM range. Cocaine is selective for the σ_1 site, since the drug affinity for the σ_2 site is about 30 σM.

To our knowledge, however, no published data described the *in vivo* affinity of cocaine for the σ_1 site, by exploring the effects of drug administration in living animals. Cocaine shows a higher affinity for the DAT, in the 0.2-0.9 σM range, but bioavailability studies must be performed for proper comparisons. Taken into account the cocaine concentration range after peripheral administration and the ubiquitous distribution of the σ_1 protein, σ_1 binding could be considered as relevant as DAT binding for the drug.

3.2 Involvement of the σ_1 Protein in the Stimulant Effects of Cocaine

The involvement of the σ_1 protein was first studied on the stimulant effects of cocaine. Acute administration of cocaine in rodents and humans induced hyperlocomotion and, at higher doses, appearance of stereotyped behaviors. Moreover, except in case of cocaine continuous infusion, these behavioral consequences of cocaine administration increased with the repetition of injections. This phenomenon, called reverse tolerance or sensitization, is of interest because, even after a very long period of abstinence following acquisition of behavioral sensitization, re-administration of cocaine promotes the expression of this sensitization, demonstrating persistence of modifications long time after drug consumption ceased, and suggesting involvement of these modifications in relapse.

Several studies showed that pre-administration of σ_1 protein antagonists could reduce the cocaine-induced hyperlocomotion and sensitization [Menkel *et al.*, 1991; Ujike *et al.*, 1996; McCracken *et al.*, 1999a,b; Matsumoto & McCracken, 1999]. Compounds were administered before cocaine, at doses inactive by themselves, and locomotion was recorded immediately following cocaine injection, using classical actimetry tests. Selective σ_1 receptor antagonists, such as BMY-14,802, rimcazole, 6-[6-(4-hydroxypiperidinyl)hexyloxy]-3-methylflavone (NPC 16377), BD1008, BD1047 or 1-[2-(3,4-dichloro-phenyl)ethyl]-4-methylpiperazine (BD1063) decreased the locomotor stimulant effect of cocaine [Maurice *et al.*, 2002; Maurice & Romieu, 2004]. Non-selective ligands that present good affinity for both DA and σ_1 receptors, such as haloperidol and (+)-3-PPP did not significantly affect the cocaine-induced locomotor effects. Moreover, an interaction with σ_2 sites may also be involved in the efficacy of drugs to block the cocaine-induced hyperlocomotor effects. First, 3σ-tropanyl-2-(4-chlorophenoxy)butyrate ((±)-SM21), a compound with high and preferential affinity for σ_2 sites, blocked cocaine-induced locomotor activity [Matsumoto & Mack, 2001]. Second, at a moderate dose (10 mg/kg ip), the σ_1 receptor antagonist BD1047 did not affect the cocaine-induced acute hyperlocomotion or locomotor sensitization in C57BL/6 mice [Romieu & Maurice, unpublished data]. McCracken *et al.* [1999b] reported that BD1047 was efficient only at 30 mg/kg ip. The drug displayed a moderate selectivity betwen σ_1 and σ_2 sites. Considering that all σ antagonists able, at low doses, to reduce the cocaine hyperlocomotion, are not really selective among the two sites or even display a higher affinity for σ_2 site, involvement of σ sites in cocaine-induced hyperlocomotion or sensitization may predominantly concern the σ_2 site, even if an efficacy of σ_1 antagonism could not be completely excluded.

3.3. Cocaine-Induced Neuronal Activation: C-Fos Expression Studies

One of the most prominent effort made by scientific community in addiction field concerned the elucidation of the neural circuitry underlying processi leading to dependence and uncontrolled consumption of drug, despite the nocive consequences arising from abuse behavior. The finding that most of drugs shared the ability to increase extracellular levels of dopamine in the nucleus accumbens, directly by promoting firing of dopaminergic neurons (via direct activation or indirect deshinibition) or indirectly by blocking the reuptake of the neurotransmitter, sustains the interest in examining the involvement of dopaminergic mesocorticolimbic pathways in drug addiction. Mesocorticolimbic pathways include dopaminergic neurons which originate in the ventral tegmetal area (VTA), within mesencephalon, and which innervate neurons of many cortical and subcortical regions, such as cortex (mainly prefrontal part), ventral striatum (nucleus accumbens), amygdala, bed nucleus of the stria terminalis and in a lesser extent hippocampus. The dopaminergic transmission overactivation after acute and mostly repeated cocaine administration in all of this regions is widely recognized. Mesoaccumbens dopaminergic pathways are thought to mediate the uphoria and pleasant well-being induced by cocaine [Wise & Hoffman, 1992; Volkow *et al.*, 1997, 2002; McBride *et al.*, 1999; Deadwyler *et al.*, 2004; DiChiara *et al.*, 2004]. The prefrontal cortex plays a major role in decision-making and triggering of behavior leading to renew positive feelings [Weiss, 2005; Goldstein & Volkow, 2002]. Amygdala and hippocampus would ensure the association of emotion and context with drug consumption and would be, together with cortex, particularly important in context-, cue- and stress-induced relapse to cocaine [McLaughlin & See, 2003; See *et al.*, 2003; Fuchs *et al.*, 2004a,b]. But, dopaminergic neurotransmission in the whole striatum, including the dorsal part, in a second time, plays a major role of gating behavior associated to drug consumption, both as a motivation-motion interface and in the recall of behavior implicitely and proceduraly memorized with drug administration [Berke & Hyman, 2000].

The neuronal activation of several target regions for dopaminergic neurons, in response to cocaine acute intraperitoneal administration, was examined in C57BL/6 mice through the measure of the proto-oncogene protein c-Fos using immunohistochemistry [Maurice & Romieu, 2004]. The c-fos protein is a transcription factor considered as a marker of evoked neuronal activity. Consequently to acute cocaine administration, increased c-Fos immunolabeling was observed within the striatum, ventral and dorsal parts, hippocampus, amygdala and bed nucleus of the stria terminalis (BNST). Pre-administration of BD1047 was able to block the cocaine-induced c-Fos surexpression in all the regions examined, as illustrated in the dorsal striatum and nucleus accumbens (Fig. 1).

In conclusion, σ_1 protein antagonism could drastically reduce the cocaine-induced enhancement of c-Fos expression in central regions known to play a key role in mediating the rewarding and reinforcing properties of cocaine. Therefore, σ_1 receptor activation could be an important step to allow cocaine seeking behavior, and compounds, endogenous or synthetic, modulating the σ_1 protein functionality could alter initiation of processes leading to dependence state.

3.4. Involvement of σ_1 Receptor and Related Neuro(Active) Steroids in Cocaine-Induced Appetitive Effect: Conditioned Place Preference Studies

One of the most popular behavioral procedure in laboratory rodents to assess addictive potential of drugs is the conditioned place preference (CPP) paradigm [Tzschentke, 1998]. This test allows to assess hedonic state induced by any substance, *i.e.*, the rewarding, neutral or aversive properties of the compound. The procedure consists in conditioning animals to associate the drug-induced chemical state and a particular environment, like one of the compartments of a two-compartment box. After conditioning, the time spent in each compartment during a drug-free session (post-conditioning) is compared to the time spent by the animal in each compartment before the conditioning phase (pre-conditioning). It has been demonstrated that all drugs of abuse in humans generate in rodents a place preference for the compartment associated to the drug-induced chemical state, suggesting that they endowed appetitive, rewarding properties. Reinforcing properties have to be assessed in self-administration paradigms, and, if results are synergistic, abuse liability in humans. Moreover, compounds able to alter the rewarding properties of a drug present anti-addictive potentials but must be investigated in self-administration models and in human therapy against drug addiction.

Several σ_1 ligands were examined on acquisition and expression of cocaine-induced place preference. Cocaine administration induced a dose-dependent place preference after four days of conditioning in C57Bl/6 mice. The selective σ_1 antagonists NE-100 and BD1047 did not induce any place preference or avoidance but, pre-administered to cocaine during conditioning, both reduced acquisition of cocaine appetitive properties, BD1047 being more effective (Fig. 2) [Romieu *et al.*, 2000, 2002]. Moreover, intracerebroventricular administration of an antisense oligodeoxynucleotide probe targeting the σ_1 protein during the conditioning phase but with a different schedule than cocaine, also led to complete abolition of the cocaine-induced place preference (Fig. 2) [Romieu *et al.*, 2000]. The σ_1 protein blockade only during the post-conditioning session was able to significantly diminish the expression of cocaine rewarding properties, suggesting that σ_1 protein activation is a requisite for both acquisition and expression of cocaine-induced place preference [Romieu *et al.*, 2002]. Neither igmesine nor PRE-084, two selective σ_1 agonists, promoted place preference. However, igmesine, pre-administered before cocaine during conditioning, enhanced the cocaine efficacy to induce place preference [Romieu *et al.*, 2002]. In turn, activation of the σ_1 protein is not able *per se* to induce appetence, but is necessary to the hedonic properties of cocaine. It is also able to pre-sensitize cocaine target neurons to exposure to the drug.

To examine whether the activation of σ_1 protein could be directly induced by cocaine, able to bind directly to the σ_1 protein, we examined the ability of σ_1 antagonists to interact with the place preference induced by N-[1-(2-benzo(b)thiophenyl)cyclohexyl]piperidine (BTCP), a PCP derivative highly selective for the DAT with no affinity for σ_1 sites. As expected, BTCP induced a strong place preference in C57BL/6 mice. Pre-administration of the σ_1 antagonists drastically reduced acquisition of BTCP appetitive properties [Romieu *et al.*, 2002], suggesting that even if cocaine binds to the σ_1 receptor, the increasing extracellular dopamine concentration may be sufficient to promote the σ_1 protein activation.

A modulatory role for neuro(active)steroids on acquisition of cocaine-induced place preference was of interest, since these steroids could act through the σ_1 protein, in the vicinity of neurons exposed and reacting to cocaine. DHEA or pregnenolone, administered prior to cocaine during conditioning, potentiated the cocaine efficacy to induce place preference [Romieu *et al.*, 2003]. In contrast, exogenous administration of progesterone or endogenous accumulation, through inhibition of the 5σ-reductase enzyme with finasteride, significantly

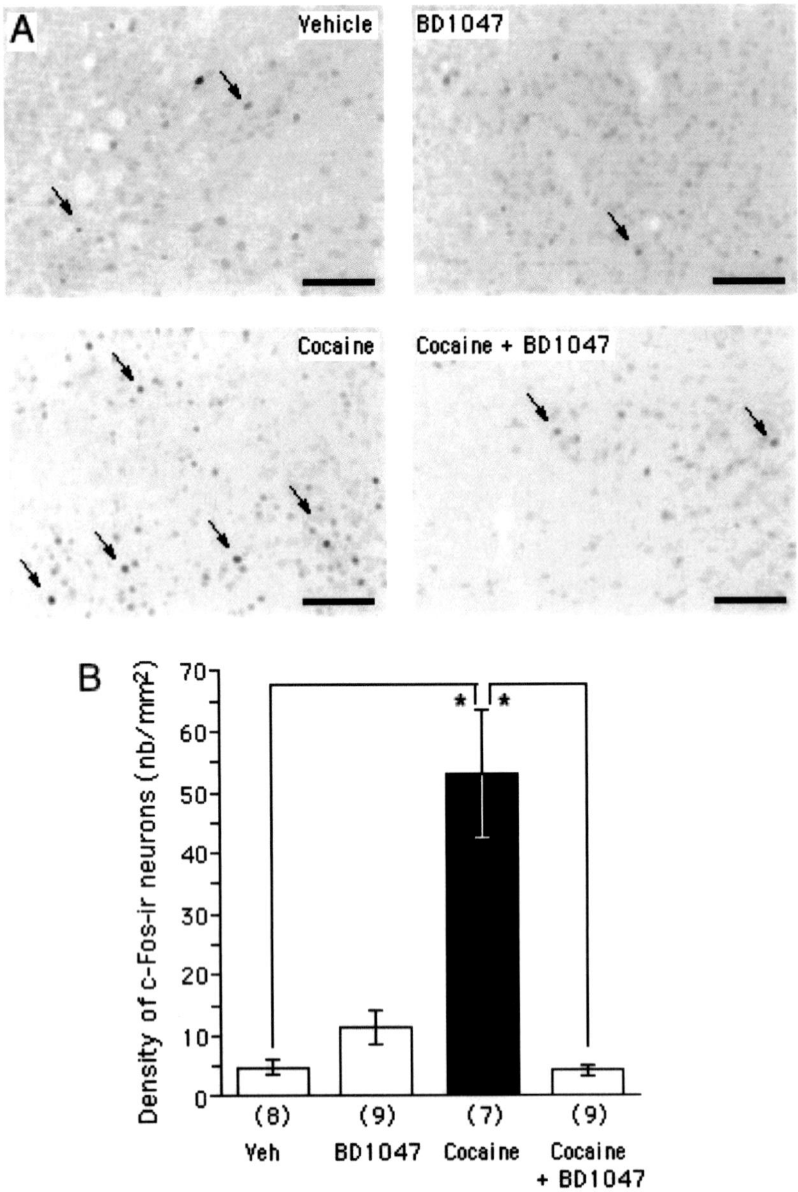

Fig. 1. (A) Typical photomicrographs showing the c-Fos immunoreactivity in the shell part of the nucleus accumbens in cocaine and/or BD1047-treated C57BL/6 mice. (B) Averaged measures of the density of c-Fos immunoreactivity. Mice received either saline solution (vehicle), cocaine (20 mg/kg ip), BD1047 (10 mg/kg ip) or cocaine + BD1047, 2 hr before sacrifice. After transcardiac perfusion with paraformaldehyde 4%, coronal sections (40 μm thickness) were cut and incubated with a c-Fos antibody (SC-52, Santa Cruz, dilution 1:5000) and then with a peroxydase-conjugated goat anti-rabbit IgG (Jackson ImmunoResearch, diluted 1:500). Slices were then rinsed, mounted and observed under light miscroscopy. c-Fos immunostaining was measured with a microcomputer imaging device (SAMBA analyse Software, Alcatel, France) capturing the image through a CCD camera connected to a light microscope (Axioskop, Zeiss, Germany). Immunoreactive cells were detected and standardized with NIH image© analysis. Arrows outline dotted c-Fos immunoreactive neurons. Scale bars = 100 μm. * $p < 0.05$, Newman-Keuls' test after two-way ANOVA. Adapted from [Romieu *et al.*, submitted article].

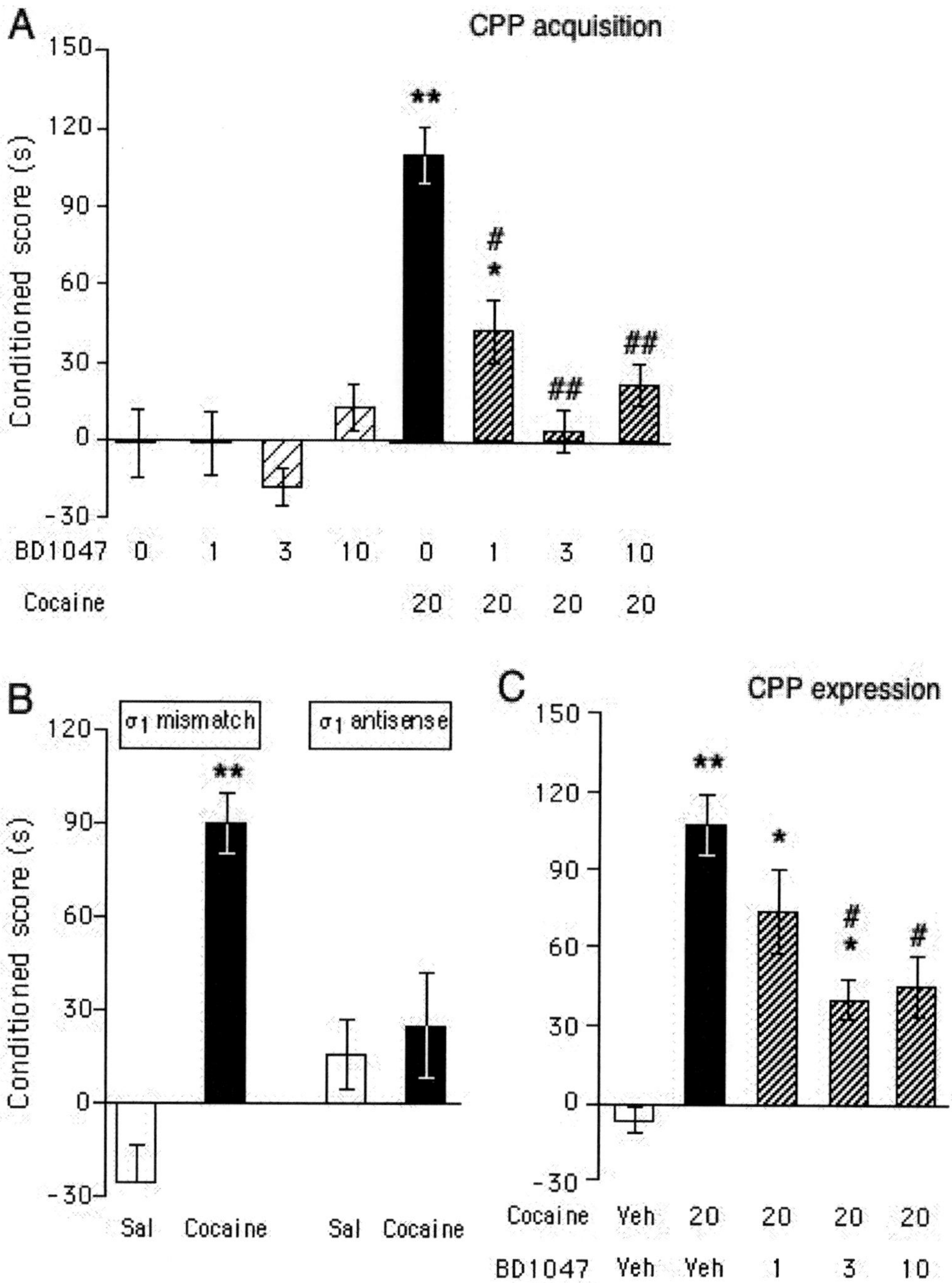

Fig. 2. Effect of the σ_1 receptor antagonist BD1047 on: (A) acquisition and (B) expression of cocaine-induced CPP. (A) BD1047 was administered 10 min before cocaine, which was given immediately before placement in the compartment during the conditioning test (n = 10-18). (B) BD1047 was administered before the post-conditioning test (n = 12). The conditioned score represents the difference in time spent in the drug-paired compartment between the post- and pre-conditioning sessions. * $p < 0.05$, ** $p < 0.01$ vs. the (vehicle+vehicle)-treated group, # $p < 0.05$, ## $p < 0.01$ vs. the (cocaine+vehicle)-treated group, Newman-Keuls' test. Adapted from [Romieu *et al.* 2002].

reduced cocain-induced place preference [Romieu *et al.*, 2003]. To examine the importance of the σ_1 receptor/steroids relationship, crossed pharmacology experiments were done and progesterone inhibited the igmesine-induced potentiation of cocaine place preference, whereas BD1047 abolished the DHEA- or pregnenolone-enhancing effect of cocaine rewarding properties [Romieu *et al.*, 2003]. Therefore, DHEA and pregnenolone acting as σ_1 agonists, and progesterone behaving as a σ_1 antagonist, modulate cocaine-induced hedonic properties, through their interaction with the σ_1 protein, effective *in vivo*. Noteworthy, the steroids also modulate NMDA- and $GABA_A$-receptors, effect that could also be involved in this behavioral effects. Moreover, these data outlined the importance in cocaine rewarding effects of steroids upstream to glucocorticoids or sexual hormones in the steroids synthesis cascade. The steroidal neuroendocrine state may influence consequence of exposure to cocaine before terminal steroids intervention. Therefore, according to plasma or cerebral concentrations in precursor steroids, cocaine efficacy may be more or less important and central neurosteroid levels and particularly the DHEA/progesterone ratio could represent a factor of vulnerability and interindividual variability counterpart to cocaine hedonic properties. It has been demonstrated in humans that oral administration of progesterone attenuated some of somatic effects of cocaine, such as the increase in diastolic blood pressure, and subjective hedonic effects in males and females [Sofuoglu *et al.*, 2004].

3.5. Reactivation of Cocaine-Induced Place Preference by Drug Priming: Key Role for the σ_1 Protein Activation

More than acute exposure to drug, the main problem concerning drug abuse and particularly cocaine addicition is the high rate of relapse in drug consumption, even after weeks, months or years of abstinence. Procedures adequately measuring reinstatement of cocaine-seeking have been developed in self-administration paradigms. These models confirmed in laboratory animals what has been clinically observed in humans: relapse is frequent after a extinction or abstinence period, and can be induced either by cocaine priming, cocaine-associated cues or context, or acute stress. Role of central regions and neural circuitry involved in reinstatement of cocaine-seeking begins to be analyzed, confering crucial role to dopaminergic mesocorticolimbic neurons in cocaine- and cues-induced reinstatement and to amygdala-BNST connections in stress-induced relapse [Weiss, 2005]. The conditioned place preference procedure could also be used to examine the reinstatement of cocaine-seeking [Mueller & Stewart, 2000; Itzhack & Martin, 2002; Lu *et al.*, 2002; Romieu *et al.* 2004]. After conditioning, the place preference could be extinguished by administering saline before confinment in the compartment previously associated with the drug, and then reactived by cocaine priming [Romieu *et al.*, 2004].

In order to examine the role of σ_1 protein in the reactivation of cocaine-seeking behavior, conditioned place preference was induced in Swiss mice using 30 mg/kg cocaine during 4 days. The behavioral response was then extinguished by substituting saline for cocaine during a four-day period. Several days after extinction, a cocaine priming injection, 15 mg/kg, reactivated the place preference for the cocaine-associated compartment. Cocaine, presumably via reactivation of mesocorticolimbic dopaminergic pathways, reinstated previous cocaine-seeking behavior in mice [Romieu *et al.*, 2004]. The σ_1 antagonist BD1047 was devoid of any effect when injected prior to reactivation session but the blockade of the σ_1 receptor activation led to complete abolition of cocaine-induced reactivation (Fig. 3). It must be noted that BD1047 was really effective, at this time point, at 30 mg/kg ip, whereas it reduced acquisition of cocaine place preference during the first days since 3 and 10 mg/kg ip doses. This shift in effective dose could be explained by the ability of cocaine to increase σ_1 protein expression after repeated injections. Indeed, after 4 days treatement, cocaine enhanced the σ_1 gene expression, measured by semi-quantitative RT-PCR, in nucleus accumbens [Romieu *et al.*, 2002], and increased the *in vivo* bioavailability of the σ_1 binding site, measured using *in vivo* [^{3}H]-SKF-10,047 binding [Romieu *et al.*, 2004]. The σ_1 protein availability being increased, for example by cocaine, or any putative endogenous activator released by cocaine, higher σ_1 antagonist doses could be necessary to block cocaine effects during the reactivation session. In addition, mice with decreased expression of the σ_1 protein, using the central administration of σ_1 antisense probe, did not display any cocaine-seeking behavior following cocaine injection during the reactivation session [Romieu *et al.*, 2004]. Moreover, administration of a selective σ_1 protein agonist, sch as igmesine, effectively reactivated cocaine-induced place preference. Similarly, DHEA, through its interaction with the σ_1 protein, reactivated the cocaine-induced place preference. Therefore, activation of the σ_1 protein plays an important permissive role in the renewal of place preference and reactivation of cocaine-seeking behavior [Romieu *et al.*, 2004]. Finally, other drugs of abuse induced a crossed reactivation cocaine-induced place preference after extinction. Indeed, nicotine, morphine, phencyclidine or alcohol administered before the reactivation session reactivated the place preference for the cocaine-associated compartment, and their effects, with the notable exception of alcohol, were also blocked by BD1047 [Romieu *et al.*, 2004]. The σ_1 protein activation may thus be a common step for drugs of abuse necessary the reactivation of cocaine place preference and maybe that σ_1 receptor activation is a key mechanism in retrieval of rewarding properties within the brain.

At the behavioral level, the σ_1 system, devoid of effect in the conditioned place preference procedure when it is selectively activated, now sparks off a real cocaine-seeking behavior. Therefore, the σ_1 protein activation became sufficient to induce drastic modification in mice behavior. Together with an increase in σ_1 receptor bioavailability, these results strongly suggest that the repeated activation of dopaminergic mesolimbic system during the place preference procedure induced an important neuronal plasticity sustained changes in reactivity of the σ_1 protein and/or the neuronal intracellular pathways involved in its activation.

3.6. Cocaine-Induced Toxicity and Lethality

Cocaine is known to interfere with vegetative functions, such as cardiac activity or respiratory system. The mechanism of action of the drug is not fully understood, but it is conceivable that cocaine acts directly on muscle cells, cardiac or skeleton muscle cells, and indirectly through central nuclei controlling these rythmic activities. It's well established that, especially in case of overdose situations, cocaine can induce convulsions and death. Although medical emergency departments did not report plethory of cases of cocaine overdose, it remains that cocaine overdose represents the major cause of emergency entries in hospital due to drug complications. Some dramatic issues have been described and, until now, no real efficacious therapy has been developed. Since cocaine binds the σ_1 protein and this protein being present in peripheral systems, it could be hypothezised that agents able to block the σ_1 protein activation may represent good candidates for alleviating cocaine-induced toxicity and lethality. Indeed, experiments conducted in rodentsshowed real convincing protective actions.

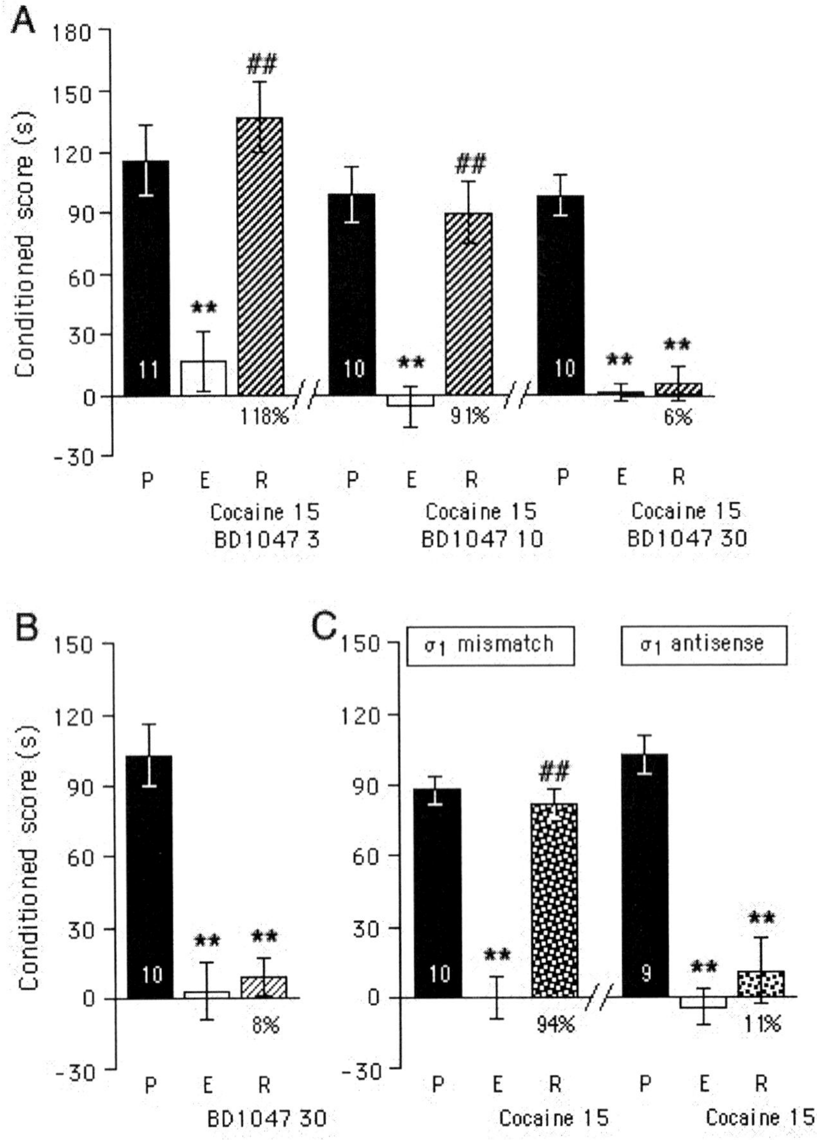

Fig. 3. Blockade of the drug-induced reactivation of cocaine-induced CPP by the σ_1 receptor antagonist BD1047. CPP was established with cocaine (30 mg/kg ip) between days 2 to 5 and then extinguished with saline solution injected in the drug-paired compartment between days 7 to 10. Reactivation was tested with BD1047 (3-30 mg/kg ip), administered 10 min before cocaine (15 mg/kg). The number of animals per group is indicated within the black bars. ** $P < 0.01$ vs. the post-conditioning measure, ## $P < 0.01$ vs. the extinction measure, Newman-Keuls' test. Adapted from [Romieu *et al.*, 2004].

Almost all σ_1 receptor antagonists tested so far could significantly reduced the percentage of mice entering in convulsions following acute cocaine overdose administration [Ritz & George, 1993; McCracken *et al.*, 2000; Matsumoto *et al.*, 2001a,b,c, 2004]. Administration of a σ_1 antisense oligodeoxynucleotide probe presented similar protective effects against cocaine-induced convulsions. In contrast, and as expected, σ_1 receptor agonists are able, when pre-administered to the drug, to worsen convulsive effects of cocaine [Matsumoto *et al.*, 2001a,b].

The σ_1 antagonists were also tested against cocaine-induced lethality. They also showed a significant protective activity in mice when administered prior to the lethal dose of cocaine [Matsumoto *et al.*, 2001a,b; McCracken *et al.*, 1999a]. Moreover, and more interestingly regarding the therapeutic outcomes in medical emergency, σ_1 antagonists could also significantly prevent the fatal issue in mice when they were administered after cocaine, when convulsions started to occur [McCracken *et al.*, 2000; Matsumoto *et al.*, 2001c]. The protective action of σ_1 antagonists could be due to their role in central neurons, maybe controlling the balance between excitatory and inhibitory inputs to these cells. To our knowledge, no study examined the potential effects of central administration of a σ_1 antisense probe on lethal consequences of cocaine administration. But, even if central activity of σ_1 receptor activation could participate, one must consider that heart contains large amounts of σ sites, among them about 80% are of the σ_1 subtype [Matsumoto *et al.*, 2001c]. The direct peripheral blockade of σ_1 receptors by antagonists could constitute a predominant part of the benefic properties of these compounds. The mode of action of the σ_1 protein in cocaine toxic consequences also remains unexplained at the cellular level, on neuronal or muscular cells. The main vriable controlled by σ_1 protein activation within the cell and able to account for the effective protective ability of the σ_1 antagonists is the modulation of $[Ca^{2+}]_i$ and Ca^{2+} fluxes through the membrane. But, still now, no report explored this mechanism of action in this model of σ_1 receptor involvement.

In conclusion, although more studies are needed to understand the role of σ_1 protein in the convulsive and lethal consequences of cocaine overdose, the effective protective action of σ_1 protein blockade by selective antagonists has been demonstrated and such compounds can be considered as promising therapeutic solution in emergency cases.

4. Intracellular Activation of the σ1 Protein as a Key Component of Cocaine-Induced Plasticity

The involvement of σ_1 protein in not only the cocaine-induced reward but also psychostimulant and toxic effects raises the question of the intracellular mechanisms underlying such effects. As described, activation of the σ_1 protein potentiates most of cocaine's effects, while blocking the the σ_1 protein expression or pharmacological antagonism of its activation inhibits cocaine-induced behavioral responses. Two mechanisms may account for the involvement of the σ_1 protein in the acute and long-term effects of cocaine: modulation of intracellular Ca^{2+} homeostasis and remodelling of the intracellular lipid rafts microdomains [Su & Hayashi, 2003].

As described above (paragraph 2.2), the σ_1 protein has been shown to be, under resting physiological conditions, part of an intracellular macromolecular complex including the $InsP_3$ receptor and an ankyrin B anchor protein on the surface of the smooth endoplasmic reticulum. The binding of σ_1 agonists to the protein result in the dissociation of the σ_1 protein/ankyrin complex from the $InsP_3$ receptor and translocation towards other organelles and plasma membranes, leading to the facilitation of intracellular Ca^{2+} mobilizations driven by the $InsP_3$ receptor [Hayashi & Su, 2001; Su & Hayashi, 2001]. Cocaine, by indirectly or directly activating the □$_1$ protein, has been shown to exert such facilitory effects on $[Ca^{2+}]_i$ [Hayashi & Su, 2001; Su & Hayashi, 2001]. The drug may also increase $[Ca^{2+}]_i$ *via* suractivation of the phospholipase C-linked dopamine D_1-type receptor [Felder *et al.*, 1989; Undie *et al.*, 2000; Su & Hayashi, 2001]. Therefore, cocaine administration, and even more preadministration of σ_1 protein agonists before the drug, results in a supersensitization of post-synaptic dopaminergic neurons. Antagonists of σ_1 receptor, which delocalize only the σ_1 protein from the $InsP_3$ receptor/ankyrin complex, prevent the σ_1 protein-mediated facilitation of $[Ca^{2+}]_i$ mobilization and thus the subsequent sensitization to cocaine, as observed at the behavioral level in terms of place preference conditioning, for instance. Such mode of action is also in accordance with functional morphological observations, such as c-Fos immunohistochemical measures in target dopaminergic structures. Indeed, σ_1 antagonists could disrupt pathways leading to CREB phosphorylation known to activate c-fos gene expression, such as intracellular pathways from dopaminergic D_1 receptors, serotonergic $5HT_2$ and glutamatergic NMDA receptors, the two formers moreover activating phospholipase C [Raymond *et al.*, 2001]. In addition, and although direct modulations could not yet been excluded, direct and effective effects on $[Ca^{2+}]_I$ and may account for the apparently non-selective neuromodulatory effects of σ_1 ligands on neurotransmitter responses [for review, see Maurice *et al.*, 2002].

Long-term effects of the cocaine interaction with the σ_1 protein may be the consequences of the regulation of the σ_1 protein expression and re-localization at the intracellular level. Indeed, the role of the σ_1 protein in the remodelling of lipid microdomains composition suggest not only their role in cellular differentiation, as proposed by Hayshi & Su [2003a,b, 2004], but also in the functional plasticity of the neuron. The σ_1 protein appears to be necessary for the precise lipid composition and correct drive of these rafts through the cell. The lipid rafts are involved in the transport of lipids within the cell and play a momentous role in the formation of new dendrites, *i.e.*, in the morphologic plasticity processes which is important for long-term adaptations of the brain to new stimuli, informations or changes in the environment. The morphological plasticity induced by self-administration of cocaine, demonstrated in dendritic spines of accumbal neurons and in dendrites of neocortical neurons [Robinson & Kolb, 1999; Robinson *et al.*, 2001], would play a major role in the persistance and robustness of dependence to cocaine. It is therefore conceivable to suggest that cocaine could promote this morphological plasticity through its effect on σ_1 proteins and thus through improved transport of new lipids and membrane constituants promoting neurite outgrowths. Administration of σ_1 antagonist blocks this mechanism and thus lead to a lack of adaptation of neurons to cocaine exposure. Such compounds may thus prevent the development of behavioral manifestations of dependence.

5. Forthcoming Issues to be Addressed Regarding the Interaction of Cocaine with the σ_1 Protein

Despite the fact that evidences have been accumulated involving the σ_1 protein activation, and resulting intraneuronal plasticity, as one of the important vectors of cocaine-induced plastictity after acute and repeated administration, studies must still be conducted to validate the protein as a potential target for therapeutic intervention. In particular, numerous questions arise from the observations conducted until now.

First, the involvement of the σ_1 protein, *i.e.*, the effects of selective agonists or antagonists, in cocaine-induced self-administration has not been reported yet. The sensibility of animals to cocaine (fixed-ratio protocols), their motivation to self-administer the drug (progressive ratio protocols), or the degree of vulnerability to relapse must be examined after pharmacological manipulations of the σ_1 protein. Preliminary studies have been conducted and suggest an involvement of the protein activation in relapse to drug seeking, particularly after drug priming or re-presentation of the cocaine-associated stimuli [Martin-Fardon *et al.*, manuscript in preparation]. These results will be necessary to firmly establish the involvement and role of the σ_1 protein in cocaine-induced addiction.

Second, it could be interesting to examine more precisely the influence of neuro(active)steroids, through their interaction with the σ_1 protein, on cocaine dependence. A first series of experiments must examine the eventual effect of cocaine, acute or chronic, administration on central neurosteroid contents, including DHEA, pregnenolone (as σ_1 agonists), progesterone (as σ_1 antagonist) and progesterone metabolites like allopregnanolone (inactive at the σ_1 protein) in order to correlate any variation with inter-individual vulnerability to cocaine. Any relationship between levels of these endogenous σ_1 ligands and the efficacy of cocaine in development and reactivation of its rewarding properties could open a new pharmacological approach to cocaine dependence in humans.

Third, clinical studies must be conducted. Taken into account the poor toxicity shown by selective σ_1 ligands, their efficacy could rapidly be assessed in clinical trials. It must be kept in mind the disappointment consequent to results obtained in clinical tests with dopaminergic antagonists, proportional to the enthousiasm due to their potent efficacy in several aspects of cocaine dependence models in rodents. Currently, the strategy to develop a dopaminergic antagonist in human cocaine addiction is clearly abandoned and agonist-like replacement pharmacotherapy seems to be largely more attractive [Grabowski *et al.*, 2004], although some authors concluded to their lack of efficacy [Soares *et al.*, 2003]. Regarding σ_1 ligands, further data are still necessary, particularly using self-administration paradigms, before proposing any agonist or antagonist strategy. However, selective σ_1 antagonists such as BD1047 could be effective in reducing the positive subjective effects of cocaine clearly reported after cocaine administration. The limitation of such a strategy appears clearly linked to the fact that cocaine users feeling no more euphoric effects would discontinue the treatment or increase their cocaine dose. However, the protective effects of σ_1 antagonists against the toxic effects of cocaine, suggest that they could be used for excessive self-administration indications. The σ_1 agonists are exciting candidates for a substitution therapeutic strategy. The experiments examining the reactivation of cocaine-induced place preference clearly suggested that when the exposure to cocaine is sufficiently repeated, the cocaine-induced plasticity switches the σ_1

protein system from a pure modulatory to an effective component. Self-administration procedures will allow to to confirm and analyze the mechanism of action of σ_1 agonists in cocaine-induced relapse, *i.e.*, to determine whether substitution of cocaine by a σ_1 agonist mimicks the cocaine chemical state and allow a pure priming effect action or, on the contrary, promotes craving, that may correspond to an increase of the time spent in the drug-associated compartment in the place preference paradigm.

6. CONCLUSION

The past and current literature clearly confers to σ_1 protein a crucial role in several cocaine exposure effects, such as neuronal evoked activity or acquisition, expression and reactivation of place preference. The latter paradigm being used to study the hedonic properties of substances, it could be considered that the σ_1 protein is critically involved in subjective effects of cocaine. Noteworthy, σ_1 antagonists could also reduce conditioned place preference induced by BTCP, morphine and alcohol in mice suggesting a pivotal permissive role for this system in brain sustaining the appetitive properties of several drug of abuse. Moreover, activation of the σ_1 protein, or the intracellular pathway implicating it, could represent a key step in recognition and seeking of cocaine and other drugs chemical states. Therefore, this protein interferes with the neuronal plasticity of systems acting in the central structures involved in pleasure, mood state and in drug addiction. Although preclinical studies have still to be extended, to better evaluate the potential of σ_1 protein in models of drug dependence, selective ligands, agonists or antagonists, undoubtedly will offer promising new therapeutic opportunities against cocaine and, maybe more generally, drug addiction.

REFERENCES

Alonso G, Phan VL, Guillemain I, Saunier M, Legrand A, Anoal M, Maurice T, (2000). Immunocytochemical localization of the σ_1 receptor in the adult rat central nervous system. *Neuroscience 97*:155-170

Baulieu EE, (1981). Steroid hormones in the brain: Several mechanisms? *In Steroid Hormone Regulation of the Brain*, Edited by Fuxe K, Gustafson JA and Wettenberg L, Pergamon Press, Oxford, pp 3-14

Bergeron R, de Montigny C, Debonnel G, (1996). Potentiation of neuronal NMDA response induced by dehydroepiandrosterone and its suppression by progesterone: effects mediated via sigma receptors. *J Neurosci 16*:1193-1202

Berke JD, Hyman SE, (2000). Addiction, dopamine, and the molecular mechanisms of memory. *Neuron 25*:515-532

Bermack JE, Debonnel G, (2005) The role of sigma receptors in depression. *J Pharmacol Sci 97*:317-336

Chien CC, Pasternak GW, (1994). Selective antagonism of opioid analgesia by a sigma system. *J Pharmacol Exp Ther 271*:1583-1590

Contreras PC, Quirion R, O'Donohue TL, (1996). Autoradiographic distribution of phencyclidine receptors in the rat brain using [^{3}H]1-(1-(2-thienyl)cyclohexyl)piperidine ([^{3}H]TCP). *Neurosci Lett 67*:101-106

Deadwyler SA, Hayashizaki S, Cheer J, Hampson RE, (2004). Reward, memory and substance abuse: functional neuronal circuits in the nucleus accumbens. *Neurosci Biobehav Rev. 27*, 703-711.

Di Chiara G, Bassareo V, Fenu S, De Luca MA, Spina L, Cadoni C, Acquas E, Carboni E, Valentini V, Lecca D, (2004). Dopamine and drug addiction: the nucleus accumbens shell connection. *Neuropharmacology* 47 S1:227-241

Ela C, Barg J, Vogel Z, Hasin Y, Eilam Y, (1994). Sigma receptor ligands modulate contractility, Ca^{2+} influx and beating rate in cultured cardiac myocytes. *J Pharmacol Exp Ther 269*:1300-1309

Felder CC, Jose PA, Axelrod J, (1989). The dopamine-1 agonist, SKF 82526, stimulates phospholipase-C activity independent of adenylate cyclase. *J Pharmacol Exp Ther 248*:171-175

Fuchs RA, Evans KA, Ledford CC, Parker MP, Case JM, Mehta RH, See RE, (2004b). The role of the dorsomedial prefrontal cortex, basolateral amygdala, and dorsal hippocampus in contextual reinstatement of cocaine seeking in rats. *Neuropsychopharmacology 30*, 296-309

Fuchs RA, Evans KA, Parker MP, See RE, (2004a). Differential involvement of orbitofrontal cortex subregions in conditioned cue-induced and cocaine-primed reinstatement of cocaine seeking in rats. *J Neurosci 24*, 6600-6610

Goldstein RZ, Volkow ND, (2002). Drug addiction and its underlying neurobiological basis: neuroimaging evidence for the involvement of the frontal cortex. *Am J Psychiatry 159*, 1642-1652

Gonzalez-Alvear GM, Werling LL, (1994). regulation of [^{3}H]dopamine release from rat striatal slices by sigma ligands. *J Pharmacol Exp Ther 271*:212-219

Gonzalez-Alvear GM, Werling LL, (1995). Sigma$_1$ receptors in rat striatum regulate NMDA-stimulated [^{3}H]dopamine release via a presynaptic mechanism. *Eur J Pharmacol 294*:713-719

Grabowski J, Shearer J, Merrill J, Negus SS, (2004). Agonist-like, replacement pharmacotherapy for stimulant abuse and dependence. *Addict Behav 29*:1439-1464

Graybiel AM, Besson MJ, Weber E, (1989). Neuroleptic-sensitive binding sites in the nigrostriatal system: evidence for differential distribution of sigma sites in the substantia nigra, pars compacta of the cat. *J Neurosci 9*:326-338

Gundlach AL, Largent BL, Snyder SH, (1986). Autoradiographic localization of sigma receptor binding sites in guinea pig and rat central nervous system with (+)^{3}H-3-(3-hydroxyphenyl)-N-(1- propyl)piperidine *J Neurosci 6*:1757-1770

Hanner M, Moebius FF, Flandorfer A, Knaus HG, Striessnig J, Kempner E, Glossman H, (1996). Purification, molecular cloning, and expression of the mammalian sigma$_1$-binding site. *Proc Natl Acad Sci USA 93*:8072-8077

Hayashi T, Maurice T, Su TP, (2000). Ca^{2+} signaling via sigma$_1$-receptors: novel regulatory mechanism affecting intracellular Ca^{2+} concentration. *J Pharmacol Exp Ther 293*: 788-798

Hayashi T, Su TP, (2001). Regulating ankyrin dynamics: Roles of sigma-1 receptors. *Proc Natl Acad Sci USA 98*:491-496

Hayashi T, Su TP, (2003a). Sigma-1 receptors (sigma(1) binding sites) form raft-like microdomains and target lipid droplets on the endoplasmic reticulum: roles in endoplasmic reticulum lipid compartmentalization and export. *J Pharmacol Exp Ther 306*:718-725

Hayashi T, Su TP, (2003b). Intracellular dynamics of sigma-1 receptors (sigma(1) binding sites) in NG108-15 cells. *J Pharmacol Exp Ther 306*:726-733.

Hayashi T, Su TP, (2004). Sigma-1 receptor ligands: potential in the treatment of neuropsychiatric disorders. *CNS Drugs 18*:269-284

Hellewell SB, Bruce A, Feinstein G, Orringer J, Williams W, Bowen WB, (1994). Rat liver and kidney contain high densities of σ_1 and σ_2 receptors: characterization by ligand binding and photoaffinity labeling, *Eur J Pharmacol 268*:9-18

Higgins ST, (1997). The influence of alternative reinforcers on cocaine use and abuse: a brief review. *Pharmacol Biochem Behav 57*:419-427

Itzhak Y, Martin JL, (2002). Cocaine-induced conditioned place preference in mice: Induction, extinction and reinstatement by related psychostimulants. *Neuropsychopharmacology 26*: 130-134

Jbilo O, Vidal H, Paul R, De Nys N, Bensaid M, Silve S, Carayon P, Davi D, Galiegue S, Bourrie B, Guillemot JC, Ferrara P, Loison G, Maffrand JP, Le Fur G, Casellas P, (1997). Purification and characterization of the human SR 31747A-binding protein. A nuclear membrane protein related to yeast sterol isomerase. *J Biol Chem 272*, 27107-27115

Kekuda R, Prasad PD, Fei YJ, Leibach FH, Ganapathy V. (1996) Cloning and functional expression of the human type 1 sigma receptor (hSigmaR1). *Biochem Biophys Res Commun, 229*:553-558

Kuhar MJ, (1992). Molecular pharmacology of cocaine: a dopamine hypothesis and its implications. *Ciba Found Symp 166*:81-89

Largent BL, Gundlach AL, Snyder SH, (1986). Pharmacological and autoradiographic discrimination of sigma and phencyclidine receptor binding sites in brain with (+)-[^{3}H]SKF 10,047, (+)-[^{3}H]-3-[3-hydroxyphenyl]-N-(1-propyl)piperidine and [^{3}H]-1-[1-(2-thienyl)cyclohexyl] piperidine. *J Pharmacol Exp Ther 238*:739-748

Lu L, Zhang B, Liu Z, Zhang Z, (2002). Reactivation of cocaine conditioned place preference induced by stress is reversed by cholecystokinin-B receptors antagonist in rats. *Brain Res 954*: 132-140

Marinelli M, Piazza PV, (2002). Interaction between glucocorticoid hormones, stress and psychostimulant drugs. *Eur J Neurosci 16*:387-94

Martin WR, Eades CG, Thompson JA, Huppler RE, Gilbert PE, (1976). The effects of morphine- and nalorphine- like drugs in the nondependent and morphine-dependent chronic spinal dog. *J Pharmacol Exp Ther 197*:517-532

Matsumoto RR, Gilmore DL, Pouw B, Bowen WD, Williams W, Kausar A, Coop A., (2004). Novel analogs of the sigma receptor ligand BD1008 attenuate cocaine-induced toxicity in mice. *Eur J Pharmacol. 492*, 21-26.

Matsumoto RR, Hewett KL, Pouw B, Bowen WD, Husbands SM, Cao JJ, Hauck Newman A., (2001c). Rimcazole analogs attenuate the convulsive effects of cocaine: correlation with binding to sigma receptors rather than dopamine transporters. *Neuropharmacology. 41*, 878-886.

Matsumoto RR, Mack AL, (2001). (±)-SM 21 attenuates the convulsive and locomotor stimulatory effects of cocaine in mice. *Eur J Pharmacol 417*: R1-R2

Matsumoto RR, McCracken KA, (1999). Antisens oligodeoxynucleotides against sigma-1 receptors reduce the convulsive and locomotor stimulatory effects of cocaine in mice. *Society of Neurosciences Abstract 25*, 203.

Matsumoto RR, McCracken KA, Friedman MJ, Pouw B, De Costa BR, Bowen WD., (2001b). Conformationally restricted analogs of BD1008 and an antisense oligodeoxynucleotide targeting sigma1 receptors produce anti-cocaine effects in mice. *Eur J Pharmacol. 419*, 163-174.

Matsumoto RR, McCracken KA, Pouw B, Miller J, Bowen WD, Williams W, De Costa BR., (2001a). N-alkyl substituted analogs of the sigma receptor ligand BD1008 and traditional sigma receptor ligands affect cocaine-induced convulsions and lethality in mice. *Eur J Pharmacol. 411*, 261-273.

Maurice A, Privat A, (1997). SA4503, a novel cognitive enhancer with sigma$_1$ (σ_1) receptor agonist properties, facilitates NMDA receptor-dependent learning in mice, *Eur J Pharmacol 328*:9-18

Maurice T, Lockhart BP, (1997). Neuroprotective and anti-amnesic potentials of sigma (σ) receptor ligands. *Prog Neuropsychopharmacol Biol Psychiatry 21*: 69-102

Maurice T, Martin-Fardon R, Romieu P, Matsumoto RR, (2002). Selective sigma$_1$ (σ_1) receptor antagonists as a new promising strategy to prevent cocaine-induced behaviors and toxicity. *Neurosci Biobehav Res 26*: 499-527

Maurice T, Phan VL, Urani A, Kamei H, Noda Y, Nabeshima T, (1999). Neuroactive neurosteroids as endogenous effector for the sigma$_1$ (σ_1) receptor: Pharmacological evidences and therapeutic opportunities. *Jpn J Pharmacol 81*:125-155

Maurice T, Romieu P, (20040 Involvement of the sigma$_1$ receptor in the appetitive effects of cocaine. *Pharmacopsychiatry* 37 Suppl 3:S198-207

Maurice T, Urani A, Phan VL, Romieu P, (2001). The interaction between neuroactive steroids and the sigma$_1$ (σ_1) receptor function: Behavioral consequences and therapeutic opportunities. *Brain Res Rev 37*:116-132

McBride WJ, Murphy JM, Ikemoto S, (1999). Localization of brain reinforcement mechanisms: intracranial self-administration and intracranial place-conditioning studies. *Behav Brain Res. 101:* 129-152.

McCracken KA, Bowen WD, De Costa BR, Matsumoto RR, (1999a). Two novel sigma receptor ligands, BD1047 and LR172, attenuate cocaine-induced toxicity and locomotor activity. *Eur J Pharmacol. 370*, 225-232.

McCracken KA, Bowen WD, Matsumoto RR., (1999b). Novel sigma receptor ligands attenuate the locomotor stimulatory effects of cocaine. *Eur J Pharmacol. 365*, 35-38.

McCracken KA, Miller J, Bowen WD, Zhang Y, Matsumoto RR, (2000). Brain sigma-1 receptor are involved in behavioral effects of cocaine. NIDA Res Monogr. 180, 291.

McLaughlin J, See RE, (2003). Selective inactivation of the dorsomedial prefrontal cortex and the basolateral amygdala attenuates conditioned-cued reinstatement of extinguished cocaine-seeking behavior in rats. *Psychopharmacology 168*:57-65

McLean S, Weber E, (1988). Autoradiographic visualization of haloperidol-sensitive sigma receptors in guinea-pig brain. *Neuroscience 25*:259-269

Menkel M, Terry M, Pontecorvo M, Katz JL, Witkin JM, (1991). Selective σ ligands block stimulant effects of cocaine. *Eur J Pharmacol 201*: 251-252

Moldow RL, Fischman AJ, (1987). Cocaine-induced secretion of ACTH, beta-endorphin and corticosterone. *Peptides 8*:819-822

Monnet FP, (2002). Sigma receptors and intracellular signaling: Impact on synaptic plasticity? *XXIII CINP Meeting Abstr* S.29.3

Monnet FP, Debonnel G, de Montigny C, (1992). In vivo electrophysiological evidence for a selective modulation of N-methyl-D-aspartate-induced neuronal activation in rat CA3 dorsal hippocampus by sigma ligands. *J Pharmacol Exp Ther 261*:123-130

Monnet FP, Debonnel G, Junien JL, De Montigny C, (1990). N-methyl-D-aspartate-induced neuronal activation is selectively modulated by sigma receptors. *Eur J Pharmacol 179*:441-445.

Monnet FP, Mahe V, Robel P, Baulieu EE, (1995). Neurosteroids, via sigma receptors, modulate the [^{3}H]norepinephrine release evoked by N-methyl-D-aspartate in the rat hippocampus. *Proc Natl Acad Sci USA 92*: 3774-3778

Mueller D, Stewart J, (2000). Cocaine-induced conditioned place preference: reinstatement by priming injections of cocaine after extinction. *Behav Brain Res 115*: 39-47

Okuyama S, Imagawa Y, Sakagawa T, Nakazato A, Yamaguchi K, Katoh M, Yamada S, Araki H, Otomo S, (1994). NE-100, a novel sigma receptor ligand: effect on phencyclidine-induced behaviors in rats, dogs and monkeys. *Life Sci 55*:PL133-138

Palacios G, Muro A, Vela JM, Molina-Holgado E, Guitart X, Ovalle S, Zamanillo D, (2003). Immunohistochemical localization of the s1-receptor in oligodendrocytes in the rat central nervous system. *Brain Res 961*:92–99

Pan YX, Mei J, Xu J, Wan BL, Zuckerman A, Pasternak GW, (1998). Cloning and characterization of a mouse σ_1 receptor. *J Neurochem 70*:2279-2285

Paul IA, Basile AS, Rojas E, Youdim MB, De Costa B, Skolnick P, Pollard HB, Kuijpers GA, (1993). Sigma receptors modulate nicotinic receptor function in adrenal chromaffin cells. *FASEB J 7*:1171-1178

Paul SM, Purdy RH, (1992) Neuroactive steroids. *FASEB J 6*:2311-2322

Phan VL, Su TP, Privat A, Maurice T, (1999). Modulation of steroidal levels by adrenalectomy/castration and inhibition of neurosteroid synthesis enzymes affect sigma$_1$ (σ_1) receptor-mediated behaviour in mice. *Eur J Neurosci 11*:2385-96

Prasad PD, Li HW, Fei YJ, Ganapathy ME, Fujita T, Plumley LH, Yang-Feng TL, Leibach FH, Ganapathy V, (1998). Exon-intron structure, analysis of promoter region, and chromosomal localization of the human type 1 sigma receptor gene. *J Neurochem 70*:443-451

Quirion R, Bowen WD, Itzhak Y, Junien JL, Musacchio JM, Rothman RB, Su TP, Tam SW, Taylor DP, (1992). A proposal for the classification of sigma binding sites. *Trends Pharmacol Sci 1992*;13:85-86.

Quirion R, Chicheportiche R, Contreras PC, Johnson KM, Lodge D, Tam SW, Woods JH, Zukin SR, (1987). Classification and nomenclature of phencyclidine and sigma receptor sites. *Trends Neurosci 10*:444-446

Raymond JR, Mukhin YV, Gelasco A, Turner J, Collinsworth G, Gettys TW, Grewal JS, Garnovskaya MN,(2001). Multiplicity of mechanisms of serotonin receptor signal transduction. *Pharmacol Ther 92*:179-121

Ritz MC, George FR, (1993). Cocaine-induced seizures and lethality appear to be associated with distinct central nervous system binding sites. *J Pharmacol Exp Ther 264*:1333-1343

Ritz MC, Lamb RJ, Goldberg SR, Kuhar MJ, (1987). Cocaine receptors on dopamine transporters are related to self-administration of cocaine. *Science 237*:1219-1223

Robinson TE, Gorny G, Mitton E, Kolb B, (2001). Cocaine self-administration alters the morphology of dendrites and dendritic spines in the nucleus accumbens and neocortex. *Synapse 39*:257-66

Robinson TE, Kolb B, (1999). Alterations in the morphology of dendrites and dendritic spines in the nucleus accumbens and prefrontal cortex following repeated treatment with amphetamine or cocaine. *Eur J Neurosci 11*:1598-604

Romieu P, Martin-Fardon R, Bowen WD, Maurice T, (2003). Sigma$_1$ (σ_1) receptor-related neuroactive steroids modulate cocaine-induced reward. *J Neurosci 23*: 3572-3576

Romieu P, Martin-Fardon R, Maurice T, (2000). Involvement of the σ_1 receptor in the cocaine-induced conditioned place preference. *Neuroreport 11*:2885-2888

Romieu P, Meunier J, Garcia D, Zozime N, Martin-Fardon R, Bowen WD, Maurice T, (2004). The sigma$_1$ (σ_1) receptor activation is a key step for the reactivation of cocaine conditioned place preference by drug priming. *Psychopharmacology 175*:154-162

Romieu P, Phan VL, Martin-Fardon R, Maurice T, (2002). The sigma$_1$ receptor involvement in cocaine-induced conditioned place preference is consequent upon dopamine uptake blockade. *Neuropsychopharmacology 26*:444-455

Sarnyai Z, Biro E, Penke B, Telegdy G, (1992). The cocaine-induced elevation of plasma corticosterone is mediated by endogenous corticotropin-releasing factor (CRF) in rats. *Brain Res 589*:154-156

Schumacher M, McEwen BS, (1989). Steroid and barbiturate modulation of the GABAa receptor. Possible mechanisms. *Mol Neurobiol 3*:275-304

See RE, Fuchs RA, Ledford CC, McLaughlin J, (2003). Drug addiction, relapse, and the amygdala. *Ann N Y Acad Sci. 985*, 294-307

Seth P, Fei YJ, Li HW, Huang W, Leibach FH, Ganapathy V, (1998). Cloning and functional characterization of a sigma receptor from rat brain. *J Neurochem 70*:922-931

Seth P, Leibach FH, Ganapathy V, (1997). Cloning and structural analysis of the cDNA and the gene encoding the murine type 1 sigma receptor. *Biochem Biophys Res Commun 241*:535-540

Sharkey J, Glen KA, Wolfe S, Kuhar MJ, (1988). Cocaine binding at sigma receptors. *Eur J Pharmacol. 149*, 171-174.

Soares BG, Lima MS, Reisser AA, Farrell M, (2003). Dopamine agonists for cocaine dependence. *Cochrane Database Syst Rev 2*:CD003352

Sofuoglu M, Mitchell E, Kosten TR, (2004). Effects of progesterone treatment on cocaine responses in male and female cocaine users. *Pharmacol Biochem Behav 78*:699-705

Su TP, (1982). Evidence for sigma opioid receptor: Binding of [^{3}H]SKF-10,047 to etorphine-inaccessible sites in guinea-pig brain. *J Pharmacol Exp Ther 223*: 284-290

Su TP, Hayashi T, (2001). Cocaine affects the dynamics of cytoskeletal proteins via sigma(1) receptors. *Trends Pharmacol Sci 22*:456-458

Su TP, Hayashi T, (2003). Understanding the molecular mechanism of sigma-1 receptors: towards a hypothesis that sigma-1 receptors are intracellular amplifiers for signal transduction. *Curr Med Chem 10*: 2075-2082

Su TP, London ED, Jaffe JH, (1988). Steroid binding at sigma receptors suggests a link between endocrine, nervous, and immune systems. *Science 240*:219-21

Taylor DP, Dekleva J, (1987). Potential antipsychotic BMY-14,802 selectively binds to sigma sites. *Drug Dev Res 11*:65-70

Tzschentke TM, 1998. Measuring reward with the conditioned place preference paradigm: a comprehensive review of drug effects, recent progress and new issues. *Prog Neurobiol.* 56, 613-672.

Ujike H, Kuroda S, Otsuki S. (1996). sigma Receptor antagonists block the development of sensitization to cocaine. *Eur J Pharmacol. 296*, 123-128.

Undie AS, Berki AC, Beardsley K, (2000). Dopaminergic behaviors and signal transduction mediated through adenylate and phospholipase C pathways. *Neuropharmacology 39*:75-87

Vaupel DB, (1983). Naltrexone fails to antagonize the sigma effects of PCP and SKF-10,047 in the dog, *Eur J Pharmacol 92*:269-274

Volkow ND, Fowler JS, Wang GJ, (2002). Role of dopaine in drug reinforcement and addiction in humans: results from imaging studies. *Behav. Pharmacol. 13*, 355-366.

Volkow ND, Wang GJ, Fischman MW, Foltin RW, Fowler JS, Abumrad NN, Vitkun S, Logan J, Gatley SJ, Pappas N, Hitzemann R, Shea CE, (1997). Relationship between subjective effects of cocaine and dopamine transporter occupancy. *Nature 386*, 827-830.

Warner EA, (1993). Cocaine abuse. *Ann Intern Med 119*:226-235

Weiss F, (2005). Neurobiology of craving, conditioned reward and relapse. *Curr Opin Pharmacol. 5*, 9-19.

Weiss F, 2005. Neurobiology of craving, conditioned reward and relapse. *Curr Opin Pharmacol* Feb;5:9-19

Wise RA, Hoffman DC, (1992). Localization of drug reward mechanisms by intracranial injections. *Synapse 10*, 247-263.

Woolverton WL, Johnson KM, (1992). Neurobiology of cocaine abuse. *Trends Pharmacol Sci 13*:193-200

In: Cocaine and Heroin Abuse Research
Editor: Lidia A. Pizzoli, pp. 61-80
ISBN 1-60021-076-7

Chapter 3

CARDIOVASCULAR COMPLICATIONS RELATED TO ACUTE AND CHRONIC COCAINE ABUSE: NECROPSY STUDIES, PATHOGENETIC MECHANISMS AND ECHOCARDIOGRAPHIC FINDINGS

Gianluca Iacobellis *
University of Texas Southwestern Medical Center, USA

ABSTRACT

Short and long-term cocaine abuse has been widely reported to induce several cardiovascular complications. Cocaine has been shown to cause angina pectoris, acute myocardial ischemia and infarction independently of amount ingested, route of administration, and frequency of use. Several pathogenetic mechanisms can be evoked to explain the cocaine-related myocardial injury. Increased myocardial oxygen demand, marked vasoconstriction of the coronary arteries, enhanced platelet aggregation, ionic currents alterations, hormones paracrine action imbalance, endothelial alterations and thrombus formation can contribute in producing myocardial ischemia or infarction. Recently, experimental and clinical studies have been performed to better clarify the mechanisms of cocaine effects on cardiovascular system. Cocaine is also well known to have an arrhythmogenic potential and to be a frequent cause of sudden cardiac death. Several cardiac dysrhythmias and conduction disturbances are correlated to a cocaine abuse. Cocaine can produce also left ventricular morphological and functional changes. In fact, several reports have described dilated and hypertrophic cardiomyopathy and left ventricular systolic dysfunction in long-term cocaine abusers. Myocarditis, pulmonary hypertension, aortic dissection or rupture and impairment of diastolic function have been also reported as consequences of both acute and chronic cocaine effect. The intravenous use of cocaine is also associated with an increased risk of bacterial endocarditis.

* Center for Human Nutrition, University of Texas Southwestern Medical Center at Dallas, 5323 Harry Hines Blvd, Dallas, Texas, USA, 75390-9052. Tel. +1 214 648 2419 FAX +1 214 648 7150, e-mail: gianluca.iaco@tin.it , gianluca.iacobellis@utsouthwestern.edu

Ultrasound techniques play a significant role in the imaging assessment and diagnosis of cocaine-associated cardiovascular complications. Thransthoracic and transesophageal echocardiography and recently the intravascular ultrasound technique provide striking and diagnostic images of cocaine-related alterations. In this report we will review the necropsy findings and the latest information on the pathogenetic mechanisms and imaging diagnostic techniques of the cardiovascular abnormalities associated with an acute and chronic cocaine abuse. Unusual and rare echocardiographic findings and images from published and unpublished case reports will be also described.

INTRODUCTION

Cocaine abuse is strongly increased in the past few years mostly in higher industrialized countries and among subject with high socio-economic level [1-2]. As the illicit use of this drug became widespread, the cocaine-related cardiovascular events, the most severe cocaine abuse side-effect, are dramatically increased. Cocaine abuse has been reported to be associated with both acute and chronic cardiovascular complications. The following cardiac disorders associated with an inappropriate cocaine use have been reported with different prevalence and incidence: acute myocardial infarction, myocardial ischemia, silent and symptomatic angina pectoris, myocarditis, dilated and hypertrophic cardiomyopathies, ventricular and sopraventricular arrhythmias, systemic and pulmonary hypertension, aortic dissection, endocarditis and thrombus formation. Several pathogenetic mechanisms can be evoked to explain the cocaine-related myocardial injury.

Increased myocardial oxygen demand, marked vasoconstriction of the coronary arteries, enhanced platelet aggregation, ionic currents alterations, hormones paracrine action imbalance, endothelial alterations and thrombus formation can contribute in producing myocardial ischemia or infarction. Cocaine can be taken by different routes: smoking, nasal, insufflation, or intravenous injection. The development of cocaine-related cardiac diseases seems to be relatively independent of cocaine amount ingested, route of administration, and frequency of use.

Ultrasound techniques play a significant role in the imaging assessment and diagnosis of cocaine-associated cardiovascular complications. Thransthoracic and transesophageal echocardiography and recently the intravascular ultrasound technique provide striking and diagnostic images of cocaine-related alterations. In this report we will review the necropsy findings and the latest information on the pathogenetic mechanisms and imaging diagnostic techniques of the cardiovascular abnormalities associated with an acute and chronic cocaine abuse. Unusual and rare echocardiographic findings and images from published and unpublished case reports will be also described.

INFLUENCE OF COCAINE ADMINISTRATION ROUTE ON CARDIOVASCULAR SYSTEM

Cocaine can be taken by different routes: smoking, nasal insufflation (“snorting”), sublingual, intravaginal and rectal administration, oral (“chewing”) or intravenous injection ("mainlining"). Cocaine is rapidly and well absorbed through the respiratory tract and all mucous membranes. Higher blood cocaine concentration can be achieved by mucous membrane administration. A positive relationship between peak plasma concentration and dose administered has been previously reported [3]. After nasal insufflation of cocaine powder, peak concentrations can be found in the blood within 30 to 60 minutes. The mucosal administration of the drug produces a slower onset of action [1-5 min], a later peak effect [15-20 min], and a longer duration of action [60-90 min] in comparison with the intravenous injection of cocaine. Intravenously administrated cocaine starts to act after 10-60 second, achieves a peak between 3 and 5 minutes and could effective until 60 minutes [4]. By the contrast, smoking cocaine has been described to have an onset of action of 3-5 seconds, a peak of action between 1 and 5 min and duration of 5-15 min. Cocaine could be taken orally, although it is poorly absorbed by the gastrointestinal tract. Cocaine and its metabolites can be detected in blood and urine. If this detection is effective only few hours after drug ingestion, hair analysis provides a very sensitive marker of cocaine abuse in the preceding weeks or months, depending on the length of the hair analyzed [5]. Differences in route of administration, drug purity, and other factors may also contribute to the cardiotoxic effects of cocaine.

Intranasal administration is one of the most common route to take cocaine. The effects of intranasal cocaine on cardiovascular performance are controversial and not completely known. Some clinical and experimental studies have been performed in order to clarify this issue. Intranasal cocaine has been reported to cause recurrent coronary vasoconstriction. This vasoconstriction effect could be due to its metabolites. In fact, the blood concentration of cocaine's main metabolites, benzoylecgonine and ethyl methyl ecgonine is increased after intranasal cocaine administration [6-7]. A small amount of intranasal cocaine (2 mg/kg) induces a modest increase in LV contractility and LV end-diastolic pressure is unchanged in humans [8].

Experimental studies indicate that cocaine, in addition to blocking norepinephrine reuptake peripherally, can exert two directionally opposite effects on central sympathetic outflow: sympathetic inhibition due to interruption of excitatory neural circuits in the brain [9-11] and sympathetic excitation due to either a direct central neural action [12-13] or inhibition of sinoaortic baroreceptor reflexes [14-15]. An elegant study on healthy volunteers analyzed the blood pressure and sympathetic nerve discharge to the skeletal muscle vasculature during intranasal cocaine administration. The Authors concluded the primary effect of intranasal cocaine seems to increase, not decrease, sympathetic nerve discharge to the skeletal muscle bed. They suggested that sinoaortic baroreflexes play a pivotal role in modulating the cocaine induced sympathetic excitation. The interplay between these excitatory and inhibitory neural influences determines the net effect of cocaine on sympathetic discharge targeted to the human skeletal muscle circulation. [16]

Nevertheless, there are some studies reporting no cardiovascular side-effect of cocaine intranasally administrated. Intranasal cocaine in a dose similar to that used medicinally or "recreationally" does not exert a deleterious influence on intracardiac pressures and left ventricular performance [8].

No evidence of thoracic aorta or coronary artery vasoconstriction after i.v. cocaine administration has been reported. [17] In fact, the immediate effects of cocaine on the thoracic aorta and coronary arteries were evaluated. If the arterial vasoconstriction is thought to play a role in the etiology of cocaine-induced cardiovascular complications, the potential effect on the structure and blood flow regulation of aorta and coronary arteries is not completely clear. The authors used transesophageal echocardiography to examine the thoracic aorta and coronary arteries before and immediately after intravenous (i.v.) cocaine (1.2 mg/kg). The diameters of thoracic aorta and the left main coronary artery have been described to be unchanged and a trend for augmentation of coronary artery blood flow has been observed. [17]

Necropsy Cardiovascular Findings

Cocaine-related chronic and acute myocardial and coronary arteries lesions have been reported. Several studies described coronary arterial alteration at necropsy in cocaine abusers. Mostly, one among these studies carefully described the coronary arterial findings in cocaine addicts [18]. The authors found that a large number of young cocaine abusers had significant coronary artery disease at necropsy. Smoking and snorting were the most common routes of cocaine administration. Severe (>75% cross-sectional area) narrowing of 1 or more of the epicardial coronary arteries by atherosclerotic plaque was the most common necropsy findings, consistently with previous reports [19-22]. Occluding thrombus superimposed on atherosclerotic plaque and grossly visible acute myocardial infarct were found only in a small number of subjects. Atherosclerosis has been detected also in young cocaine abusers. The authors suggested that chronic cocaine abuse can accelerate coronary atherosclerosis in young people. The severe coronary narrowing could explain the death due to cocaine overdose in these young subjects. The severity of coronary obstructive lesions has been associated with chronic intimal proliferation and acute platelet thrombosis, mostly in young chronic intravenous cocaine abuser. Cocaine-induced coronary artery spasm may have occurred and produced focal endothelial injury and platelet aggregation. Premature atherosclerotic coronary artery disease has been observed in postmortem studies of long-term cocaine abusers and may provide the nidus for such thrombus formation [23].

Cocaine abuse can also cause degenerative and inflammatory alterations of the myocardium. Cocaine-induced myocarditis has been reported [24-26]. The cardiotoxic effects of catecholamines have been proposed to play an important role in producing myocarditis and toxic cardiomyopathies in cocaine abusers [27].

Some studies suggested that cocaine may cause direct toxicity to the myocardium. Myocardial specimens from endomyocardial biopsies performed in cocaine abusers showed different patterns of myocardial damnage [28]. Multifocal myocyte necrosis, focal myocarditis and dilated cardiomyopathy have been described. Cocaine has been reported also to increase the severity and mortality of viral myocarditis in experimental studies [28]. Ultrastructurally, extensive loss of myofibrils and sarcoplasmic vacuolization were observed. The pathogenesis of acute cocaine-induced toxicity is due by a direct destruction of myofibrils resulting in myocyte necrosis. If these changes are associated with interstitial inflammatory cell infiltrates is not completely known. The occurrence of lymphocytic myocarditis has been also reported. Lymphocytic invasion and interstitial fibrosis have been associated with the long-term cocaine abuse [30].

This review reports macroscopic and microscopic findings from an unpublished case of cocaine-induced myocarditis. (Figure 1)

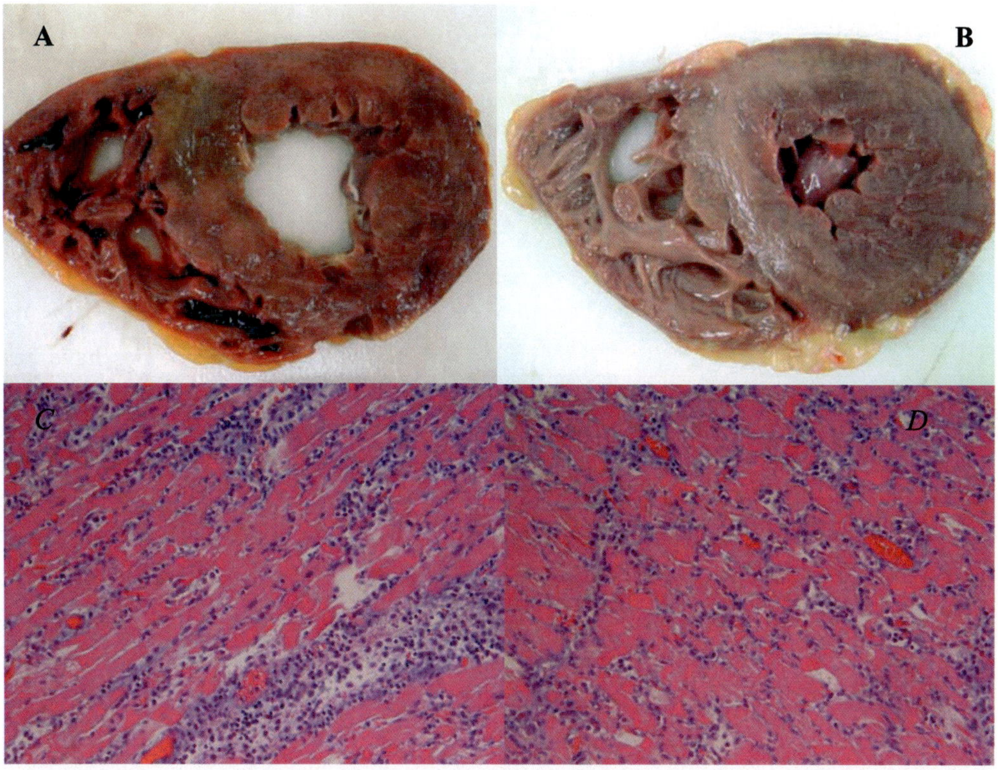

Figure 1 Legend: Cocaine-associated myocarditis in 42 year old male with sudden death 3 days after use of cocaine and with cocaine-metabolites identified in the postmortem blood. [A] and [B]: Cross sections of heart, fresh. The myocardium has a mottled appearance [variation in color from light tan to dark brown], most prominent in the interventricular septum in [A], and more patchy in [B]. [C] and [D]: Contraction band necrosis and mixed mononuclear cell inflammatory infiltrate of myocardium, 200x, hematoxylin and eosin stain. Both [C] and [D] have contraction band necrosis [most prominent in [D] and a mixed mononuclear cell inflammatory infiltrate [macrophages and lymphocytes], with a few, other, scattered inflammatory cells, including a few eosinophils.
Clinical case and photograms are reported with the permission of Dr. Walter Kemp, Department of Pathology, University of Texas Southwestern Medical Center at Dallas, Texas, USA

Cocaine is also well know to induce infective endocarditis. Necropsy studies have been peformed to understand the prevalence and types of cocaine-induced valve damnage. The tricuspid and mitral valves are the most common sites of vegetations. Most of the infection caused sufficient damage to cause dysfunction. Gross examination of the valves at necropsy indicated that the infected valve were anatomically normal in most of studied specimens. Most of the subjects died during their first episode of active infectious endocarditis [31].

Coronary Artery Disease Risk Related to Cocaine Abuse

The Onset Study showed that users of cocaine sustained a transient 24-fold increase in risk of myocardial infarction in the hours immediately after cocaine use and that the elevated risk rapidly decreased thereafter [32]. In addition, cocaine addicts have a risk of no fatal myocardial infarction 7 times more than no cocaine users. The Third National Heath and Nutrition Examination Survey (NHANES III) survey reported that frequent cocaine users, mostly younger subjects, have a significantly higher likelihood of no fatal myocardial infarction than nonusers [33]. In the past few years the incidence of new cocaine users increased among subjects aged 45 and older, but could be underestimated. A large epidemiological study showed that the prevalence of elder subjects using cocaine is higher [2%] than that previously estimated [34]. Several mechanisms can be invoked to explain the increase triggering of myocardial infarction induced by cocaine. Cocaine has been reported to cause acute myocardial infarction both in patients with normal coronary tree [35] and more frequently in patients with underlying coronary disease [33, 36-40].

Pathogenetic Mechanisms of Cocaine-Induced Cardiovascular Complications

a. Coronary Artery Disease

Cocaine has been shown to cause angina pectoris, acute myocardial ischemia and infarction independently of amount ingested, route of administration, and frequency of use. The pathogenesis of cocaine-related myocardial ischemia and infarction is probably multifactorial and includes one or more of the following elements: an increased myocardial oxygen demand in the face of a limited or fixed supply, marked vasoconstriction of the coronary arteries, and enhanced platelet aggregation and thrombus formation. Cocaine induces an increase in the three major determinants of the myocardial oxygen demand: the heart rate, the systemic arterial pressure, and left ventricular contractility. At the same time, the ingestion of even small amounts of the drug causes vasoconstriction of the epicardial coronary arteries, so-called inappropriate vasoconstriction, in that the myocardial oxygen supply decreases even as the demand increases [41-42]. Although cocaine induces vasoconstriction in both normal and diseased segments of the coronary arteries, its effects are more pronounced in the diseased segments [43]. As a result, cocaine users with atherosclerotic coronary artery disease are probably at greater risk for an ischemic event after cocaine use than are cocaine users without coronary artery disease. Cocaine administration induces a vasoconstriction "status" according to several mechanisms. First, cocaine causes a high concentration of norepinephrine and dopamine at postsynaptic receptor sites by blocking their presynaptic reuptake. This effect produces an adrenergic hyperactivity leading to an increase in heart rate, blood pressure, and left ventricular contractility. Second, cocaine induces coronary vasoconstriction in both stenotic and nonstenotic segments through stimulation of α-adrenergic receptors [7]. Cocaine-induced vasoconstriction of the coronary arteries is primarily a result of the stimulation of coronary arterial a -adrenergic receptors, since it may be reversed with phentolamine (an α -adrenergic antagonist) and is exacerbated by propranolol (β-adrenergic antagonist) [44-45]. Labetalol, which has both a- and b-adrenergic–blocking activity, reverses the cocaine-induced increase in systemic arterial pressure but exerts no demonstrable effect on cocaine-induced vasoconstriction of the coronary arteries [46-47]. As the concentrations of cocaine's major metabolites [benzoylecgonine and ecgonine methyl ester] rise, delayed vasoconstriction of the coronary arteries occurs. Thus, the delayed or recurrent vasoconstriction of the coronary arteries appears to be caused by cocaine's major metabolites, which explains why myocardial ischemia or infarction may occur several hours after the ingestion of cocaine.

Third, cocaine has been found to increase the endothelial release of endothelin, (a potent vasocontrictor agent, probably through stimulation of σ-receptors) and decreased production of nitric oxide (a potent vasodilator) [48-49]. Both effects can promote vasoconstriction. The cocaine-induced vasoconstriction/vasospasm may therefore be facilitated by the release of endothelin-1. Cocaine has been suggested to be an exogenous stimulator at endothelial σ-receptors. Moreover, asymptomatic alveolar hemorrhage has been reported in otherwise healthy crack cocaine smokers. These findings seem to be associated with elevated levels of endothelin-1, suggesting a cocaine-induced pulmonary microvascular injury. [50]. Fourth, experimental studies showed that cocaine cause a rapid rise in intracellular free Ca^{2+} [51] and a concomitant loss of intracellular Mg^{2+} [52-53] in vascular smooth muscle cells.

In addition to vasoconstriction, cocaine may induce thrombus formation in the coronary arteries. In fact, cocaine consumption has been associated with thrombosis of coronary arteries. Hemodynamic changes can alter stenotic atherosclerotic plaque, resulting in occlusive thrombus formation. Angiographic studies have shown that cocaine addicts who developed acute myocardial infarction showed occlusive thrombi at nonstenotic sites within their coronary arteries. Cocaine use is associated with enhanced platelet activation and aggregability [23, 53-56] as well as increases in the concentration of plasminogen-activator inhibitor, [23] which may promote thrombus formation. Cocaine has been reported to increase platelet aggregability both in vivo [57] and in vitro experiments. Nevertheless, the mechanism by which cocaine causes platelet activation is still unclear [58]. Cocaine could be not directly responsible of platelet activation and its metabolites may be also involved in this process. Cocaine has been shown to reduce the threshold of rabbit [59] and human platelets to aggregation. [23]. In addition, intravenous cocaine infusion has been documented to activate circulating platelets in dogs. This study reported a significant expression of P-selectin on the surface of circulating platelets after intravenous cocaine infusion. Cocaine-induced up-regulation of local complement expression, possibly via the production of reactive oxygen species has been also suggested to explain the increase platelet aggregability due to the cocaine. [59]. Cocaine has been described to increase membrane attack complex (MAC) formation in the myocardium [60]. Cocaine modifies immune cell function and expression of cytokines and adhesion molecules [60-61]. Cocaine induced a transient erythrocytosis that may increase blood viscosity while maintaining tissue oxygenation during vasoconstriction. An increase in von Willebrand factor without a compensatory change in endogenous fibrinolysis may trigger platelet adhesion, aggregation, and intravascular thrombosis. [62]. Cocaine may also induce a blood doping effect and alter plasma constituents that influence thrombogenicity [63]. In vitro studies have shown that cocaine causes structural defects in the endothelial-cell barrier [64-65], increasing its permeability to low-density lipoprotein and enhancing the expression of endothelial adhesion molecules and leukocyte migration, [66] all of which are associated with the progression of atherosclerosis.

Intracoronary infusion of cocaine has been performed in animals [67] and humans [68-69]. In dogs, a large amount of intravenous cocaine causes a worsening of LV systolic function [67] and a rise in LV end-diastolic pressure. Human studies have been described to be safe and cause no change in coronary arterial blood flow. The achieved intracoronary cocaine concentration was similar in magnitude to that reported in cocaine abusers dying of intoxication, with minimal systemic effects. Intracoronary infusion of cocaine in coronary sinus blood induces severe left ventricular systolic and diastolic function deterioration [69].

b. Left Ventricular Dysfunction

Chronic cocaine exposure has been associated with left ventricular dysfunction. Cocaine may affect left ventricular systolic function by several pathogenetic mechanisms. Cocaine-related myocardial ischemia and infarction are the major cause of left ventricular dysfunction. The sympathetic stimulation induced by cocaine can also contribute to left ventricular function impairment and significant left ventricular morphological changes. The frequent occurrence of myocarditis, observed in postmortem studies of intravenous cocaine users can be an additional cause of left ventricular dysfunction [21]. Recently, experimental studies have shown that cocaine alters cytokine production inducing morphological changes. In fact, it has been reported that cocaine inhibits human endothelial cell IL-8 in the endothelium, [70] induces the transcription of genes responsible for changes in the composition of myocardial collagen and myosin, [71] and causes myocyte apoptosis in fetal myocardial cells [72-74].

Cocaine intoxication can induce LV dysfunction by a direct action or by the concomitant metabolic and acid–base disturbances. Cocaine has been described to alter the physiological calcium handling by cardio-myocytes [75]. In isolated myocardial tissue, cocaine-induced alterations in calcium ion handling result in an increase in the intracytosolic calcium concentration, causing prolongation of the calcium transient and a negative lusitropic effect [76-78]. Other authors proposed a different mechanism that implies a cocaine-induced change in myofilament calcium ion sensitivity leading to impaired LV systolic or diastolic performance.

c. Arrhythmogenic Effects

Cocaine is known to have an arrhythmogenic potential, but the mechanisms of this effect are still unclear and poorly evaluated in humans [79-80]. The risk to develop lethal arrhythmias with cocaine use seems to be related to an abnormal myocardium substrate. Studies in animals showed that cocaine precipitates ventricular arrhythmias and fibrillation in the presence of myocardial ischemia [81]. By the contrast, in absence of myocardial ischemia no arrhythmogenic effect of cocaine has been reported. The sympathomimetic effect of cocaine may increase ventricular irritability and lower the threshold for fibrillation. Cocaine increases the intracellular calcium concentration, resulting in after depolarizations and triggered ventricular arrhythmias [82]. Cocaine blocks the sodium channels and induces an enhanced sympathetic state. Inhibition of cardiac Na current by cocaine is voltage- and frequency dependent. Reduced Na current leads to a depression of Vmax in the action potential that reduces its propagation in the heart, consistent with the finding of a prolonged QRS complex. This effect inhibits the generation and conduction of the action potential inducing QRS and QT intervals prolongation [83]. Prolongation of the action potential duration may be due to reduction of repolarizing K currents [84-85]. This is in accordance with the finding that cocaine is an antagonist of human HERG channels [84-87]. The shortening of the action potential duration obtained at higher concentration may be explained by a reduction of L-type Ca current and blockade of non-inactivated TTX- sensitive Na channels [88-89].

Cocaine abuse has been also described to reduce vagal activity producing a reduction in the variability of the heart rate [90]. Myocardial ischemia and reperfusion and the direct effect of catecholamines on cardiomyocytes have been also invoked to explain the cocaine-induced arrhythmias. These alterations have been described to cause an enhanced cytoplasmic calcium levels, inducing delayed after-potentials, repetitive action-potential generation and premature ventricular beats. Additionally, cocaine can alter conduction velocity by its local anesthetic properties. These effects can produce repolarization phenomena related to potassium channel inhibition inducing a substrate for re-entrant circuits inducing ventricular fibrillation.

ECHOCARDIOGRAPHIC FINDINGS

Several experimental studies reported that cocaine abuse produce left ventricular dysfunction. Long-term cocaine abuse has been shown to cause left ventricular hypertrophy, dilated cardiomyopathy and systolic dysfunction. [90–95] Evidence of left ventricular systolic dysfunction in asymptomatic long-term cocaine users has been also reported. Cocaine has been reported to induce dose-related hemodynamic changes, such as increased heart rate and/or arterial pressure. Some studies suggested that cocaine depresses myocardial function, [96-98] but the effect of cocaine on myocardial contractility is still not completely clear. In fact, some studies have reported a cocaine-induced reduced coronary flow and spasm [99], whereas others described vasodilatation or no vascular changes, [100-101] or LV performance dysfunction not related to myocardial depression [102]. The impaired LV function has been suggested to be associated with the cocaine-induced myocardial depression [103-104]. Nevertheless, the results are still controversial. The reduction in ejection-phase indexes of LV function has been reported to be due to increased wall stress without change in the relation between wall stress and fractional shortening. [103]. Other studies on closed-chest, sedated dogs indicated that the primary effects of infused cocaine seem to be due to altered loading conditions. The ejection fraction and fractional shortening decrease in proportion to increases in end-systolic wall stress. These data support the lack of important myocardial depression, at least as a consequence of local ischemia. Nevertheless, these authors did not exclude the possibility of a transient decrease in myocardial contractility very early in the infusion. [102]

Systolic parameters, such as fractional shortening and ejection fraction have been found decreased in experimental studies. Intravenous cocaine infusion induced also an increase of LV end-diastolic pressure end-systolic dimension. LV end-systolic wall thickness was reduced, suggesting also impairment on midwall systolic function. Cocaine has been reported to reduce LV positive dP/dt in some studis [96-97,105], but was found to be unchanged in others [98].

Significant LV hypertrophy or regional wall motion abnormalities have been described in nonhospitalized cocaine users. Cocaine-associated LV hypertrophy and dysfunction may be restricted to certain high-risk groups of chronic cocaine users [106].

Newborn infants exposed to cocaine in utero have been reported to show left ventricular diastolic segmental abnormalities [107-108]. It is unknown whether these abnormalities are transient because of short-term effects or persist in older infants, possibly reflecting a teratogenic effect of cocaine. These studies showed that prenatal cocaine exposure in asymptomatic infants leads to higher global and segmental fractional area changes and asynchrony during diastole.

Cocaine-Related Chest Pain

Large observational studies on the management of the cocaine-related chest pain have been performed [109-110]. These studies suggested that a 9-to-12 hour period in chest pain observation is a sufficient period to have a very low risk of death or myocardial infarction in cocaine users with out evidence of previous cardiovascular diseases.

Since nitroglycerin [111-112] and verapamil [113] reverse cocaine-induced hypertension and vasoconstriction of the coronary arteries, they are the agents of choice for patients with cocaine-associated chest pain. By the contrast propranolol a b adrenergic–blocking agent — exacerbates cocaine-induced vasoconstriction of the coronary arteries, and therefore it should not be used in patients with cocaine-related chest pain [40]. Aspirin should be administered to patients with cocaine induced myocardial ischemia to inhibit platelet aggregation. Benzodiazepines may attenuate cocaine's toxic effects on the heart and the nervous system. Because of the limited experience with thrombolytic therapy in patients with cocaine-related infarction, [114-115] reports of catastrophic complications associated with its use in cocaine users and the difficulty involved in using standard electrocardiographic criteria to identify myocardial infarction, we caution against the routine use of thrombolytic therapy in patients who may have cocaine-related infarction.

Case Reports from the Literature

Some usual and unusual cocaine-related cardiovascular complications cases are reported in this paragraph.

Aortic Dissection

Cocaine has been described to induce aortic dissection representing a severe clinical and surgical emergency [116-122]. Acute aortic dissection was associated with recent crack cocaine use in more than one third of all cases. The typical patient with cocaine-related aortic dissection is younger and more likely to be black, compared with other patients with aortic dissection, and has untreated hypertension and left ventricular hypertrophy. Aortic dissection should be considered as a possible diagnosis in recent cocaine users who have severe chest pain. The resulting increases in heart rate, blood pressure, and myocardial contractility would theoretically increase the risk of aortic dissection, particularly if baseline arterial pressure were elevated. Several cases of aortic dissections have been reported and some of them have been detected by transesophageal echocardiography [123-125].

Unusual Cardiac Thrombus Formation

Chronic abuse of cocaine can induce endothelial alterations allowing thrombus formation. A worm-shaped thrombus mimicking Chiari's network in a cocaine user has been reported (Figure 2) [126]. Serpiginous and mobile thrombus can simulate Chiari's network causing a difficult differential diagnosis.

A rare case of biventricular myocardial infarction induced by cocaine and a large left and a smaller right ventricular apical thrombus, detected by serial multiplane transesophageal echocardiography, has been reported [127]. A case of renal infarction, uncommonly described, and aortic thrombus in a patient who used nasal cocaine has been reported [128].

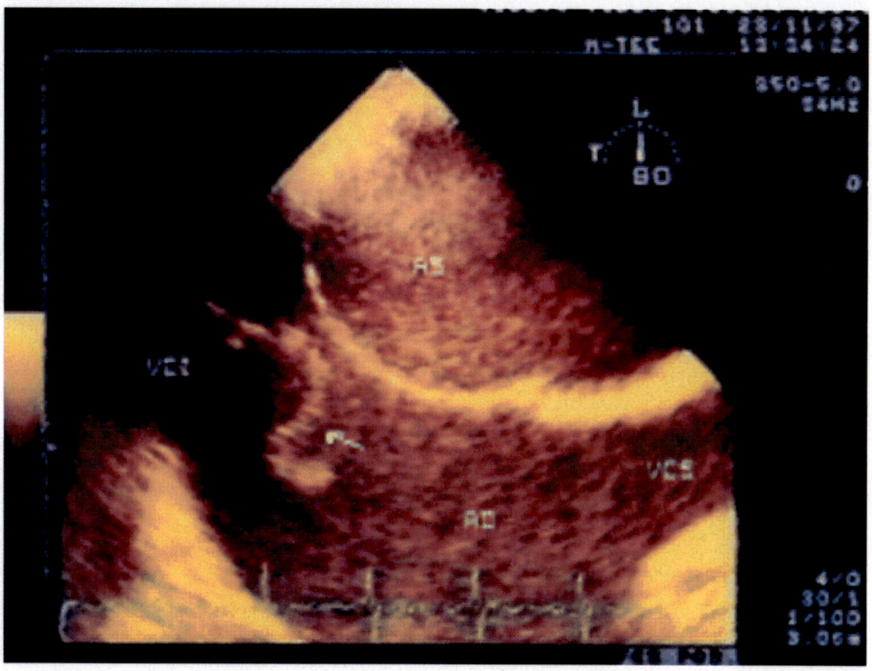

Figure 2 legend Transesophageal echocardiogram. Worm-shaped thrombus mimicking Chiari's network in a young cocaine user (Iacobellis et al Heart. 2002; 88:4)

Intravascular Ultrasound Imaging

A case of acute myocardial infarction in a young cocaine abuser was reported. The left anterior descending coronary artery lesion was described as eccentric by angiography studies and confirmed by intravascular ultrasound (IVUS) images, with positive remodeling and hypoechoic features. The authors suggested that IVUS imaging could be an useful diagnostic tool characterizing the extent and morphology of coronary atherosclerosis in patients suffering cocaine-associated acute myocardial infarction [129].

Endocarditis

Cocaine, especially when administered intravenously, can produce infectious endocarditis and valvular endothelium damages. The prevalence of valvular has been reported to be significantly higher in patients with intravenous cocaine addiction compared to nasal insufflation addicts. Tricuspid valve is the most frequently involved, and this could be due to previous tricuspid valve damage, frequently observed in intravenous drug-addicts [130].

Anaesthesiological Emergency

Cocaine abuse could represent also an emergency during surgery. In the literature, anaesthesia is regarded as safe for patients with chronic cocaine misuse after abstinence of 24 hours, but a deep anaesthesia and a cocaine-free interval of at least one week before elective surgical procedures is strongly recommended. Clinically, cocaine is used topically in ophthalmology due to its local analgesic and strong vasoconstrictive properties. Cocaine has a similar effect on the CNS as amphetamines and produces euphoria and hallucinations. Cocaine acts indirectly on sympathetic stimulation, release of dopamine and inhibition of catecholamine metabolism. Intoxication with cocaine leads to respiratory depression, arrhythmias, ventricular fibrillation and death [131].

Acknowledgments

I thank Dr. Walter Kemp, Department of Pathology at the University of Texas Southwestern Medical Center, Dallas, Texas for his precious expertise and for providing the striking cocaine-associated myocarditis pictures.

References

[1] Office of Applied Studies. Year-end 1999 emergency department data from the Drug Abuse Warning Network. Rockville, Md.: Substance Abuse and Mental Health Services Administration, August 2000. (DHHS publication no. (SMA) 00-3462.)

[2] Summary of findings from the 1999 National Household Survey on Drug Abuse. Rockville, Md.: Substance Abuse and Mental Health Services Administration, August 2000. (DHHS publication no. (SMA) 00-3466)

[3] Javaid JI, Fischman MW, Schuster CR, Dekirmenjian H, Davis JM Cocaine plasma concentration: relation to physiological and subjective effects in humans. *Science.* 1978; 202: 227-8.

[4] Lange RA, Hillis LD. Cardiovascular complications of cocaine use. *N Engl J Med,* 2001; 345: 351-358

[5] Ness RB, Grisso JA, Hirschinger N, et al. Cocaine and tobacco use and the risk of spontaneous abortion. *N Engl J Med* 1999; 340:333-9

[6] Brogan WC 3rd, Lange RA, Glamann DB, Hillis LD Recurrent coronary vasoconstriction caused by intranasal cocaine: possible role for metabolites. Ann *Intern Med.* 1992 1; 116:556-61

[7] Moliterno DJ, Willard JE, Lange RA, Negus BH, Boehrer JD, Glamann DB, Landau C, Rossen JD, Winniford MD, Hillis LD. Coronary-Artery Vasoconstriction Induced by Cocaine, Cigarette Smoking, or Both *N Engl. J Med,* 1994; 330: 454 – 459

[8] Boehrer JD, Moliterno DJ, Willard JE, Snyder RW II, Horton RP, Glamann DB, Lange RA, Hillis LD. Hemodynamic effects of intranasal cocaine in humans. *J Am Coll Cardiol.* 1992;20:90–93

[9] Raczkowski, V.F.C., Y.M. Hernandez, H.K. Erzouki, T.P. Abrahams, A.K. Mandal, P. Hamosh, E. Friedman, J.A. Quest, K.L. Dretchen, and R.A. Gillis. Cocaine acts in the central nervous system to inhibit sympathetic neural activity. *J. Pharmacol. Exp. Ther.* 1991. 257:511–519.

[10] Gantenberg, N.S., and G.R. Hageman. Cocaine depresses cardiacsympathetic efferent activity in anesthetized dogs. *J. Cardiovasc. Pharmacol;* 1991. 17:434–439.

[11] Hageman, G.R., and T. Simor. Attenuation of the cardiac effects of cocaine by dizocilpine. *Am. J. Physiol.* 1993. 264:H1890–H1895.

[12] Knuepfer, M.M., Branch CA Cardiovascular responses to cocaine are initially mediated by the central nervous system. *J. Pharmacol. Exp.Ther.* 1992; 263:734–741.

[13] Wilkerson, R.D. Cardiovascular effects of cocaine in conscious dogs: importance of fully functional autonomic and central nervous systems. *J Pharmacol. Exp. Ther.* 1988; 246:466–471.

[14] Andresen, M.C., M. Yang, S.H. Nelson, and O.S. Steinsland. Cocaine inhibits baroreflex control of arterial pressure by action at arterial baroreceptor.baroreflex buffering of sympathetic activation during exercise-induced elevations in arterial pressure. *J. Clin. Invest.* 1990; 86:1855–1861

[15] Trouve, R., Nahas G, Latour C. Inhibition by cocaine of the baroreflex in the rat. *Proc. Soc. Exp. Biol. Med.* 1992; 201:215–218.

[16] Jacobsen TN, Grayburn PA, Snyder II RW, Hansen J, Chavoshan B, Landau C, Lange RA, Hillis LD, Victor RG. Effects of Intranasal Cocaine on Sympathetic Nerve Discharge in Humans *J. Clin. Invest.* 1997. 99:628–634

[17] Eisenberg MJ, Yakel DL, Mendelson J, Redberg RF, Jones RT, Foster E. Immediate effects of intravenous cocaine on the thoracic aorta and coronary arteries. A transesophageal echocardiographic study. *Chest.* 1996 ;110:147-54.

[18] Dressler FA, Malekzadeh S, Roberts WC Quantitative analysis of amounts of coronary arterial narrowing in cocaine addicts. *Am J Cardiol* 1990;65:303-308

[19] Simpson RW, Edwards WD. Pathogenesis of cocaine-induced ischemic heart disease. Autopsy findings in a 21-year-old man. *Arch Pathol Lab Med* 1986; 110:479-484

[20] Isner JM, Estes NAM III, Thompson PD, Costanzo-Nordin MR, Subramanian R, Miller G, Katsas G, Sweeney K, Sturner WQ. Acute cardiac events temporally related to cocaine abuse. *N Engl J Med* 1986;315:1438-1443

[21] Virmani R, Robinowitz M, Smialek JE, Smyth DF. Cardiovascular effects of cocaine: an autopsy study of 40 patients. *Am Heart J* 1988;115:1068-1076

[22] Stemberg RG, Winniford MD, Hillis LD, Dowling GP, Buja LM. Simultaneous acute thrombosis of two major coronary arteries following intravenous cocaine use. *Arch Pathol Lab Med* 1989; 113:521-524

[23] Rezkalla SH, Mazza JJ, Kloner RA, Tillema V, Chang SH. Effects of cocaine on human platelets in healthy subjects. *Am J Cardiol* 1993;72:243-6

[24] Welch RD Ischemia, contraction band necrosis and myocarditis. *Ann Emerg Med.* 1991; 20:591-2.

[25] Jentzen JM Cocaine-induced myocarditis. *Am Heart J.* 1989; 117:1398-9

[26] Kloner RA, Hale S, Alker K, Rezkalla S The effects of acute and chronic cocaine use on the heart. *Circulation.* 1992; 85:407-19.

[27] Rump AF, Theisohn M, Klaus W The pathophysiology of cocaine cardiotoxicity. *Forensic Sci Int.* 19950; 71:103-15

[28] Peng SK, French WJ, Pelikan PC Direct cocaine cardiotoxicity demonstrated by endomyocardial biopsy. *Arch Pathol Lab Med.* 1989; 113:842-5

[29] Wang JF, Zhang J, Min JY, Sullivan MF, Crumpacker CS, Abelmann WH, Morgan JP Cocaine enhances myocarditis induced by encephalomyocarditis virus in murine model. *Am J Physiol Heart Circ Physiol.* 2002 ;282:H956-63

[30] Simpson RW, Edwards WD Pathogenesis of cocaine-induced ischemic heart disease. Autopsy findings in a 21-year-old man. *Arch Pathol Lab Med.* 1986;110:479-84

[31] Dressler FA, Roberts WC Infective endocarditis in opiate addicts: analysis of 80 cases studied at necropsy. *Am J Cardiol.* 1989; 63:1240-57

[32] Mittleman MA, Mintzer D, Maclure M, Tofler GH, Sherwood JB, Muller JE Triggering of Myocardial Infarction by Cocaine *Circulation.* 1999; 99 :2737-2741

[33] Qureshi AI, Suri MF, Guterman LR, Hopkins LN, Cocaine use and the likelihood of nonfatal myocardial infarction and stroke: data from the Third National Health and Nutrition Examination Survey. *Circulation.* 2001 103:502-6

[34] Rivers E, Shirazi E, Aurora T, Mullen M, Gunnerson K, Sheridan B, Eichhorn L, Tomlanovich M. Cocaine use in elder patients presenting to an inner-city emergency department. *J Acad Emerg* 2004; 11:874-877

[35] Minor RL Jr, Scott BD, Brown DD, Winniford MD. Cocaine-induced myocardial infarction in patients with normal coronary arteries. *Ann Intern Med.* 1991; 115:797–806

[36] Smith HW III, Liberman HA, Brody SL, Battey LL, Donohue BC, Morris DC. Acute myocardial infarction temporally related to cocaine use. Clinical, angiographic, and pathophysiologic observations. *Ann Intern Med.* 1987; 107:13–18;

[37] Williams MJ, Stewart RA. Serial angiography in cocaine-induced myocardial infarction. *Chest.* 1997; 111:822–824; Hollander JE, Hoffman RS. Cocaine-induced myocardial infarction: an analysis and review of the literature. *J Emerg Med.* 1992; 10:169–177;

[38] Cheng TO Risk of acute myocardial infarction in cocaine abusers. *Circulation.* 2000; 101:E227

[39] Siegel AJ Risk of cocaine-induced myocardial infarction during sport. *Circulation.* 2000; 102:E17;

[40] Cregler LL, Mark H. Relation of acute myocardial infarction to cocaine abuse. *Am J Cardiol.* 1985; 56:794

[41] Lange RA, Cigarroa RG, Yancy CW Jr, Willard JE, Popma JJ, Sills MN, McBride W, Kim AS, Hillis LD. Cocaine-induced coronary-artery vasoconstriction. *N Engl J Med.* 1989; 321:1557–1562

[42] Benzaquen BS, Cohen V, Eisenberg MJ Effects of cocaine on the coronary arteries *Am Heart J.* 2001; 142:402-10

[43] Flores ED, Lange RA, Cigarroa RG, Hillis LD. Effect of cocaine on coronary artery dimensions in atherosclerotic coronary artery disease: enhanced vasoconstriction at sites of significant stenoses. *J Am Coll Cardiol* 1990; 16:74-9

[44] Hollander JE, Carter WA, Hoffman RS. Use of phentolamine for cocaine- induced myocardial ischemia. *N Engl J Med* 1992;327:361

[45] Boehrer JD, Moliterno DJ, Willard JE, Hillis LD, Lange RA. Influence of labetalol on cocaine-induced coronary vasoconstriction in humans.*Am J Med* 1993;94:608-10

[46] Sofuoglu M, Brown S, Babb DA, Pentel PR, Hatsukami DK. Effects of labetalol treatment on the physiological and subjective response to smoked cocaine. *Pharmacol Biochem Behav* 2000; 65:255-9

[47] Lange RA, Cigarroa RG, Flores ED, et al. Potentiation of cocaine induced coronary vasoconstriction by beta-adrenergic blockade. *Ann InternMed* 1990; 112:897-90

[48] Wilbert-Lampen U, Seliger C, Zilker T, Arendt RM. Cocaine increases the endothelial release of immunoreactive endothelin and its concentrations in human plasma and urine: reversal by coincubation with sigmareceptor antagonists. *Circulation* 1998; 98:385-90

[49] Mo W, Singh AK, Arruda JA, Dunea G. Role of nitric oxide in cocaine-induced acute hypertension. *Am J Hypertens* 1998; 11:708-1

[50] Baldwin GC, Choi R, Roth MD, Shay AH, Kleerup EC, Simmons MS, Tashkin DP Evidence of chronic damage to the pulmonary microcirculation in habitual users of alkaloidal ["crack"] cocaine. *Chest.* 2002; 121:1231-8

[51] Zhang A, Cheng TP, Altura BT, Altura BM. Acute cocaine results in rapid rises in intracellular free calcium concentration in canine cerebral vascular smooth muscle cells: possible relation to etiology of stroke. *Neurosci Lett.* 1996; 215:57–59

[52] Altura BM, Zhang A, Cheng TP, Altura BT. Cocaine induces rapid loss of intracellular free Mg^{2+} in cerebral vascular smooth muscle cells. *Eur J Pharmacol.* 1993; 246:299–301

[53] Huang QF, Gebrewold A, Altura BT, Altura BM. Cocaine-induced cerebral vascular damage can be ameliorated by Mg^{2+} in rat brain. *Neurosci Lett.* 1990; 109:113–116

[54] Stenberg RG, Winniford MD, Hillis LD, Dowling GP, Buja LM. Simultaneous acute thrombosis of two major coronary arteries following intravenous cocaine use. *Arch Pathol Lab Med* 1989; 113:521-4

[55] Kugelmass AD, Oda A, Monahan K, Cabral C, Ware JA. Activation of human platelets by cocaine. *Circulation* 1993; 88:876-83

[56] Rinder HM, Ault KA, Jatlow PI, Kosten TR, Smith BR. Platelet alpha- granule release in cocaine users. *Circulation* 1994; 90:1162-7

[57] Kugelmass AD, Shannon RP, Yeo EL, Ware JA. Intravenous cocaine induces platelet activation in the conscious dog. *Circulation.* 1995; 91:1336–1340

[58] Togna G, Tempesta E, Togna AR, Dolci N, Cebo B, Caprino L. Platelet responsiveness and biosynthesis of thromboxane and prostacyclin in response to in vitro cocaine treatment. *Haemostasis.* 1985; 15:100–107

[59] Tanhehco EJ, K. Yasojima, P. L. McGeer,. Lucchesi BR. Acute Cocaine Exposure Up-Regulates Complement Expression in Rabbit Heart *J. Pharmacol. Exp. Ther.,* , 2000; 292: 201 – 208

[60] Pellegrino T, Bayer BM In vivo effects of cocaine on immune cell function. *J Neuroimmunol* 1998; 83: 139-147

[61] Gan XH, Zhang L, Berger O, Stins MF, Way D, Taub DD, Chang SL, Kim KS, House SD, Weinand M, Witte M, Graves MC and Fiala M Cocaine enhances brain endothelial adhesion molecules and leukocyte migration. *Clin Immunol* 1999; 91: 68-76

[62] Siegel AJ, Sholar MB, Mendelson JH, Lukas SE, Kaufman MJ, Renshaw PF, McDonald JC, Lewandrowski KB, Apple FS, Stec JJ, Lipinska I, Tofler GH, Ridker PM.Cocaine-induced erythrocytosis and increase in von Willebrand factor: evidence for drug-related blood doping and prothrombotic effects. *Arch Intern Med.* 1999; 159:1925-9

[63] Shannon RP, Manders WT, Shen YT. Role of blood doping in the coronary vasoconstrictor response to cocaine. *Circulation.* 1995; 92:96-105

[64] Kolodgie FD, Virmani R, Cornhill JF, Herderick EE, Smialek J. Increase in atherosclerosis and adventitial mast cells in cocaine abusers: an alternative mechanism of cocaine-associated coronary vasospasm and thrombosis. *J Am Coll Cardiol* 1991; 17:1553-60

[65] Kolodgie FD, Wilson PS, Mergner WJ, Virmani R. Cocaine-induced increase in the permeability function of human vascular endothelial cell monolayers. *Exp Mol Pathol* 1999; 66:109-22

[66] Gan X, Zhang L, Berger O, et al. Cocaine enhances brain endothelial adhesion molecules and leukocyte migration. *Clin Immunol* 1999; 91:68-76

[67] Bedotto JB, Abel FL, Wilson SP, Zhao R, Fennell WH. Cocaine depresses the canine myocardium. *Circ Shock.* 1989;28:309–319

[68] Daniel WC, Lange RA, Landau C, Willard JE, Hillis LD. Effects of the intracoronary infusion of cocaine on coronary arterial dimensions and blood flow in humans. *Am J Cardiol.* 1996;78:288–291

[69] Pitts WR, Vongpatanasin W, Cigarroa JE, Hillis LD, Lange RA. Effects of the intracoronary infusion of cocaine on left ventricular systolic and diastolic function in humans. *Circulation* 1998; 97:1270-1273

[70] Mao JT, Zhu LX, Sharma S, et al. Cocaine inhibits human endothelial cell IL-8 production: the role of transforming growth factor-beta. *Cell Immunol* 1997; 181:38-43

[71] Besse S, Assayag P, Latour C, et al. Molecular characteristics of cocaine-induced cardiomyopathy in rats. *Eur J Pharmacol* 1997; 338:123-129

[72] Xiao Y, He J, Gilbert RD, Zhang L. Cocaine induces apoptosis in fetal myocardial cells through a mitochondria-dependent pathway. *J Pharmacol Exp Ther* 2000; 292:8-14

[73] Li G, Xiao Y, Zhang L Cocaine Induces Apoptosis in Fetal Rat Myocardial Cells through the p38 Mitogen-Activated Protein Kinase and Mitochondrial/Cytochrome c Pathways. *J Pharmacol Exp Ther.* 2004 Sep 13

[74] Xiao Y, Xiao D, He J, Zhang L Maternal cocaine administration during pregnancy induces apoptosis in fetal rat heart. *J Cardiovasc Pharmacol.* 2001; 37:639-48

[75] Perreault CL, Hague NL, Morgan KG, Allen PD, Morgan JP. Negative inotropic and relaxant effects of cocaine on myopathic human ventricular myocardium and epicardial coronary arteries in vitro. *Cardiovasc Res* 1993; 27:262-268

[76] Perreault CL, Morgan KG, Morgan JP. Effects of cocaine on intracellular calcium handling in cardiac and vascular smooth muscle. In: Thadani P, ed. Cardiovascular toxicity of cocaine: underlying mechanisms. *Research monograph* 108. Washington, D.C.: Government Printing Office, 1991:139-53. [DHHS publication no. [ADM] 91-1767.]

[77] Perreault CL, Hague NL, Ransil BJ, Morgan JP. The effects of cocaine on intracellular Ca^{2+} handling and myofilament Ca^{2+} responsiveness of ferret ventricular myocardium. *Br J Pharmacol.* 1990; 101:679–685

[78] Huang L, Woolf JH, Ishiguro Y, Morgan JP. Effect of cocaine and methylecgonidine on intracellular Ca2+ and myocardial contraction in cardiac myocytes. *Am J Physiol* 1997; 273:H893-H901

[79] Inoue H, Zipes DP. Cocaine-induced supersensitivity and arrhythmogenesis. *J Am Coll Cardiol* 1988; 11:867-74.

[80] Kerns W II, Garvey L, Owens J. Cocaine-induced wide complex dysrhythmia. *J Emerg Med* 1997; 15:321-9

[81] Kanani PM, Guse PA, Smith WM, Barnett A, Ellinwood EH Jr. Acute deleterious effects of cocaine on cardiac conduction, hemodynamics, and ventricular fibrillation threshold: effects of interaction with a selective dopamine D1 antagonist SCH 39166. *J Cardiovasc Pharmacol* 1998; 32:42-8

[82] Wit AL, Rosen MR. After depolarizations and triggered activity. In: Fozzard HA, Haber E, Jennings RB, Katz AM, Morgan HE, eds. *The heart and cardiovascular system: scientific foundations*. Vol. 2. New York: Raven Press, 1986:1449-90

[83] Perera R, Kraebber A, Schwartz MJ. Prolonged QT interval and cocaine use. *J Electrocardiol* 1997; 30:337-9

[84] Zhang S, Rajamani S, Chen Y, Gong Q, Rong Y, Zhou Z et al. Cocaine blocks HERG, but not KvLQT11mink, potassium channels. *Mol Pharmacol* 2001; 59:1069–1079.

[85] Karle CA, Kiehn J. An ion channel 'addicted' to ether, alcohol and cocaine: the HERG potassium channel. *Cardiovasc Res* 2002; 53:6

[86] O 'Leary ME. Inhibition of HERG potassium channels by coca ethylene: a metabolite of cocaine and ethanol. *Cardiovasc Res* 2002; 53:59–67.

[87] Z hang S, Rajamani S, Chen Y, Gong Q, Rong Y, Zhou Z et al. Cocaine blocks HERG, but not KvLQT11mink, potassium channels. *Mol Pharmacol* 2001; 59:1069–1079.

[88] Clarkson CW, Xu Y-U, Chang C, Follmer CH. Analysis of the ionic basis for cocaine's biphasic effect on action potential duration in guinea pig ventricular myocytes. *J Mol Cell Cardiol* 1996; 28:667

[89] Premkumar LS. Selective potentiation of L-type calcium channel currents by cocaine in cardiac myocytes. *Mol Pharmacol* 1999; 56:1138–1142.

[90] Billman GE, Lappi MD. Effects of cocaine on cardiac vagal tone before and during coronary artery occlusion: cocaine exacerbates the autonomic response to myocardial ischemia. *J Cardiovasc Pharmacol* 1993; 22: 869-76.

[91] Bertolet BD, Freund G, Martin CA, Perchalski DL, Williams CM, Pepine CJ. Unrecognized left ventricular dysfunction in an apparently healthy cocaine abuse population. *Clin Cardiol.* 1990; 13:323-328

[92] Om A, Warner M, Sabri N, Cecich L, Vetrovec G. Frequency of coronary artery disease and left ventricular dysfunction in cocaine users. *Am J Cardiol.* 1992; 69:1549-1552

[93] Brickner ME, Willard JE, Eichhorn EJ, Black J, Grayburn PA. Left ventricular hypertrophy associated with chronic cocaine abuse. *Circulation* 1991;84:1130-1135

[94] Wiener RS, Lockhart JT, Schwartz RG. Dilated cardiomyopathy and cocaine abuse: report of two cases. *Am J Med* 1986; 81:699-701

[95] Chokshi SK, Moore R, Pandian NG, Isner JM. Reversible cardiomyopathy associated with cocaine intoxication. *Ann Intern Med* 1989; 111:1039-1040

[96] Wilkerson RD. Cardiovascular effects of cocaine in conscious dogs: importance of fully functional autonomic and central nervous systems. *J Pharmacol Exp Ther.* 1988; 246:466-471

[97] Hale SL, Alker KJ, Rezkalla S, Figures G, Kloner RA. Adverse effects of cocaine on cardiovascular dynamics, myocardial blood flow and coronary artery diameter in an experimental model. *Am Heart J.* 1989; 118:927-933

[98] Bedotto JB, Lee RW, Lancaster LD, Olajos M, Goldman S. Cocaine and cardiovascular function in dogs: effects on heart and peripheral circulation. *J Am Coll Cardiol.* 1988; 11:1337-1342.

[99] Chapman SF, Lust RM, Morrison RF, Etemad-Moghadam R, Chitwood WR, Austin EH. Possible mechanism of cocaine-induced sudden cardiac death. *FASEB J.* 1989; 3:A40

[100] Fraker TD, Temesy-Armos PN, Brewster PS, Wilkerson RD. Mechanism of cocaine-induced myocardial depression in dogs. *Circulation.* 1990; 81:1012-1016

[101] Friedrichs GS, Wei H-M, Merrill GF. Coronary vasodilation caused by intravenous cocaine in the anesthetized beagle. *Can J Physiol Pharmacol.* 1990; 68:893-897

[102] Mehta PM, Grainger TA, Lust RM, Movahed A, Terry J, Gilliland M.G.F, Jolly SR, Effect of Cocaine on Left Ventricular Function Relation to Increased Wall Stress and Persistence After Treatment *Circulation.* 1995; 91:3002-3009

[103] Liu C-P, Tunin C, Kass DA. Transient time course of cocaine-induced cardiac depression versus sustained peripheral vasoconstriction. *J Am Coll Cardiol.* 1993; 21:260-268

[104] Stambler BS, Komamura K, Ihara T, Shannon RP. Acute intravenous cocaine causes transient depression followed by enhanced left ventricular function in conscious dogs. *Circulation.* 1993; 87:1687-1697

[105] Abel FL, Wilson SP, Zhao RR, Fennell WH. Cocaine depresses the canine myocardium. *Circ Shock.* 1989; 28:309-319

[106] Eisenberg MJ, Jue J, Mendelson J, Jones RT, Schiller NB. Left ventricular morphologic features and function in nonhospitalized cocaine users: a quantitative two-dimensional echocardiographic study. *Am Heart J.* 1995; 129:941-6

[107] Mehta SK, Super DM, Connuck D, Kirchner HL, Salvator A, Singer L, Fradley LG, Thomas JD, Sun JP. Diastolic alterations in infants exposed to intrauterine cocaine: a follow-up study by color kinesis. *J Am Soc Echocardiogr.* 2002; 15:1361-6

[108] Mehta SK, Super DM, Salvator A, Singer L, Connuck D, Fradley LG, Harcar-Sevcik RA, Thomas JD, Sun JP Diastolic filling abnormalities by color kinesis in newborns exposed to intrauterine cocaine. *J Am Soc Echocardiogr.* 2002; 15:447-53.

[109] Amin M, Gabelman G, Karpel J, Buttrick P. Acute myocardial infarction and chest pain syndromes after cocaine use. *Am J Cardiol* 1990; 66:1434-7

[110] Weber JE, Shofer FS, Larkin GL, Kalaria AS, Hollander JE. Validation of a brief observation period for patients with cocaine-associated chest pain. *N Engl J Med* 2003; 348:510-7

[111] Baumann BM, Perrone J, Hornig SE, Shofer FS, Hollander JE. Randomized, double-blind, placebo-controlled trial of diazepam, nitroglycerin, or both for treatment of patients with potential cocaine-associated acute coronary syndromes. *Acad Emerg Med* 2000; 7:878-85

[112] Brogan WC III, Lange RA, Kim AS, Moliterno DJ, Hillis LD. Alleviation of cocaine-induced coronary vasoconstriction by nitroglycerin. *J Am Coll Cardiol* 1991; 18:581-6

[113] Negus BH, Willard JE, Hillis LD. Alleviation of cocaine-induced coronary vasoconstriction with intravenous verapamil. *Am J Cardiol* 1994; 73:510

[114] Hollander JE, Burstein JL, Hoffman RS, Shih RD, Wilson LD. Cocaine-associated myocardial infarction: clinical safety of thrombolytic therapy. *Chest* 1995; 107:1237-41.

[115] Hoffman RS, Hollander JE. Thrombolytic therapy and cocaine induced myocardial infarction. *Am J Emerg Med* 1996; 14:693-5

[116] Chang RA, Rossi NF. Intermittent cocaine use associated with recurrent dissection of the thoracic and abdominal aorta. *Chest.* 1995; 108: 1758–1762

[117] Perron AD, Gibbs M. Thoracic aortic dissection secondary to crack cocaine ingestion. *Am J Emerg Med.* 1997; 15: 507–509

[118] Rashid J, Eisenberg MJ, Topol EJ. Cocaine-induced aortic dissection. *Am Heart J.* 1996; 132: 1301–1304

[119] Madu EC, Shala B, Baugh D. Crack-cocaine-associated aortic dissection in early pregnancy: a case report. *Angiology.* 1999; 50: 163–168

[120] Famularo G, Polchi S, Di Bona G, et al. Acute aortic dissection after cocaine and sildenafil abuse. *J Emerg Med.* 2001; 21: 78–79

[121] Eskander KE, Brass NS, Gelfand ET. Cocaine abuse and coronary artery dissection. *Ann Thorac Surg.* 2001; 71: 340–341

[122] Jaffe BD, Broderick TM, Leier CV. Cocaine-induced coronary-artery dissection. *N Engl J Med.* 1994; 330: 510–511

[123] Hsue, PY, Salinas PY, Bolger AF, Benowitz NL, Waters DD Acute Aortic Dissection Related to Crack Cocaine *Circulation.* 2002; 105:1592

[124] Sherzoy A, Sadler D, Brown J Cocaine-related acute aortic dissection diagnosed by transesophageal echocardiography. *Am Heart J.* 1994 ; 128:841-3

[125] Om A, Porter T, Mohanty PK Transesophageal echocardiographic diagnosis of acute aortic dissection complicating cocaine abuse. *Am Heart J.* 1992; 123:532-4

[126] Iacobellis G, Puletti M, Vitarelli A. Worm-shaped thrombus mimicking Chiari's network in a cocaine user. *Heart.* 2002; 88:4

[127] Espinola-Zavaleta NG, Vargas-Barron J, Vazquez-Neira J, Romero-Cardenas A, Keirns C.Echocardiographic Diagnosis of Biventricular Thrombi in a Cocaine-Induced Myocardial Infarction. *Echocardiography.* 1998; 15:499-502

[128] Mochizuki Y, Zhang M, Golestaneh L, Thananart S, Coco M.Acute aortic thrombosis and renal infarction in acute cocaine intoxication: a case report and review of literature. *Clin Nephrol.* 2003 ; 60:130-3

[129] Erwin MB, Hoyle JR, Smith CH, Deliargyris EN Cocaine and accelerated atherosclerosis: insights from intravascular ultrasound. *Int J Cardiol.* 2004; 93:301-3

[130] Gullone N, de Rosa AF, Pellegrini A, Naveira J, Muzzio E, Rigou DG. Echocardiographic detection of heart valvular disease in cocaine addict patients *Medicina (B Aires)* 2003; 63:711-4.

[131] Vagts DA, Boklage C, Galli C Intraoperative ventricular fibrillation in a patient with chronic cocaine abuse--a case report *Anaesthesiol Reanim*. 2004; 29:19-24

In: Cocaine and Heroin Abuse Research
Editor: Lidia A. Pizzoli, pp. 81-95
ISBN 1-60021-076-7

Chapter 4

COGNITIVE DYSFUNCTION IN COCAINE ABUSE: EVIDENCE FOR IMPAIRMENTS IN IMPULSE CONTROL AND DECISION-MAKING

***Laurie M. Rilling*[*,†] *and Bryon Adinoff*[†,‡]**
[†]University of Texas Southwestern Medical Center, USA
[‡]VA North Texas Health Care System,USA

ABSTRACT

Cocaine is one of the most widely abused psychoactive substances in the United States, with an estimated 1.3 million Americans using the drug on a regular (at least monthly) basis. Even occasional cocaine use can result in serious medical complications, such as cardiac damage, vascular ischemia, respiratory failure, and persistent alterations in neural function. In this chapter, we will examine the most recent research on impulsivity and decision-making in cocaine use. First, we will present a brief overview of the cognitive processes affected by cocaine use. Next, we will review the relevant literature detailing the status of inhibitory control and decision-making in cocaine users, as well as their proposed neuroanatomical correlates. Finally, we will attempt to integrate these findings with the current view of cocaine addiction and relapse, with an emphasis on the role of impulsivity and decision-making in continued cocaine use despite the elevated risk of negative consequences

Cocaine is one of the most widely abused psychoactive substances in the United States, with an estimated 1.3 million Americans using the drug on a regular (at least monthly) basis (Department of Health and Human Services, 1994). Even occasional cocaine use can result in serious medical complications, such as cardiac damage, vascular ischemia, respiratory failure, and persistent alterations in neural function (Bartzokis et al, 1999; Bolouri and Small, 2004; Frishman et al, 2003; Neiman, Haapaniemi, and Hillbom, 2000; Qureshi et al, 2001; Su et al.,

[*] Correspondence: Laurie M. Rilling, Ph.D., UT Southwestern Medical Center, 5323 Harry Hines Blvd., Dallas Texas 75390-8846; Telephone: (214) 648-4646; E-mail: laurie.rilling@utsouthwestern.edu

2003; Vallee et al., 2003; Velasquez, et al., 2004; Wilson and Saukkonen, 2004). The neurologic sequelae associated with these serious medical complications can include seizures, hypertensive encephalopathy, cerebral vasculitis, ischemic stroke and cerebral hemorrhage, and may result in severe and permanent cognitive disability in those who survive the acute phase of these potentially fatal conditions (Bolouri and Small, 2004; Keller and Chappell, 1997; Konzen et al., 1995; Nolte et al., 1996; Reeves, McWilliams, Fitz-Gerald, 1995; Strickland, Miller, Kowell, and Stein, 1998; Tolat, O'Dell, Golamco-Estrella, and Avella, 2000, Valee et al, 2003).

In addition to an acute medical event, alterations in neural structure, receptor action and cerebral blood flow occur with repeated exposure (Franklin et al, 2002; Matochik et al, 2003), leading to the persistent cognitive and functional declines that accompany the state of addiction (Ardila et al., 1991; Bolla, Cadet, and London, 1998; Franken, 2003; Di Sclafani et al., 2002; Strickland and Stein, 1995; see also Neiman, Haapaniemi, and Hillborn, 2000). Together, these neurophysiological and neurocognitive changes likely account for the reduced impulse control and poor decision-making that perpetuates the abuse and undermines attempts at prolonged abstinence.

In this chapter, we will examine the most recent research on impulsivity and decision-making in cocaine use. First, we will present a brief overview of the cognitive processes affected by cocaine use. Next, we will review the relevant literature detailing the status of inhibitory control and decision-making in cocaine users, as well as their proposed neuroanatomical correlates. Finally, we will attempt to integrate these findings with the current view of cocaine addiction and relapse, with an emphasis on the role of impulsivity and decision-making in continued cocaine use despite the elevated risk of negative consequences.

Cocaine Use and Cognitive Impairment

There is a growing body of evidence to support the relationship between chronic cocaine use and impaired neurocognitive functioning. Varying degrees of impairment have been reported in specific cognitive domains, including memory, verbal fluency, spatial relations, psychomotor speed, and grip strength (Hoff et al., 1996; Manschreck et al., 1990; O'Malley et al., 1990; Roberts and Bauer, 1993; Strickland and Stein, 1995). In contrast, several investigators have found that cocaine users demonstrate enhanced performance on select cognitive measures (Bauer, 1993; O'Malley et al., 1990, 1992; Sevy et al., 1990; Manschreck et al., 1990), but this likely reflects methodological differences among studies, such as sample characteristics, patterns of cocaine use, or the specific task employed. Despite these conflicting findings, two areas of cognition that appear to be consistently impaired are select aspects of attention and executive functioning, namely inhibitory control and decision-making. .

Components of Attention and Executive Functions

The concept of attention is complex and engenders much debate among cognitive scientists. Several investigators have developed theoretical models of attention in which various cognitive mechanisms are identified as being responsible for the component processes of attentional function. For example, Shallice (1982) has proposed that two adaptive mechanisms underlie the process of attention: contention scheduling and supervisory attentional control. The first mechanism, *contention scheduling*, can be thought of as an automatic selection process which is elicited through external stimuli and involves little or no conscious awareness (e.g., bottom-up processing). It is ideal for handling routine behaviors which occur under well-known circumstances. In contrast, the second mechanism, *supervisory attentional control*, serves as a top-down process by which attention is modulated via inhibitory control over externally activated schemas held in working or short-term memory (see van Zomeren and Brouwer, 1994). This mechanism is similar to the *central executive* in the model of working memory proposed by Baddeley (1986). In the Baddeley model, the central executive modulates attention by exerting inhibitory control over a number of subsidiary *slave* systems (see van Zomeren and Brouwer, 1994 for a comprehensive review of attentional theories).

Although the supervisory attentional system (SAS) and central executive were conceptualized within the framework of attentional models, these complex attentional mechanisms are commonly associated with the cognitive construct of *executive functions*. This term refers set of higher-order cognitive processes involved in the monitoring and modulation of behavior. These include such functions as planning, organization, problem-solving and decision-making through the generation and implementation of strategies, the evaluation of behavioral outcomes, integration of feedback, and the consideration of response alternatives (Brandt and Blysma, 1993; Huber and Shuttlewoth, 1990). Both complex attentional mechanisms and executive functions have been neuroanatomically associated with distinct regions of the frontal cortex, as well as frontal-subcortical circuits (Salmon, Heindel, and Hamilton, 2001; Baddeley and Della Sala, 1998). This growing body of literature will be reviewed in greater detail in subsequent sections.

Inhibitory Control and Impulsivity in Cocaine Use

The process of addiction is a complex phenomenon that involves reciprocal alterations in neurochemical and behavioral responses. Historically, the mesolimbic dopamine system and motivational processes have played a dominant role in the study of drug abuse and addiction (Taylor, 1985; Salamone et al., 1997; Adinoff et al., 2004). Increasingly, however, researchers interested in the effects of chronic drug abuse are turning their attention toward regions of the frontal cortex involved in inhibitory control (Ardila et al., 1991, Biggins et al. 1997; Fillmore, Rush, and Hays, 2002; Fuchs et al., 2004; Goldstein et al., 2001; Horner et al., 1996; Moeller et al., 2004; Volkow et al., 1996).

Evidence derived from the study of rodents and primates suggests that dysfunction of the frontostriatal system may be particularly important in the compulsive reward-seeking behavior observed in chronic drug abuse (Baylis and Gaffin, 1991; Butter, 1968; Dias et al., 1996a, 1996b; Rosenkilde, 1979). Based upon these and other supporting studies (e.g., Weissenborn et al., 1997), Jentsch and Taylor (1999) have proposed a theoretical model which predicts that chronic drug use results in the disruption of normal frontostriatal function (specifically corticostriatal projections from the medial prefrontal cortex to the caudate nucleus and nucleus accumbens) which controls inhibitory modulation. Further, they propose that compulsive drug-seeking behaviors are perpetuated by the "functional synergism between impairments in inhibitory control and augmentations in conditioned reward (which) manifest as an overwhelming control of behavior by drugs and conditioned reinforcers," (p. 384). This model provides an excellent framework within which the emerging human data can be considered.

Inhibitory control serves as a top-down regulatory process through which a prepotent response can be suppressed or terminated. This control mechanism can be applied to both internal cognitive processes and overt behavioral actions. For example, in chronic cocaine use, the individual may be unable to suppress the recurrent thoughts of using cocaine, as well as the behavioral response triggered by cocaine-associated stimuli. Given the inherent difficulty in measuring internal thought processes, much of the research to date has focused on chronic cocaine use and its effect on impulsivity and behavioral inhibition.

Evidence from both animal and human research has consistently supported an association between long-term cocaine use and reduced behavioral inhibition (Ardila et al, 1991; Biggins et al, 1997; Butros et al., 1994, 1997; Fillmore, Rush, and Hays, 2002; Fuchs et al, 2994; Hester and Garavan, 2004; Horner et al, 1996; Volkow et al, 1996). Studies examining inhibitory function in humans have employed a variety of neuropsychological and cognitive paradigms, including traditional and computerized versions of the Stroop task (Stroop, 1935), continuous performance tasks, go/no-go tasks, and the stop-signal task. These tasks are commonly used to demonstrate impaired behavioral inhibition in non-substance abusing populations with impulse control disorders, such as Attention-Deficit-Hyperactivity Disorder (ADHD) and Oppositional/Defiant Disorder (e.g., Nigg, 1999; Oosterlaan and Sergeant, 1996; Schachar et al, 1995), as well as traumatic brain injury (Levin et al., 2004; O'Keeffe, et al., 2004; Whyte et al., 1998) and stroke (Reding et al., 1993).

Due to their excellent sensitivity, substance abuse investigators are increasingly utilizing these cognitive tasks to examine the role of behavioral inhibition in chronic drug abuse and addiction. In the stop-signal paradigm, response inhibition and execution are examined using a computerized choice reaction time (RT) task that requires the participant to respond or inhibit responding to a "go-signal" or a "stop-signal," respectively. Signals are presented at different ratios and the inter-stimulus-interval (ISI) may vary from 50 to 350 ms, with the probability of inhibiting decreasing in a linear fashion as the ISI increases (Fillmore et al, 2001, Fillmore and Vogel-Sprott, 1999, 2000). Response inhibition is measured by examining the number of successfully inhibited responses relative to the total number of stop-signals presented (i.e., probability of inhibition) and the estimated mean latency to inhibit a response (e.g., stop-signal RT; see Logan, 1994 for calculation details). Fillmore and colleagues (2002a, 2002b) employed the stop-signal task in a series of studies examining inhibitory control in adults with a history of chronic cocaine use. Results from these studies indicated that inhibitory control was reduced relative to non-cocaine using controls, both in terms of their ability to inhibit a response and the amount of time required to do so. Furthermore, inhibitory deficits were similar for chronic cocaine users who had used cocaine within one week of testing (Fillmore et al, 2002a) and those who received oral cocaine immediately prior to testing as part of a placebo-controlled inpatient design (Fillmore, Rush, and Hays, 2002b), independent of the inhibitory response latencies. Speed and accuracy performance to go-signals, as opposed to stop-signals, was unaffected in both cocaine groups. Taken together, these findings suggest that while cocaine has a negative effect on inhibitory control, it is not necessarily due to slowed inhibitory function but rather a disruption of the inhibitory process itself.

Similar to the stop-signal task, the go/no-go task requires the individual to inhibit a prepotent motor response to environmentally triggered stimuli (see Rubia et al, 2003 for a review of how these two tasks differ). Using a standard go/no-go paradigm, Kaufman and colleagues (2003) examined inhibitory control in sample of 13 active cocaine users with an average of 11 years of use. Compared to age-matched healthy controls, the cocaine users demonstrated significantly worse inhibitory control as measured by the number of commission errors (i.e., failure to inhibit a response to a non-target). . When this task was employed in conjunction with event-related functional magnetic imaging (fMRI), a neuroimaging technique used to assess brain function, cocaine users showed reduced activation following both successful STOPS and ERRORS in frontal and midline areas, including the anterior cingulate cortex (ACC) or Brodmann areas (BAs) 6 and 32. These areas are believed to be involved in error-detection and have been implicated in inhibitory dysfunction in other populations, such as schizophrenia (Carter et al, 2001) and obsessive-compulsive disorder (Ursu et al, 2001). Using a somewhat modified version of the go/no-go task, Hester and Garavan (2004) found that, relative to healthy controls, the magnitude of the cocaine users' inhibitory impairment tended to increase proportionally with the demand on executive (or inhibitory) control. Under even-related fMRI conditions, the inhibitory control deficit in cocaine users was associated with reduced activation in the ACC (BAs 32/34), pre-supplementary motor cortex (BA 6), and right superior frontal gyrus (BAs 10/9), relative to controls. Furthermore, unlike the controls, the cocaine users did not demonstrate any increased ACC activation in response to the increased executive demand; rather they exhibited an unexpected hyperactivation of the left cerebellum. This latter finding highlights the disruption of not only frontal cortical regions in chronic cocaine users, but perhaps the entire network of frontal-subcortical-cerebellar connections. Other brain regions that have been implicated in cocaine-related reductions in inhibitory control include the orbitofrontal cortex (Goldstein et al, 2001; Fuchs et al, 2004) and the anterior corpus callosum (Moeller et al, 2005).

In summary, the evidence supporting an association between chronic cocaine use and impaired inhibitory control is quite compelling, though admittedly still preliminary in nature. Replication of these results would provide additional support for this important link between impulsivity and the difficulties such individuals encounter when faced with the environmental triggers that entice them to use again. Moreover, although there is some evidence that ACC dysfunction may serve as the neural substrate for this impairment, the extent to which habitual cocaine use may disrupt other frontal, subcortical, and even cerebellar regions is yet to be determined. Clearly, this is an area of research that deserves continued attention from the scientific community.

Cocaine Use and Decision Making

One of the most difficult challenges substance abusers face when attempting to remain abstinent is resisting the urge to use when they encounter drug-related cues in the environment (Luborsky et al., 1995). In this situation, the individual is presented with the choice of whether they will resume their drug use or maintain their abstinence. This decision will undoubtedly be associated with positive and negative consequences, some of which will be short-lived and others which will be long-lasting. For those who have not developed a chemical addiction (or dependency), the decision to abstain from drug use in order to avoid potentially adverse consequences may seem relatively logical and straightforward. However, one of the hallmarks of addiction is the persistent use of chemical substances despite the likelihood of seriously negative long-term effects (Grant et al, 2000; WHO, 1992).

Individuals who engage in drug use are often described as "risk-takers" or "sensation seekers," both of which highlight the some of the variables involved in this decision-making process. For those who are able to postpone their response long enough to engage in the decision-making process (i.e., those with relatively preserved impulse control), they are compelled to engage in a spontaneous cost/benefit analysis. In other words, they must ask themselves, "What are the costs and benefits of returning to drug use versus maintaining abstinence?" This decision is highly influenced by multiple factors, including prior experiences, the expected rewards, and possible punishments. In the case of drug use, the reward typically involves a rapid transition from an unpleasant to a pleasant physiological (and perhaps psychological) state. Thus, the temptation of the immediate reward must be weighed against the reality of the delayed cost. There is a substantial scientific literature devoted to the study of decision-making in healthy individuals (see Tversky and Kahneman, 1981). The relationship between impaired decision-making and chronic cocaine use, however, is still somewhat preliminary and continues to be an area of intense study.

One of the most common paradigms used to examine human risk-taking and decision-making is the gambling task (GT). This measure was developed to assess behavioral patterns in the context of a reward-punishment situation and has proven to be quite sensitive to decision-making deficits in patients with ventromedial prefrontal cortex lesions (Bechara et al., 1994, 1999, 2000) as well as individuals with a history of chronic substance abuse (Grant et al., 2000; Petry et al., 1998; Mazas et al., 2000). In the computerized version of this task, subjects are required to choose between two options; one with the possibility of large immediate rewards and a risk of large punishments and a second with the possibility of small rewards and a risk of small punishments. Reward-punishment ratios are fixed so that the first option will result in a net loss and the second option will result in a net gain upon completion of the task. Optimal performance on this measure requires the subject to make conservative choices (e.g., smaller rewards) and delay the gratification achieved by receiving a larger payout until the end of the task.

There is a strong tendency, however, for humans (and animals) to "discount" delayed outcomes (Monterosso et al., 2001). As such, those who seek immediate gratification will more often choose a larger immediate reward despite the greater risk of long-term negative consequences. Indeed, findings from studies of drug-abusing individuals suggest that those who more steeply discount the future suffer from a kind of "temporal myopia," in which the overwhelming desire for immediate gratification interferes with their ability to contemplate future consequences (Bickle, Odum, & Madden, 1999; Kirby et al., 1999; Madden, Bickle, & Jacobs, 1999; Mitchell, 1999; Vuchinch & Simpson, 1998). This myopic perspective may predispose these individuals to problematic drug use even before they are exposed to their drug of choice (Bechara et l., 1994; Bickel & Marsch, 2001; Herrnstein & Prelec, 1992; Monterosso et al., 2001; Vuchinich & Tucker, 1988). It has also been suggested that chronic under-arousal in a subset of drug abusing individuals may serve to increase their tendency toward "risk-seeking" behavior. This phenomenon, combined with a myopic outlook, may elevate the risk of recurrent relapse following chemical dependency treatment (Bartzokis et al., 2000; Quay, 1965; Zuckerman, 1979, 1994). The interaction between perception of risk (e.g., risk-discounting) and the preference for risk (e.g., sensation-seeking) in the perpetuation of drug abuse has not been well studied however, and warrants further systematic examination.

Despite the controversies surrounding the role of risk-taking versus sensation-seeking, there is growing support in the scientific literature for an association between impaired decision-making and chronic drug abuse. Numerous studies have reported that drug-dependent individuals are impaired on the GT relative to matched controls (Bartzokis et al., 2000; Bechara et l., 2001; Ernst et al., 2003; Fishbein, 2000; Grant, Contoreggi & London, 2000; Mazas, Finn, & Steinmetz, 2000; Rotheram-Fuller, et al., 2004). For example, Grant and colleagues (2000) utilized the GT in conjunction with the Wisconsin Card Sorting Test (WCST) to examine decision-making in a group of active polysubstance abusers and drug-naïve controls. The majority of substance abusers acknowledged using cocaine (28/30 subjects) and over half endorsed using heroin (19/30 subjects). Most substance-abusing subjects also endorsed using marijuana, alcohol, and nicotine, while the only substance a majority of controls endorsed using was alcohol (16/24 subjects). After controlling for IQ differences, results indicated that drug abusers performed significantly worse than controls in terms of their net score on the GT, with almost 50% of the drug abusing subjects yielding net scores in the negative range as compared to only 8% of the controls. In a subsequent study, Ernst and colleagues (2003) examined GT performance over five blocks of 20-card choices and found that a similar sample of active substance abusers performed significantly worse than controls during the third block. The authors interpreted this finding as reflecting a critical "hunch" time-period when respondents should begin to internalize the reward/penalty differences between decks. Similar decision-making deficits have also been reported using a somewhat different version of the gambling task paradigm (Heyman & Dunn, 2002).

In contrast, several recent studies that examined cocaine-dependent individuals reported no differences in GT performance between these individuals and control subjects (Adinoff et al, 2003; Bolla et al., 2003; Tucker et al, 2004). Upon closer inspection, it appears that differences in methodology and sample characteristics may at least partially explain these conflicting findings. For example, subjects in the studies with negative findings consisted of patients who identified cocaine as their drug of choice, as opposed to individuals in the earlier described studies who acknowledged concurrent use of heroin and cocaine. In addition, studies with negative findings limited their sample to subjects who were abstinent for a specified period of time, many of whom were either enrolled in a residential chemical dependency treatment program or had recently completed such a program. This is in contrast to the "active" substance abusers who were included in the studies reporting group differences. Differences in gender distribution among patient and control samples may have also contributed to discrepant findings, as there is some evidence to suggest that males perform slightly better than females on gambling tasks (LeLand et al, 1998; Reavis et al., 1998). Finally, variability in the task parameters, administration procedures, and methods for computing primary outcome variables may also contribute to the inconsistencies among studies employing the GT.

Although the GT performance data reported in the literature thus far is equivocal at best, there is emerging evidence to support an association between cocaine use and alterations in brain function as measured by neuroimaging. Several recent studies have examined resting cerebral blood flow (rCBF) in cocaine-dependent individuals using single-photon emission computed tomography (SPECT) and positron emission tomography (PET), with a focus on frontal cortical regions believed to be involved in decision-making. One area of particular interest has been the orbitofrontal cortex (OFC). This brain region is an important part of the neural networks involved in positive reinforcement in primates (Rolls and Baylis, 1994) and has reciprocal connections with many brain regions that mediate the rewarding effects of cocaine in humans (Rolls, 2000; Volkow and Fowler, 2000). Damage to the OFC may produce changes in personality, social behavior, and judgment characterized by irresponsibility and repetition of inappropriate or self-destructive behaviors.

Studies using PET to examine the role of the OFC in drug addiction have revealed increases in activation in the OFC, anterior cingulate, right insular region, and the amygdala in response to cocaine-related cues (Bonson et al., 2002, Childress et al., 1999; Grant et al., 1996; Wang et al., 1999). Alterations in the striato-thalamo-orbitofrontal network have also been reported in association with cocaine addicted individuals' performance on tasks of impulsivity and conflict monitoring (Goldstein et al., 2001). Using PET to examine the neural activation patterns associated with decision-making, Bolla and colleagues (2003) found that cocaine abusers who were abstinent for an average of 24 days showed increased right OFC activation during the GT as compared to non-drug using controls. Moreover, they reported that the amount of cocaine used (grams/week) prior to their period of abstinence was negatively correlated with activation in the left OFC. Similar increases in rCBF have been found using SPECT in a sample of abstinent cocaine-dependent individuals (Tucker et al., 2004). Others have reported no association between OFC activation and GT performance in this population (Adinoff et al., 2003), but indicate a relative decrease in resting rCBF in cocaine-dependent subjects compared to controls (Adinoff et al., 2001, Volkow et. 1992). Other brain regions associated with GT performance in cocaine users include the ACC and the dorsolateral prefrontal cortex (DLPFC) (Adinoff et al, 2003; Bolla et al., 2003; Tucker et al., 2004). Taken together, these findings suggest that chronic cocaine users show persistent functional abnormalities in prefrontal regions involved in decision-making.

SUMMARY

Based on the currently available data, it is clear that cocaine use is associated with alterations in neural activation. How these changes are manifested in terms of cognitive dysfunction and treatment outcome, however, remains unclear. Historically, models of addiction have emphasized such constructs as incentive motivation and the subjective phenomenon of craving (Bindra, 1992; Cox and Klinger, 1988; Robinson and Berridge, 2000; Toates, 1994), with a focus on mesolimbic-dopamine system. In the field of addictions research, however, there is a growing interest in the role of cognitive factors and how they may influence the addictions process, as well as the likelihood of a successful treatment outcome. Studies thus far have provided preliminary data to support an association between cocaine use and impaired inhibitory control (i.e., impulsivity), with the ACC emerging as the likely neural substrate for the observed cognitive dysfunction. Evidence for a decision-making deficit in cocaine users is equivocal, but alterations in OFC activation, as well as the

ACC and DLPC, suggest a disruption of frontal neural networks even in the absence of any overt performance decrement.

Despite these promising findings, the etiology of impaired "frontal" function and inhibitory control remains poorly delineated. For example, it is not known whether persons who engage in chronic cocaine use suffer from a preexisting neurocognitive impairment that places them at risk for addiction or whether the use of cocaine itself produces alterations in brain structure and function that ultimately result in the addiction despite an individuals' baseline susceptibility for developing such a disorder. It is likely that the truth lies somewhere between these two extremes. In other words, the majority of individuals who struggle with addiction likely carry an elevated premorbid risk due to impaired inhibitory function that is further exacerbated by alterations in neural function secondary to their prolonged use of the drug in question (e.g., cocaine). Beyond the etiology question lies a host of methodological issues that make interpretation of these intriguing findings even more challenging. Future studies would benefit from including greater detail regarding sample characteristics and drug use history (e.g., amount, duration, and method of use), as well as more comprehensive assessment of intellectual, neuropsychological, and psychosocial functioning. Such improvements in data collection and reporting would facilitate comparisons across studies and likely enhance our ability to isolate potentially critical cognitive mechanisms for successful treatment outcome. Given that prevention of relapse is a primary goal of treatment, there is clearly a need to better understand the role of impulsivity and decision-making in chronic drug use in order to tailor interventions to address these important factors.

References

Adinoff, B., Devous, M. D., Cooper, D. B., et al. Resting regional cerebral blood flow and gambling task performance in cocaine-dependent subjects and healthy comparison subjects. *American Journal of Psychiatry* (2003) 160(10):1892-1894.

Ardila, A., Rosselli, M., and Strumwasser, S. Neuropsychological Deficits in Chronic Cocaine Abusers. *International Journal of Neuroscience* (1991) 57(1-2):73-79.

Baddeley, A., and Della Sala, S. Working Memory and Executive Control. In A. C. Roberts, T. W. Robbins, and L. Weiskrantz, eds., *The Prefrontal Cortex.* Oxford University Press, 1998.

Baddeley, A. D. *Working Memory.* Oxford University Press, 1986.

Bartzokis, G., Beckson, M., Hance, D. B., et al. Magnetic resonance imaging evidence of "silent" cerebrovascular toxicity in cocaine dependence. *Biological Psychiatry* (1999) 45(9):1203-1211.

Bartzokis, G., Lu, P. H., Beckson, M., et al. Abstinence from cocaine reduces high-risk responses on a gambling task. *Neuropsychopharmacology* (2000) 22(1):102-103.

Bauer, L. O. Eye-Movements in Recovering Substance-Abusers - a Prospective-Study. *Addictive Behaviors* (1993) 18(4):465-472.

Baylis, L. L., and Gaffan, D. Amygdalectomy and Ventromedial Prefrontal Ablation Produce Similar Deficits in Food Choice and in Simple Object Discrimination-Learning for an Unseen Reward. *Experimental Brain Research* (1991) 86(3):617-622.

Bechara, A., Damasio, A. R., Damasio, H., et al. Insensitivity to Future Consequences Following Damage to Human Prefrontal Cortex. *Cognition* (1994) 50(1-3):7-15.

Bechara, A., Damasio, H., and Damasio, A. R. Emotion, decision making and the orbitofrontal cortex. *Cerebral Cortex* (2000) 10(3):295-307.

Bechara, A., Damasio, H., Damasio, A. R., et al. Different contributions of the human amygdala and ventromedial prefrontal cortex to decision-making. *Journal of Neuroscience* (1999) 19(13):5473-5481.

Bechara, A., Dolan, S., Denburg, N., et al. Decision-malting deficits, linked to a dysfunctional ventromedial prefrontal cortex, revealed in alcohol and stimulant abusers. *Neuropsychologia* (2001) 39(4):376-389.

Bickel, W. K., and Marsch, L. A. Toward a behavioral economic understanding of drug dependence: delay discounting processes. *Addiction* (2001) 96(1):73-86.

Bickel, W. K., Odum, A. L., and Madden, G. J. Impulsivity and cigarette smoking: delay discounting in current, never, and ex-smokers. *Psychopharmacology* (1999) 146(4):447-454.

Biggins, C. A., MacKay, S., Clark, W., et al. Event-related potential evidence for frontal cortex effects of chronic cocaine dependence. *Biological Psychiatry* (1997) 42(6):472-485.

Bindra, D. Motivation, the Brain, and Psychological Theory. In S. Koch and D. Leary, eds., *A Century of Psychology as Science.* American Psychological Association, 1992.

Bolla, K. I., Cadet, J. L., and London, E. D. The neuropsychiatry of chronic cocaine abuse. *Journal of Neuropsychiatry & Clinical Neurosciences* (1998) 10(3):280-9.

Bolla, K. I., Eldreth, D. A., London, E. D., et al. Orbitofrontal cortex dysfunction in abstinent cocaine abusers performing a decision-making task. *Neuroimage* (2003) 19(3):1085-94.

Bolouri, M., and Small, G. Neuroimaging of hypoxia and cocaine-induced hippocampal stroke. *J Neuroimaging* (2004) 14(3):290-1.

Bonson, K., Grant, S., Contoreggi, C., et al. Neural systems and cue-induced cocaine craving. *Neuropsychopharmacology* (2002) 26:376-386.

Brandt, J., and Blysma, F. The neuropsychology of Huntington's disease. *Trends in Neurosciences* (1993) 9:118-120.

Butros, N., Uretsky, N., Bernston, G., et al. Effects of cocaine on sensory inhibition in rats: preliminary data. *Soc Biol Psychit* (1994) 36:242-248.

Butter, C. Perseveration in extinction and in discrimination reversal following selective frontal ablations in *Macaca mulatta. Psychiol Behav* (1968) 4:163-171.

Carter, C. S., MacDonald, A. W., Ross, L. L., et al. Anterior cingulate cortex activity and impaired self-monitoring of performance in patients with schizophrenia: An event-related fMRI study. *American Journal of Psychiatry* (2001) 158(9):1423-1428.

Childress, A. R., Mozley, P. D., McElgin, W., et al. Limbic activation during cue-induced cocaine craving. *American Journal of Psychiatry* (1999) 156(1):11-18.

Cox, W. M., and Klinger, E. A Motivational Model of Alcohol-Use. *Journal of Abnormal Psychology* (1988) 97(2):168-180.

Department of Health and Human Services. HHS releases 1993 household drug survery., *HHS News*, 1994.

Di Scalfani, V., Tolou-Shams, M., Price, L., et al. Neuropsychological performance of individuals dependent on crack-cocaine or crack-cocaine and alcohol, at 6 weeks and 6 months of abstinence. *Drug and Alcohol Dependence* (2002) 66:161-171.

Dias, R., Robbins, T. W., and Roberts, A. C. Dissociation in prefrontal cortex of affective and attentional shifts. *Nature* (1996a) 380(6569):69-72.

Dias, R., Robbins, T. W., and Roberts, A. C. Primate analogue of the Wisconsin Card Sorting Test: Effects of excitotoxic lesions of the prefrontal cortex in the marmoset. *Behavioral Neuroscience* (1996b) 110(5):872-886.

Ernst, M., Grant, S. J., London, E. D., et al. Decision making in adolescents with behavior disorders and adults with substance abuse. *American Journal of Psychiatry* (2003) 160(1):33-40.

Fillmore, M. T., and Rush, C. R. Alcohol effects on inhibitory and activational response strategies in the acquisition of alcohol and other reinforcers: Priming the motivation to drink. *Journal of Studies on Alcohol* (2001) 62(5):646-656.

Fillmore, M. T., and Rush, C. R. Impaired inhibitory control of behavior in chronic cocaine users. *Drug and Alcohol Dependence* (2002) 66(3):265-273.

Fillmore, M. T., Rush, C. R., and Hays, L. Acute effects of oral cocaine on inhibitory control of behavior in humans. *Drug and Alcohol Dependence* (2002) 67(2):157-167.

Fillmore, M. T., and Vogel-Sprott, M. An alcohol model of impaired inhibitory control and its treatment in humans. *Experimental and Clinical Psychopharmacology* (1999) 7(1):49-55.

Fillmore, M. T., and Vogel-Sprott, M. Response inhibition under alcohol: Effects of cognitive and motivational conflict. *Journal of Studies on Alcohol* (2000) 61(2):239-246.

Fishbein, D. Neuropsychological function, drug abuse, and violence - A conceptual framework. *Criminal Justice and Behavior* (2000) 27(2):139-159.

Franklin, T. R., Acton, P. D., Maldjian, J. A., et al. Decreased gray matter concentration in the insular, orbitofrontal, cingulate, and temporal cortices of cocaine patients. *Biological Psychiatry* (2002) 51(2):134-142.

Frishman, W., DelVecchio, A., Sanal, S., et al. Cardiovascular manifestations of substance abuse: part 2: alcohol, amphetamines, heroin, cannabis, and caffeine. *Heart Dis* (2003) 5(4):253-71.

Fuchs, R. A., Evans, K. A., Parker, M. C., et al. Differential involvement of the core and shell subregions of the nucleus accumbens in conditioned cue-induced reinstatement of cocaine seeking in rats. *Psychopharmacology* (2004) 176(3-4):459-465.

Goldstein, R. Z., Leskovjan, A. C., Hoff, A. L., et al. Severity of neuropsychological impairment in cocaine and alcohol addiction: association with metabolism in the prefrontal cortex. *Neuropsychologia* (2004) 42(11):1447-58.

Goldstein, R. Z., Volkow, N. D., Wang, G. J., et al. Addiction changes orbitofrontal gyrus function: involvement in response inhibition. *Neuroreport* (2001) 12(11):2595-2599.

Grant, S., Contoreggi, C., and London, E. D. Drug abusers show impaired performance in a laboratory test of decision making. *Neuropsychologia* (2000) 38(8):1180-1187.

Grant, S., London, E. D., Newlin, D. B., et al. Activation of memory circuits during cue-elicited cocaine craving. *Proceedings of the National Academy of Sciences of the United States of America* (1996) 93(21):12040-12045.

Herrstein, R., and Prelec, D. A theory of addiction. In G. Lowenstein and J. Elster, eds., *Choice over Time.* Russell Sage Press, 1992.

Hester, R., and Garavan, H. Executive dysfunction in cocaine addiction: Evidence for discordant frontal, cingulate, and cerebellar activity. *The Journal of Neuroscience* (2004) 24(49):11017-11022.

Heyman, G. M., and Dunn, B. Decision biases and persistent illicit drug use: an experimental study of distributed choice and addiction. *Drug and Alcohol Dependence* (2002) 67(2):193-203.

Hoff, A. L., Riordan, H., Morris, L., et al. Effects of crack cocaine on neurocognitive function. *Psychiatry Research* (1996) 60(2-3):167-176.

Horner, B., Scheibe, K., and Stine, S. Cocaine abuse and attention-deficit hyperactivity disorder: Implications of adult symptomatology. *Psychology of Addictive Behaviors* (1996) 10(1):55-60.

Huber, S., and Shuttleworth, E. Huntington's disease. In J. Cummings, ed., *Subcortical Dementia*. Oxford University Press, 1990.

Jentsch, J. D., and Taylor, J. R. Impulsivity resulting from frontostriatal dysfunction in drug abuse: implications for the control of behavior by reward-related stimuli. *Psychopharmacology* (1999) 146(4):373-390.

Kaufman, J. N., Ross, T. J., Stein, E. A., et al. Cingulate hypoactivity in cocaine users during a GO-NOGO task as revealed by event-related functional magnetic resonance imaging. *Journal of Neuroscience* (2003) 23(21):7839-7843.

Keller, T. M., and Chappell, E. T. Spontaneous acute subdural hematoma precipitated by cocaine abuse: Case report. *Surgical Neurology* (1997) 47(1):12-14.

Kirby, K., Petry, N., and Bickel, W. K. Heroin addicts have higher discount rates for delayed rewards than non-drug using controls. *J Exp Psychol* (1999) 128:78-87.

Konzen, J., Levine, S., and Garcia, J. Vasospasm and thrombus formation as possible mechanism of stroke related to alkaloidal cocaine. *Stroke* (1995) 26(6):1114-8.

LeLand, D., Richardson, J., Vankov, A., et al. Decision-making and associated ERPS in low- and high-dependence smokers performing the Iowa gambling task. *Society for Neuroscience Abstracts* (1998) 24:1175.

Levin, H. S., Hanten, G., Zhang, L. F., et al. Selective impairment of inhibition after TBI in children. *Journal of Clinical and Experimental Neuropsychology* (2004) 26(5):589-597.

Logan, G. On the ability to inhibit thought and action: a users' guide to the stop-signal paradigm. In D. Dagenbach and T. Carr, eds., *Inhibitory Processes in Attention, Memory, and Language*. Academic Press, 1994.

Luborsky, L., McKay, J., Mercer, D., et al. To use or refuse cocaine: The deciding factors. *J Substance Abuse* (1995) 7:293-310.

Madden, G. J., Bickel, W. K., and Jacobs, E. A. Discounting of delayed rewards in opioid-dependent outpatients: Exponential or hyperbolic discounting functions? *Experimental and Clinical Psychopharmacology* (1999) 7(3):284-293.

Manschreck, T. C., Schneyer, M. L., Weisstein, C. C., et al. Freebase Cocaine and Memory. *Comprehensive Psychiatry* (1990) 31(4):369-375.

Matochik, J. A., London, E. D., Eldreth, D. A., et al. Frontal cortical tissue composition in abstinent cocaine abusers: a magnetic resonance imaging study. *Neuroimage* (2003) 19(3):1095-1102.

Mazas, C. A., Finn, P. R., and Steinmetz, J. E. Decision-making biases, antisocial personality, and early-onset alcoholism. *Alcoholism-Clinical and Experimental Research* (2000) 24(7):1036-1040.

Mitchell, S. H. Measures of impulsivity in cigarette smokers and non-smokers. *Psychopharmacology* (1999) 146(4):455-464.

Mitchell, S. L., and Lawson, F. M. E. Decision-making for long-term tube-feeding in cognitively impaired elderly people. *Canadian Medical Association Journal* (1999) 160(12):1705-1709.

Moeller, F. G., Barratt, E. S., Fischer, C. J., et al. P300 event-related potential amplitude and impulsivity in cocaine-dependent subjects. *Neuropsychobiology* (2004) 50(2):167-173.

Moeller, F. G., Hasan, K. M., Steinberg, J. L., et al. Reduced anterior corpus callosum white matter integrity is related to increased impulsivity and reduced discriminability in cocaine-dependent subjects: Diffusion tensor imaging. *Neuropsychopharmacology* (2005) 30(3):610-617.

Monterosso, J., Ehrman, R., Napier, K. L., et al. Three decision-making tasks in cocaine-dependent patients: do they measure the same construct? *Addiction* (2001) 96(12):1825-1837.

Neimann, J., Haapanieme, H., and Hillbom, M. Neurological complications of drug abuse: pathophysiological mechanisms. *Eur J Neurol* (2000) 7(6):595-606.

Nigg, J. T. The ADHD response-inhibition deficit as measured by the stop task: Replication with DSM-IV combined type, extension, and qualification. *Journal of Abnormal Child Psychology* (1999) 27(5):393-402.

Nolte, K., Brass, L., and Fletterick, C. Intracranial hemorrhage associated with cocaine abuse: a prospective autopsy study. *Neurology* (1996) 46(5):1291-6.

O'Keeffe, F., Dockree, P., and Robertson, I. Poor insight in traumatic brain injury mediated by impaired error processing? Evidence from electrodermal activity. *Cognitive Brain Research* (2004) 22(1):101-112.

O'Malley, S., Adamse, M., Heaton, R., et al. Neuropsychological impairment in chronic cocaine abusers. *Am J Drug Alcohol Abuse* (1992) 18:131-144.

O'Malley, S., and Gawin, F. Abstinence symptomatology and neuropsychological impairment in chronic cocaine abusers. *NIDA Research Monographs* (1990) 101:179-190.

Oosterlaan, J., and Sergeant, J. A. Inhibition in ADHD, aggressive, and anxious children: A biologically based model of child psychopathology. *Journal of Abnormal Child Psychology* (1996) 24(1):19-36.

Petry, N. Substance abuse, pathological gambling, and impulsiveness. *Drug and Alcohol Dependence* (2001) 63:29-38.

Quay, H. Psychopathic personality as pathological stimulation seeking. *Am J Psychiatry* (1965) 122:180-183.

Qureshi, A. I., Suri, M. F. K., Guterman, L. R., et al. Cocaine use and the likelihood of nonfatal myocardial infarction and stroke - Data from the Third National Health and Nutrition Examination survey. *Circulation* (2001) 103(4):502-506.

Reavis, R., Overman, W., Hendrix, S., et al. Possible double dissociation of function between adult males and females in two brain system. *Society for Neuroscience Abstracts* (1998) 24:1177.

Reding, M., Gardner, C., Hainline, B., et al. Neuropsychiatric problems interfering with inpatient stroke rehabilitation. *J Neurol Rehab* (1993) 7(1):1-7.

Reeves, R. R., Mcwilliams, M. E., and Fitzgerald, M. Cocaine-Induced Ischemic Cerebral Infarction Mistaken for a Psychiatric Syndrome. *Southern Medical Journal* (1995) 88(3):352-354.

Roberts, L. A., and Bauer, L. O. Reaction-Time during Cocaine Versus Alcohol-Withdrawal - Longitudinal Measures of Visual and Auditory Suppression. *Psychiatry Research* (1993) 46(3):229-237.

Robinson, T. E., and Berridge, K. C. The psychology and neurobiology of addiction: an incentive-sensitization view. *Addiction* (2000) 95(8):S91-S117.

Rolls, E. T. The orbitofrontal cortex and reward. *Cerebral Cortex* (2000) 10(3):284-294.

Rolls, E. T., and Baylis, L. L. Gustatory, Olfactory, and Visual Convergence within the Primate Orbitofrontal Cortex. *Journal of Neuroscience* (1994) 14(9):5437-5452.

Rosenkilde, C. E. Functional-Heterogeneity of the Prefrontal Cortex in the Monkey - Review. *Behavioral and Neural Biology* (1979) 25(3):301-345.

Rotheram-Fuller, E., Shoptaw, S., Berman, S., et al. Impaired performance in a test of decision-making by opiate-dependent tobacco smokers. *Drug and Alcohol Dependence* (2004) 73:79-86.

Rubia, K., Smith, A. B., Brammer, M. J., et al. Right inferior prefrontal cortex mediates response inhibition while mesial prefrontal cortex is responsible for error detection. *Neuroimage* (2003) 20(1):351-358.

Salamone, J. D., Cousins, M. S., and Snyder, B. J. Behavioral functions of nucleus accumbens dopamine: Empirical and conceptual problems with the anhedonia hypothesis. *Neuroscience and Biobehavioral Reviews* (1997) 21(3):341-359.

Salmon, D., Heindel, W., and Hamilton, J. Cognitive Abilities Mediated by Frontal-Subcortical Circuits. In D. Lichter and J. Cummings, eds., *Frontal-Subcortical Circuits in Psychiatric and Neurologic Disorders.* The Guilford Press, 2001.

Schachar, R., Tannock, R., and Marriott, M. Deficient inhibitory control in attention deficit hyperactivity disorder. *J Abnorm Child Psychol* (1995) 23:411-437.

Sevy. (1990).

Sevy, S., Kay, S. R., Opler, L. A., et al. Significance of Cocaine History in Schizophrenia. *Journal of Nervous and Mental Disease* (1990) 178(10):642-648.

Shallice, T. Specific Impairments of Planning. *Philosophical Transactions of the Royal Society of London Series B-Biological Sciences* (1982) 298(1089):199-209.

Strickland, T. L., Miller, B. L., Kowell, A., et al. Neurobiology of cocaine-induced organic brain impairment: Contributions from functional neuroimaging. *Neuropsychology Review* (1998) 8(1):1-9.

Strickland, T. L., and Stein, R. Cocaine-Induced Cerebrovascular Impairment - Challenges to Neuropsychological Assessment. *Neuropsychology Review* (1995) 5(1):69-79.

Su, J., Li, J., Li, W., et al. Cocaine induces apoptosis in cerebral vascular muscle cells: potential roles in strokes and brain damage. *Eur J Pharmacol* (2003) 482(1-3):61-6.

Taylor, J. R. Neural mechanisms of the potentiation of conditioned reinforcement by psychomotor stimulant drugs, *Department of Experimental Psychology*. University of Cambridge, 1985.

Toates, F. Comparing Motivational Systems-An Incentive Motivation Perspective. In C. Legg and D. Booth, eds., *Appetite: Neural and Behavioural Bases.* Oxford University Press, 1994.

Tolat, R. D., O'Dell, M. W., Golamco-Estrella, S. P., et al. Cocaine-associated stroke: three cases and rehabilitation considerations. *Brain Injury* (2000) 14(4):383-391.

Tucker, K. A., Potenza, M. N., Beauvais, J. E., et al. Perfusion abnormalities and decision making in cocaine dependence. *Biological Psychiatry* (2004) 56(7):527-530.

Tversky, A., and Kahneman, D. The Framing of Decisions and the Psychology of Choice. *Science* (1981) 211(4481):453-458.

Ursu, S., van Veen, V., Siegle, G., et al. Executive control and self-evaluation in obsessive-compulsive disorder: an event-related fMRI study . Presented at conference, "Cognitive Neuroscience Society Meeting." New York, NY, 2001.

Vallee, J. N., Crozier, S., Guillevin, R., et al. Acute basilar artery occlusion treated by thromboaspiration in a cocaine and ecstasy abuser. *Neurology* (2003) 61(6):839-841.

van Zomeren, A., and Brouwer, W. *Clinical Neuropsychology of Attention.* Oxford University Press, 1994.

Velasquez, E., Anand, R., Newman, W., et al. Cardiovascular complications associated with cocaine use. *J La State Med Soc* (2004) 156(6):302-10.

Volkow, N. D., Ding, Y. S., Fowler, J. S., et al. Cocaine addiction: Hypothesis derived from imaging studies with PET. *Journal of Addictive Diseases* (1996) 15(4):55-71.

Volkow, N. D., Fowler, J. S., and Wang, G. J. Imaging studies on the role of dopamine in cocaine reinforcement and addiction in humans. *Journal of Psychopharmacology* (1999) 13(4):337-345.

Vuchinich, R. E., and Simpson, C. A. Hyperbolic temporal discounting in social drinkers and problem drinkers. *Experimental and Clinical Psychopharmacology* (1998) 6(3):292-305.

Wang, G. J., Volkow, N. D., Fowler, J. S., et al. Regional brain metabolic activation during craving elicited by recall of previous drug experiences. *Life Sciences* (1999) 64(9):775-784.

Weissenborn, R., Robbins, T. W., and Everitt, B. Effects of medial prefrontal or anterior cingulate cortex lesions on responding for cocaine under fixed-ratio and second-order schedules of reinforcement in rats. *Psychopharmacology* (1997) 134:242-257.

Whyte, J., Fleming, M., Polansky, M., et al. The effects of visual distraction following traumatic brain injury. *Journal of the International Neuropsychological Society* (1998) 4(2):127-136.

Wilson, K., and Saukkonen, J. Acute respiratory failure from abused substances. *J Intensive Care Med* (2004) 19(4):183-93.

World Health Organization. International statistical classification of diseases and related health problems (10th revision). 1992.

Zuckerman, M. *Sensation Seeking: Beyond the Optimal Level of Arousal.* Lawrence Erlbaum, 1979.

Zuckerman, M. *Behavioral Expressions and Biosocial Bases of Sensation Seeking.* Cambridge University Press, 1994.

In: Cocaine and Heroin Abuse Research
Editor: Lidia A. Pizzoli, pp. 97-119
ISBN 1-60021-076-7

Chapter 5

COCAINE-DEPENDENT PATIENTS WITH ANTISOCIAL PERSONALITY DISORDER

Nena Messina**, *David Farabee and Richard Rawson
UCLA Integrated Substance Abuse Programs, USA

ABSTRACT

This study compared the efficacy of two commonly used treatment approaches (cognitive–behavioral treatment and contingency management) for the treatment of cocaine dependence among methadone-maintained patients with and without antisocial personality disorder (ASPD). This disorder is strongly associated with substance abuse and recent study findings provide a strong argument against the perception that substance abusers with ASPD are unresponsive to drug treatment.

Method: Patients were randomly assigned to four study conditions including cognitive–behavioral treatment (CBT), contingency management (CM), CBT with CM, or methadone maintenance (also the control condition). The Structural Clinical Interview for Mental Disorders–IV was administered to 108 patients to assess ASPD.

Hypotheses: We hypothesized that ASPD patients in the three treatment conditions (CBT, CM, CBT + CM) would have better treatment responsivity over the 16-week course of treatment than would ASPD patients in the control condition (MM). Moreover, we hypothesized that there would be a cumulative treatment effect among ASPD patients over the course of treatment, with good performance in the CBT condition, better performance in the CM condition, and optimum performance in the CBT + CM condition. Conversely, we hypothesized that the positive treatment effect of CM would decline for the ASPD patients once the incentive was removed (i.e., during the post-treatment outcome period).

Results: A two-way analysis of variance showed that patients with ASPD were more likely to abstain from cocaine use during treatment than patients without ASPD. The strong treatment effect for ASPD patients was primarily due to the CM condition. A

* Corresponding Author: Nena Messina, Ph.D., 1640 S. Sepulveda Blvd., Suite 200 Los Angeles, CA. 90025, Phone: (310) 445-0874 ext. 335, Fax: (310) 312-0559, nmessina@ucla.edu, dfarabee@ucla.edu, matrixex@ucla.edu

series of regression analyses showed that ASPD remained significantly related to CM treatment responsivity while controlling for other related factors.
Conclusion: Monetary incentives appear to reduce cocaine use among substance abusers with ASPD more than among those without ASPD. The results of the present study and other recent publications suggest that substance abusers with ASPD may be more responsive to treatment than previously believed.

INTRODUCTION

Antisocial personality disorder (ASPD) is a personality disorder officially recognized by the American Psychiatric Association and often associated with substance abuse and criminal behavior. The key features of the disorder are outlined in the *Diagnostic and Statistical Manual of Mental Disorders,* fourth edition, commonly known as the DSM-IV. The essential feature of this disorder is "a pervasive pattern of disregard for, and violation of, the rights of others that begins in childhood or early adolescence and continues into adulthood" (American Psychiatric Association, 1994: 645). Common signs of childhood development of ASPD are lying, stealing, fighting, resisting authority, and cruelty to animals. Aggressive sexual behavior, drinking and drug abuse are common in adolescence. Adult manifestations include illegal behavior, deceitfulness, recklessness, violence, job troubles, and marital difficulties. (For a complete description of ASPD, see Messina, 2002.)

Previous research indicates that this disorder is also strongly associated with excessive substance abuse in adulthood, with about 40% to 50% of substance abusers meeting the criteria for ASPD (Messina, Wish, & Nemes, 1999; Tims, DeLeon, & Jainchill, 1994) and approximately 90% of persons diagnosed with ASPD being substance abusers (Gerstley, Alterman, McLellan, & Woody, 1990). In light of the prevalence of ASPD among substance-abusing populations, it became imperative that effective treatment strategies be identified. Thus, the recurring association among ASPD, substance abuse, and crime led to a variety of treatment outcome evaluations for substance abusers with this disorder. Yet, there is a widely held belief among treatment providers that persons with ASPD will not respond well to treatment as a direct result of the symptoms of their disorder (e.g., habitual lying and lack of emotional insight). In fact, treatment providers and therapists alike often state that patients with ASPD will manipulate their therapy for their own self-serving needs (Abram, 1989; Davidson & Neale, 1990; Evans & Sullivan, 1990; Forrest, 1992). As one expert notes: "If it is to their advantage to act cured, they will do so, but they will return to former patterns of behavior at the first opportunity" (Coon, 1983: 465). This belief was substantiated by a frequently cited report that stated that, compared to other types of patients, antisocial opioid abusers responded poorly to both routine drug abuse counseling and specialized psychotherapy (Woody, McLellan, Luborsky, & O'Brien, 1985).

Results from more recent studies that have empirically assessed the relationship between ASPD and substance abuse treatment outcomes have not supported the previous findings regarding this disorder and treatment response (Brooner, Kidorf, King, & Stoller, 1998; Gil, Nolimal, & Crowley, 1992; Messina et al., 1999; Silverman et al., 1998). Gil et al. (1992) compared the treatment outcomes of 55 consecutively admitted methadone maintenance patients with ASPD (42%) and those without ASPD. Although the findings were limited by the small sample and ambiguous design, no significant differences were found between those with and those without ASPD on any 12-month outcome variable (e.g., treatment retention, urine test results, therapy session attendance). It appeared that ASPD patients did as well as those without ASPD in a traditional methadone maintenance program. However, a lack of difference did not necessarily imply good treatment responsivity. The authors reported low overall retention in this sample of clients.

Valliant (1975) had previously speculated that structured behavioral programs with incentives for participation might produce the best results for antisocial opioid patients. Evans and Sullivan (1990) also stated that "[it] is highly unlikely that antisocials will develop genuine remorse and altruistic reasons for staying clean and sober. However, they may be interested if it will help them win at poker, make more money, or stay out of jail" (p. 104).

Brooner and his colleagues (1998) directly tested Valliant's hypothesis regarding the use of incentives. Forty opioid abusers with co-occurring ASPD were randomly assigned to an experimental treatment condition combining methadone maintenance and contingency management techniques (i.e., a structural behavioral intervention using rapid delivery of positive and negative contingencies) or a control condition (i.e., standard methadone maintenance). In the experimental condition, take-home methadone doses and dose alterations were contingent on drug-free urine specimens and counseling session attendance. Preliminary findings did not reveal significant differences between the groups; yet, both groups showed marked reductions in heroin and cocaine use during the 17-week outcome evaluation. The authors contend that these findings are not only contrary to what is commonly thought about ASPD clients in traditional methadone treatment, but also about ASPD clients in enhanced methadone (i.e., methadone maintenance combined with contingency management) treatment programs as well. However, this study was limited by a small sample and by the absence of a non-ASPD control group.

Other contingency management approaches include giving vouchers that are exchangeable for goods and services in response to drug-free urine specimens. Silverman et al. (1998) compared the treatment responsiveness of 59 methadone maintenance patients with ASPD (19%) and without ASPD who were participating in voucher-based cocaine abstinence reinforcement therapy. Patients were randomly assigned to two levels of voucher-based interventions or a control group in which vouchers were given on a noncontingent basis. The authors found that both contingent interventions significantly increased abstinence from cocaine and opiates, compared with the control group. Moreover, a diagnosis of ASPD was unrelated to treatment outcomes. However, the small sample size (and low prevalence of ASPD) may have rendered any differences in outcomes between substance abusers with ASPD and those without ASPD difficult to detect.

Another study explored the relationship of ASPD and treatment outcomes in therapeutic communities (TCs) with random assignment of (primarily cocaine dependent) respondents to two residential programs differing primarily in length (Messina et al., 1999). TCs often rely on cognitive behavioral methods to change existing behavior patterns. Clients diagnosed as having ASPD (n=166) were compared to 172 clients with no ASPD on three outcome measures. After controlling for relevant factors, clients with ASPD were as likely to complete treatment as other clients and they exhibited the same patterns of reduced drug use and criminal activity as did non-ASPD clients.

The findings from the above recent studies could indicate that ASPD is not a strong predictor of treatment nonresponsivity, as previously believed.The implications of these findings are important in light of the fact that substance abusers with ASPD are more likely than those without ASPD to engage in violent and serious criminal behaviors (Abram, 1989; Brooner, Schmidt, Felch, & Bigelow, 1992). However, the empirical literature assessing the relationship between ASPD and substance abuse treatment outcomes is lacking, and the existing research is limited by small sample sizes, nonrandom designs, and/or the absence of an appropriate control group. The present study sought to examine the relationship between ASPD and substance abuse treatment responsivity by addressing these primary weaknesses of the literature.

This study directly compares the efficacy of two commonly used treatment approaches (cognitive behavioral treatment and contingency management) for the treatment of cocaine dependence among methadone-maintained patients *with and without* ASPD. These two treatment approaches represent two of the most promising psychological-behavioral approaches for the treatment of substance abuse. However, the rationales for these two approaches differ considerably. Cognitive behavioral treatment (CBT) strategies are based upon social learning principles (Bandura, 1977). These techniques include a wide range of treatment strategies designed to prevent relapse to drug use. The primary focus of CBT is maintaining a habit-changing process. This process is twofold: to prevent the occurrence of initial lapses to drug use after one has embarked on a program of habit change, and to prevent any lapse from escalating into total relapse (Marlatt & Gordon, 1985).

Contingency management (CM) techniques, on the other hand, are founded on principles of operant conditioning (Skinner, 1938). The CM techniques create systems of incentives and disincentives to motivate behavior change. Some positive incentive strategies include take-home methadone doses and cash incentives for drug-free urine specimens. One of the most promising applications of CBT and CM is in the area of cocaine abuse treatment. Cocaine abuse continues to be a serious public health problem and is an important factor in drug-related crime and violence (Everingham & Rydell, 1994). Moreover, cocaine abuse among methadone-maintained patients continues to be a serious challenge for treatment clinicians (Farabee, Rawson, & McCann, 2002; Rawson, Obert, McCann, & Ling, 1991; Silverman, Chutuape, Bigelow, & Stitzer, 1999). Both CBT and CM have been shown to be effective in treating cocaine-dependent patients (Carroll, 1999; Carroll et al., 1994; Farabee et al., 2002; Foote et al., 1994; Marlatt & Gordon, 1985; Silverman et al., 1996; Silverman et al., 1998; Silverman et al., 1999).

This study offers an excellent opportunity to compare the relative efficacy of an information-based "talk therapy" (CBT) with a purely operant paradigm (CM) for producing desired behavior change among substance-abusing clients with co-occurring ASPD. Furthermore, this study assesses the relative efficacy of combining these interventions (CBT+CM) for reducing cocaine use among methadone-maintained patients with ASPD. Since all patients are involved in a "platform" condition of methadone maintenance, it is possible to use a study design in which three active cocaine treatment conditions (CBT, CM, and CBT+CM) are compared to a control condition in which patients receive no additional treatment for their cocaine disorder.

Because of the limited literature (both in number and design) regarding substance abuse treatment responsivity for ASPD patients, findings are somewhat difficult to interpret. It is possible that group differences within the methadone maintenance studies have not been found because of the low power generated by the insufficient sample sizes. For example, it is likely that Brooner et al. (1998) would have found a significant difference between the ASPD patients in the experimental (CM) condition and the ASPD patients in the control condition had they used a larger sample. (By our calculations, their preliminary study generated a power of only .07, with an effect size of .15). The ASPD patients in the CM condition had a larger number of drug-free urine specimens, on average, than did the ASPD patients in the control condition. Monetary incentives for cocaine abstinence could be a strong external motivator for patients with ASPD.

Monetary incentives *combined* with drug-relapse education and peer support (i.e., CBT) might prove to be a strong treatment intervention for co-disordered patients.

Therefore, we hypothesized that ASPD patients in the three treatment conditions (CBT, CM, CBT+CM) would have better treatment responsivity over the 16-week course of treatment than would ASPD patients in the control condition (i.e., methadone maintenance only). Moreover, we hypothesized that there would be a cumulative treatment effect among ASPD patients over the course of treatment, with good performance in the CBT condition, better performance in the CM condition, and optimum performance in the CBT+CM condition.

$$[CBT] < [CM] < [CBT + CM]$$

Conversely, we hypothesized that the positive treatment effect of CM would decline for the ASPD patients once the incentive is removed (i.e., during the posttreatment outcome period). Because it has been speculated that ASPD patients have little internal motivation, it is reasonable to hypothesize that they will be less likely to remain abstinent in the absence of external incentives. Because the available literature assessing the relationship between ASPD and treatment outcomes is lacking, we also posed the more general research question: Is a diagnosis of ASPD a significant predictor of treatment outcomes?

METHOD

The data for this study is from the "Behavioral/Cognitive Behavioral Trial for Cocaine Abuse Project", a treatment outcome study for methadone-maintained, cocaine-dependent patients. The main treatment outcome report for this project can be found in Rawson et al. (2002). The current chapter focuses on the ASPD diagnosis and its relation to treatment outcomes.

Patients

Study participants were volunteers from two licensed narcotic treatment programs in Los Angeles, California (Matrix Institute and West Los Angeles Treatment Program). To be eligible for the study, all candidates were required: (1) to have been on methadone maintenance treatment at one of the two clinics for a minimum of 90 days; (2) to meet DSM-IV criteria for cocaine dependence; and (3) to show evidence of cocaine use (cocaine-metabolite positive urine sample) during the month prior to study enrollment. Individuals were ineligible if they (1) were also dependent upon alcohol or benzodiazepines to the point of requiring withdrawal medication; (2) if they had received specific treatment for cocaine in the previous 30 days; or (3) if they were court-mandated to treatment.

During a 30-month recruitment period, 120 individuals met study eligibility criteria, were enrolled in the study, and were randomly assigned into one of the four study conditions (CBT, CM, CBT+CM, or MM). † At admission, slightly more than half (56%) of the sample was male and the mean age was 43. With respect to race/ethnicity, 38% of the sample were White, 31% African American, 28% Hispanic, and 6% "other." The majority of patients (72%) had completed at least 12 years of school. A small percentage (15%) of the sample reported that they had steady employment over the past 3 years. Among the four conditions, none of the between-group differences in patient characteristics was statistically significant. Similar to the demographic profiles, self-reported prevalence of past-month drug and alcohol use did not vary significantly by study condition.

Procedures

Random assignment into one of the four study conditions (30 patients in each condition) took place following informed consent procedures and a 2-week baseline data collection period.

Demographic and background information was captured using the Addiction Severity Index (ASI). The ASI is a semi-structured interview instrument used for both clinical and research purposes to determine service needs (McLellan et al., 1992). It is a comprehensive instrument consisting of questions pertaining to demographics, employment, living situation, past and current health status, past and current drug use, past and current drug treatment history, past and current criminal and criminal justice involvement, and past and current mental health status and treatment.

The Structural Clinical Interview for Mental Disorders-IV (SCID) was administered during the first 30 days of study participation by a trained masters- or Ph.D.-level staff person to confirm the substance use diagnosis and to determine the presence of ASPD. The SCID is a semi-structured interview for making Axis I and Axis II diagnoses based on DSM-IV criteria (Kranzler, Rounsaville, & Tennen, 1995). SCID interviews were supervised and reviewed by a Ph.D.-level staff member. A total of 108 clients were evaluated by the SCID diagnostic interview and are the focus of this study (12 patients dropped-out of treatment prior to administration of the SCID). Forty-four percent of the target sample met the DSM-IV criteria for ASPD. The frequency of ASPD among the study patients is consistent with other reports on the psychiatric co-morbidity among methadone maintained-individuals (Rounseville, Eyre, Weissman, & Kleber, 1983; Sievewright & Daly, 1997).

† Only four individuals volunteered for study participation in the first 60 days of recruitment. The two study clinics operated on a fee-for-service basis in which patients paid either $140 (Matrix Clinic) or $180 (West LA Clinic) per month for methadone maintenance treatment services. Only after a $40 per month methadone program fee-reduction was offered as an incentive for study participation did study recruitment become adequate. Thus, the group of individuals who participated in this study can be characterized as having relatively low motivation to stop their cocaine use as defined by the requirement of a $40 per month incentive to encourage study participation.

Treatment Interventions

CBT procedures. The CBT procedure consisted of a total of 48 group sessions (3 per week for 16 weeks). Typical groups had four to eight patients. Each group session was scheduled to be 90 minutes in duration, and the material for each session was provided in a workbook. Each workbook presented a concept or a brief written exercise that explained or illustrated an aspect of cognitive-behavioral therapy. This method has been found in previous work by Rawson, Obert, McCann, Smith, and Scheffey (1989) to help stimulant users achieve and maintain abstinence. Many of the concepts were distilled from Marlatt and Gordon (1985) and/or are consistent with the National Institute on Drug Abuse manual on CBT (Carroll, 1999). Each session was led by a master's level therapist who had received 40-60 hours of supervised training in delivering the materials in a standardized manner. All sessions were audiotaped and reviewed by a counseling supervisor. Feedback was given to the therapist to shape and reinforce consistency.

The session format consisted of the topic being introduced by the staff member/group leader, the sheet being read aloud by the leader or a participant volunteer, and group members being given approximately 5 to 10 minutes to discuss the relevance of the topic to him/herself. Those individuals who were unwilling to discuss the topic were allowed to sit and listen. At the end of the topic discussion (typically 45-60 minutes into the session), each individual was asked to discuss his/her drug use/nonuse over the previous time period since the last group. The group leader and other group members verbally reinforced those reporting no use, less use, and/or the initiation of some new prosocial behavior. Finally, each member was asked to describe his/her behavioral plan for the time period leading up to the next session. Plans that included activities based upon the cognitive behavioral principles presented in the treatment groups received praise from the group leader and other members.

CM procedures. Patients in the CM-only condition were required to provide three urine samples per week and meet briefly (2-5 minutes) with the CM technician. The meetings with the CM technician covered four topics: (1) a review of the results of the urine test (tested immediately using enzyme multiplied immunoassay tests [EMIT]); (2) the delivery of the appropriate paper voucher certificate, if earned; (3) a discussion of how the voucher or accumulated voucher account could be redeemed; and (4) the delivery of the earned items when the vouchers were redeemed. On occasions when vouchers were earned, the CM technician provided praise and encouragement for successful performance. Patients who provided samples positive for stimulants (there were no contingencies for drug use other than stimulants) were not "scolded" or punished (other than the punishment of withholding the voucher).

The voucher value was based upon an escalating schedule that was similar to that used in previous studies (Higgins et al., 1993, 1994). The initial voucher value started at $2.50 per stimulant-negative sample, increasing in value by $1.25 with each successive negative sample, and with a $10 bonus for three consecutive stimulant-negative samples. The maximum voucher value was $46.25 per sample (excluding the $10 bonus). Across the course of the entire 16 weeks, the maximum possible earning (48 consecutive stimulant-free samples) was $1,277.50. Cash was never given to patients. As the voucher account increased in value as a result of stimulant-free urine samples, patients were encouraged to "spend" their savings on items that could support drug-free activities.

Patients in all study conditions received identical methadone maintenance (MM) services. The average dose of methadone at baseline was 72 milligrams for the CBT group, 62 milligrams for the CM group, 68 milligrams for the CBT+CM group, and 71 milligrams for the MM-only group. Participation in the study had no effect on the nature of their MM treatment. There were very clear rules for the termination of patients from the study. Termination could be a result of: (1) study completion (16-weeks); (2) missing two consecutive weekly data collection visits; or (3) missing either six consecutive CBT groups or six consecutive urine samples. Therefore, a consistent 2-week absence from protocol participation was the criterion for study termination across all study conditions.

Study Measures

The cocaine treatment intervention lasted 16 weeks for all conditions. Cocaine use, as measured by urinalysis, was the principal dependent measure during and after treatment. All study patients were required to give three urine samples per week throughout the 16-week study period and at each of the three follow-up interviews (17, 26, and 52 weeks). All samples were analyzed for metabolites of cocaine (benzoylecognine, BE) and methamphetamine. (Methamphetamine was included as a target along with cocaine to prevent "stimulant switching"; however, the frequency of methamphetamine use in this population was almost nonexistent. Hence, the study findings are specific to cocaine). A 300 ng/ml urinary BE cutoff was used to define a positive sample. All samples were analyzed on-site using EMIT (SYVA) reagent test procedures. All samples were monitored (i.e., collected in bottles equipped with temperature strips, and the bathrooms where samples were collected did not have hot water to prevent tampering). In addition, approximately 33% of all samples were collected under observation. Observation of urine specimens was conducted on a random basis. All subjects were breath alcohol tested at the time of the collection of each urine sample.

Follow-up urine specimens were analyzed for cocaine, methamphetamine, metabolites of illicit opiates, benzodiazepines, barbiturates, and cannabinoids. Ninety percent of the sample provided urine specimens at the 17-week follow-up, 83% provided specimens at the 26-week follow-up, and 83% provided specimens at the 52-week follow-up. There were no significant differences in follow-up rates between those with and those without ASPD across the four study conditions at any of the follow-up periods (percentages shown below).

- *17-Week Follow-Up*: Non-ASPD CBT = 86%; ASPD CBT = 93%; Non-ASPD CM = 92%; ASPD CM = 93%; Non-ASPD CBT+CM = 89%; ASPD CBT+CM = 100%; Non- ASPD control = 87%; ASPD control = 83%.
- *26-Week Follow-Up*: Non-ASPD CBT = 79%; ASPD CBT = 93%; Non-ASPD CM = 83%; ASPD CM = 87%; Non-ASPD CBT+CM = 89%; ASPD CBT+CM = 86%; Non-ASPD control = 73%; ASPD control = 75%.

Table 1 Sample Characteristics at Admission, by ASPD Status (N = 108)

	No ASPD (N = 60)	ASPD (N = 48)	Total (N = 108)
Characteristics	%	%	%
Gender			
Male	43**	71**	56
Female	*57*	*29*	*44*
	100%	100%	100%
Race/Ethnicity			
White	43	31	38
Black	40**	21**	31
Hispanic/Other	*17*	*48*	*31*
	100%	100%	100%
Mean Age at Admission (SD)	43.7 (7.6)	43.5 (8.1)	43
Education			
Less than 12 years	18*	40*	28
High-school Degree or more	*82*	*60*	*72*
	100%	100%	100%
Full Time Employment Past 3 Years	17	13	15
Study Condition			
CBT	23	29	26
CM	20	31	25
CBT+CM	32	15	24
MM	*25*	*25*	*25*
	100%	100%	100%

*p < .05. **p < .01.

52-Week Follow-Up: Non-ASPD CBT = 79%; ASPD CBT = 86%; Non-ASPD CM = 75%; ASPD CM = 93%; Non-ASPD CBT+CM = 95%; ASPD CBT+CM = 71%; Non-ASPD control = 73%; ASPD control = 83%.

Data Analysis

The distribution of demographic and drug-use characteristics by ASPD status was evaluated using chi-square analysis and t-tests. Similarly, the distribution of SCID-I and II diagnoses across study conditions was evaluated by chi-square analysis. In-treatment cocaine use measures were analyzed using a Two-Way Analysis of Variance (ANOVA). To control for inflated alpha error, Tukey-Kramer tests were used for all post hoc comparisons. In addition, a series of regression analyses were conducted to assess in-treatment cocaine use while controlling for pre-existing differences between those with and those without ASPD. To assess cocaine and heroin use following treatment, separate chi-square analyses were conducted for those with and those without ASPD at each of the follow-up time periods. All statistical tests were considered significant at $p \leq .05$ and were two-tailed.

RESULTS

Demographic characteristics for ASPD and non-ASPD patients were similar across the four study conditions; however, small cell sizes limited reliable statistical inference. Although patients were randomly assigned to the study conditions, they were not randomly assigned by ASPD diagnosis. To further explore any pre-existing differences, all ASPD patients were compared with all non-ASPD patients with regard to their demographic and drug use characteristics.

Table 2 Self-Reported Drug/Alcohol Use 30 Days Prior to Admission, by ASPD Status (N = 108)

Substance Use 30 Days Prior to Admission	No ASPD (N = 60) %	ASPD (N = 48) %	Total (N = 108) %
Alcohol Use	57	60	58
Alcohol Use to Intoxication	23	35	29
Marijuana	30	27	29
Heroin Use	58*	79*	68
Other Opiates	08**	31**	18
Cocaine Use	100	98	99
Amphetamines	03	08	06

*p < .05. **p < .01.

Table 3 SCID-I and II Diagnoses, by Study Condition (N = 108)[a]

Diagnoses[b]	CBT (N=28) %	CM (N=27) %	CBT+CM (N=26) %	MM (N=27) %	Total (N=108) %
SCID-I					
Substance Use Disorder	100	100	100	100	100
Mood Disorder	18	33	23	19	23
Anxiety Disorder	18	37	27	19	25
SCID-II					
Antisocial Personality Disorder (ASPD)	50	56	27	44	44
All Diagnoses					
Substance Use Disorder Only	29	23	50	36	34
Substance Use and Other Axis I Disorders	21	22	23	19	21
Substance Use and ASPD	36	22	12	26	24
Substance Use, ASPD, and Other Axis I Dis.	14	33	15	19	21
	100%	100%	100%	100%	100%

[a] N's vary slightly due to missing data.
[b] Only diagnoses prevalent in 5% or more of the sample are shown.
Note. Differences are not significant.

Consistent with previous literature, patients diagnosed with ASPD were significantly more likely to be male (71% vs. 43%, $p < .01$) and to have less than a high school education (40% vs. 18%, $p < .05$) than non-ASPD patients (see Table 1). With regard to ethnicity, patients with ASPD were significantly more likely than non-ASPD patients to be Hispanic (48% vs. 17%, $p < .01$). No significant differences between those with and those without ASPD were found with regard to age or employment, and patients with ASPD were equally distributed among the study conditions.

Comparisons of demographic characteristics of *ASPD-patients only* across the four study conditions were also conducted. No significant differences were found with regard to age, gender, race/ethnicity, or high school education (results are not shown).

Table 2 displays the self-reported drug and alcohol use patterns by ASPD status during the 30 days prior to study admission. Those with ASPD were significantly more likely to have used heroin (79% vs. 58%, $p < .05$) and other opiates (31% vs. 8%, $p < .01$) during this time period, than non-ASPD patients. No other substance-use differences were found. Cocaine (99%) and heroin (68%) were most likely to be used during the 30 days prior to study admission, followed by alcohol (58%), marijuana (29%), other opiates (18%), and amphetamines (6%).

Table 3 displays the prevalence of ASPD, substance use disorder, and other SCID-I psychiatric disorders by study condition. Only those diagnoses prevalent in more than 5% of the sample are shown. There were no significant differences among the four study conditions with regard to prevalence of psychiatric disorders. All subjects met the criteria for substance use disorder and almost half (44%) had co-occurring ASPD. Of those evaluated by the SCID, 34% had no disorders other than substance use, 21% had substance use and other Axis I disorders, 24% had substance use with co-occurring ASPD, and 21% had substance use disorder, co-occurring ASPD, and other Axis I disorders. (All analyses combine clients with substance use disorder only and those with other Axis I disorders into the non-ASPD group.)

In-Treatment Performance

Treatment retention. Treatment retention is frequently an important outcome indicator and is sometimes used as one measure of treatment efficacy. In this study, the value of treatment retention as a dependent measure was compromised by the necessity to reduce patients' monthly methadone program fees by $40 to promote study enrollment. Therefore, not surprisingly, there was no significant difference in study retention for patients with and those without ASPD across four study conditions. The average number of weeks in treatment for the ASPD group was 14.7 (SD = 3.4), ranging from 12 to 16. The average number of weeks in treatment for the non-ASPD group was 13.2 (SD = 4.9), ranging from 10 to 15 weeks.

Cocaine-abstinence during treatment. The primary dependent measure in this study was cocaine use as measured by urine toxicology. Since retention in treatment was not significantly different for those with and without ASPD across study conditions, the most direct measure of cocaine use across the 16 weeks of the trial was the number of *cocaine-negative* urine samples given by each participant during their 48 opportunities to give samples (3 times per week for 16 weeks). There were no significant differences between those with and those without ASPD across the four study conditions with regard to the rates of missing urines.

Table 4 Treatment Effectiveness Scores for In-Treatment Cocaine-Free Urine Samples, by Study Condition and ASPD Status

ASPD Status	CBT	CM*	CBT+CM	MM
No ASPD				
Mean TES for Cocaine (s.d)	17.6 $(17.9)_a$	25.5 $(20.7)_a$	24.2 $(21.1)_a$	14.5 $(16.9)_a$
ASPD				
Mean TES for Cocaine (S.D.)	24.8 $(15.6)_a$	39.4 $(11.4)_b$	37.7 $(13.3)_{ab}$	9.3 $(11.3)_c$

Note. Subscripts represent the results of pairwise comparisons between study conditions; means that *do not* have a subscript in common are significantly different from each other (p < .05).

*The CM condition was the only condition with a significant difference between those with and without ASPD (p < .05).

A Two-Way ANOVA was performed to determine differences in the mean number of cocaine-negative samples (CNS) provided by ASPD status and by study condition. The possibility of an interaction effect (ASPD status X study condition) was also explored. We initially asked if ASPD would be a significant predictor of in-treatment responsivity. There was a significant main effect for ASPD status. The mean number of CNS for patients with ASPD (CNS = 27.4, SD = 17.5) was significantly higher than the mean number of CNS for those without ASPD (CNS = 20.5, SD = 19.4) [F (1,107) = 4.74, $p < .05$), suggesting that ASPD patients performed better during the 16-week treatment course than non-ASPD patients. However, there was no interaction effect between ASPD status and study condition.

We also hypothesized that ASPD patients in the three cocaine treatment conditions (CBT, CM, CBT+CM) would have better outcomes than ASPD patients in the control condition (MM). This hypothesis was supported. Pairwise comparisons of the mean number of CNS indicated that ASPD patients in each of the treatment conditions had significantly higher scores than those in the control condition (CBT = 24.8; CM = 39.4; CBT+CM = 37.7; vs. MM = 9.3, $p < .05$). The same pattern was found among the study conditions for the non-ASPD group, but differences were not statistically significant (see Table 4).

The above findings indicate that ASPD patients responded positively to the three cocaine treatment conditions; however, we also hypothesized a cumulative treatment effect for ASPD patients, with optimum performance in the CBT+CM condition (CBT< CM < CBT+CM). This hypothesis was not supported. Pairwise comparisons did show that the mean number of CNS for the ASPD patients in the CM condition was significantly higher than the mean number of CNS for the ASPD patients in the CBT-only condition (CBT = 24.8 vs. CM = 39.4, $p < .05$). However, no differences were found for the ASPD patients in the CBT+CM condition compared with the ASPD patients in the CM or CBT-only groups (shown in Table 4).

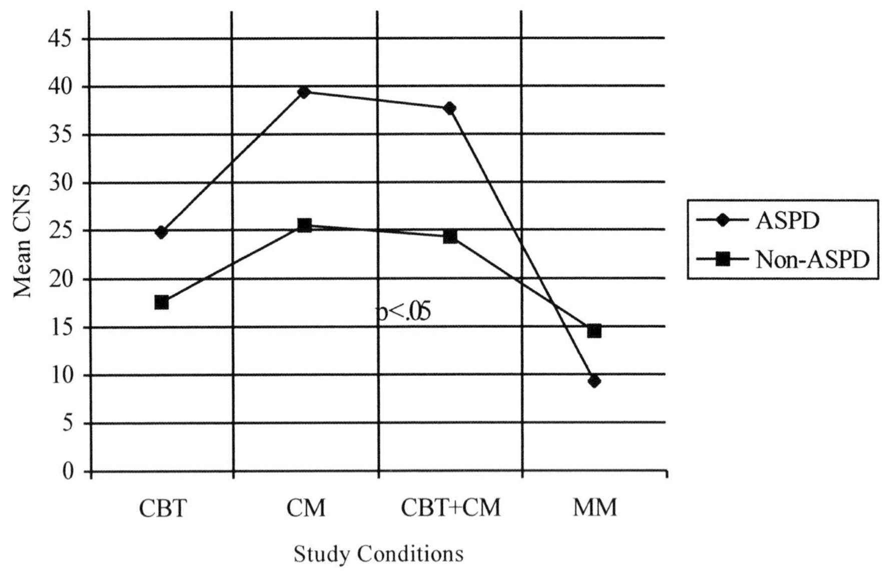

Figure 1: Cocaine-Negative Specimens Provided During Treatment (N=108)

Moreover, ASPD patients in the CM condition performed significantly better than the non-ASPD CM patients (ASPD/CM CNS = 39.4 vs. non-ASPD/CM CNS = 25.5, $p < .05$). The differences in CNS means were not significant for ASPD and non-ASPD patients in any of the other study conditions (shown in Figure 1).

The above bivariate analyses, however, do not take into account pre-existing differences between those with and without ASPD that might be related to in-treatment performance. Initially, no demographic differences were found between those with and those without ASPD in any of the treatment conditions; however, when we compared *all* of the ASPD patients with *all* of the non-ASPD patients (see Tables 1 and 2), some pre-existing differences were evident (i.e., gender, race, high school education, and opiate use). Therefore, we decided to further explore the association of ASPD with CM treatment using multivariate analyses. Because the total number of patients in the CM condition fell below 30, we were limited in the number of independent variables (or predictors) that could be included in the multivariate analyses (Keppel, 1991). Thus, we conducted a series of regressions pairing ASPD with each of the above characteristics. In all of these pairings, a diagnosis of ASPD remained significantly related to the mean number of CNS ($p<.01$). We further confirmed the *lack* of an association of ASPD to in-treatment performance among the other study conditions (analyses not shown).

Post-Treatment Performance

Cocaine urinalysis results for ASPD patients at each follow-up period. We hypothesized that the positive treatment effect of CM would decline for the ASPD patients once the incentives were removed (i.e., no vouchers were given during the posttreatment outcome periods). This hypothesis was not supported. ASPD patients in the CM conditions continued to abstain from cocaine use throughout the three follow-up time periods. Figure 2 shows that ASPD patients in the CM-only condition were as likely as those in the other study conditions to have cocaine-free urine specimens at weeks 17, 26, and 52. In fact, over 70% of the CM-only group provided cocaine-free specimens at each follow-up time period. Overall, differences in percentages of cocaine-free specimens between the treatment groups and the control group were not significant at weeks 17 and 26. However, percentages were significantly different at week 52, indicating that between 65% and 80% of the ASPD patients in any of the three treatment conditions were abstaining from cocaine use at the 52-week follow-up period, compared to 20% in the control condition ($p < .05$).

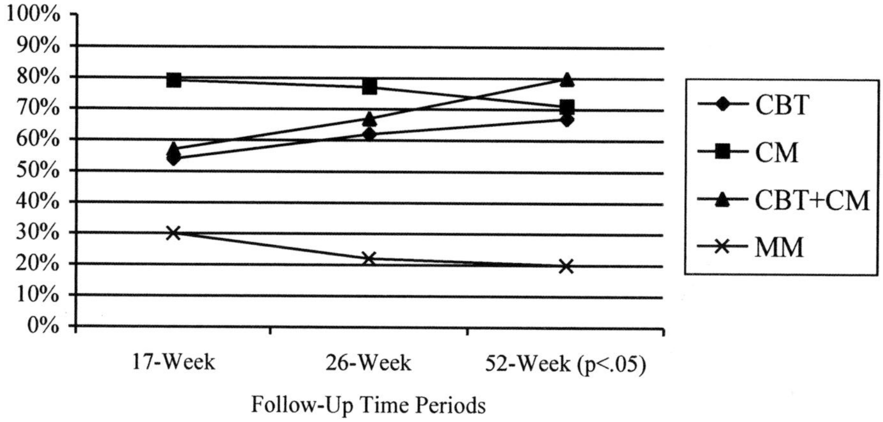

Figure 2 Cocaine-Free Urine Specimens During Follow-Up [ASPD Patients]

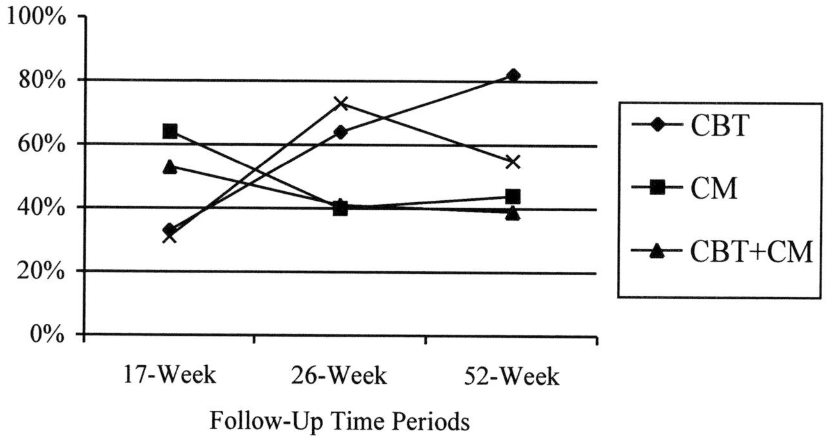

Figure 3 Cocaine-Free Urine Specimens During Follow-Up [Non-ASPD Patients]

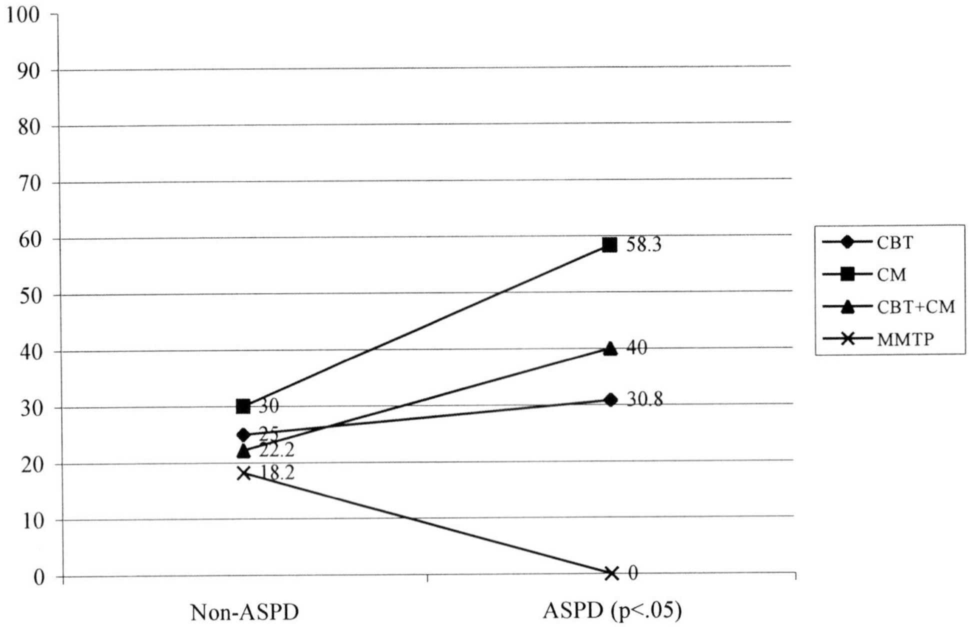

Figure 4: Percentage of Cocaine-Free Urine Specimens at All Three Follow-Up Periods (N=91)

Cocaine urinalysis results for non-ASPD patients at each follow-up period. The rates of cocaine abstinence for the non-ASPD patients did not follow the same trends as those for the ASPD patients. Figure 3 shows that the percentages of cocaine-free specimens were similar across the four study groups for each follow-up time period (i.e., no significant differences were found). However, the CBT-only group was the only treatment group that showed substantial increases in abstinence over the three follow-up time periods (33%, 64%, and 81% respectively).

Post-treatment responsivity. To assess overall differences in posttreatment performance between those with and those without ASPD, we created a posttreatment responsivity measure that totaled the percentages of patients who had cocaine-free urine specimens at all three of the follow-up periods. Figure 4 shows the posttreatment results by study condition for those with and those without ASPD. Among non-ASPD patients, there were no significant differences in cocaine negative specimens at each of the three follow-up time periods.

In contrast, the ASPD patients in the three cocaine treatment conditions showed large differences in continued abstinence from cocaine compared with those in the control condition ($p < .05$). Over half of the ASPD patients in the CM-only condition had cocaine-free urine results at each follow-up interview (58%), followed by those in the CBT+CM condition (40%), and those in the CBT-only condition (31%). None of the MM-only group had three consecutive cocaine-free urine results.

Because the posttreatment findings regarding cocaine use were not as expected, we explored the possibility that ASPD patients were more likely than non-ASPD patients to be using heroin at the follow-up time periods. These results are shown below.

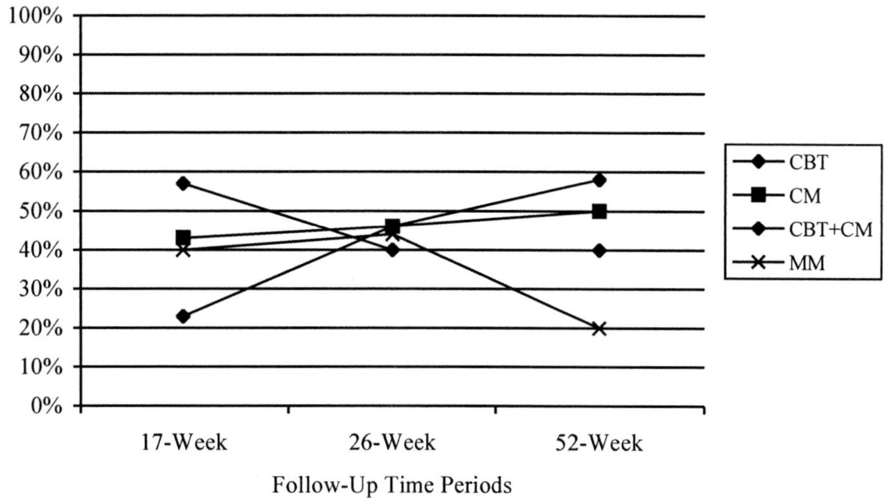

Figure 5: Heroin-Free Urine Specimens During Follow-Up [ASPD Participants]

Post-treatment heroin urinalysis results. Overall, study patients were less likely to abstain from heroin use, compared to cocaine use, at the three follow-up time periods regardless of treatment group or ASPD status (see Figures 5 and 6). However, abstinence rates were not trivial. At the 26-week follow-up, between 40% and 50% of the ASPD patients tested negative for heroin, whereas between 50% and 60% of the non-ASPD patients tested negative for heroin. In addition, non-ASPD patients in the CBT-only condition were significantly more likely to abstain from heroin at the 17-week follow-up compared with those in the other treatment conditions (CBT = 75% vs. CM = 36% vs. CBT+CM = 35% vs. MM = 23%, $\underline{p} < .05$).

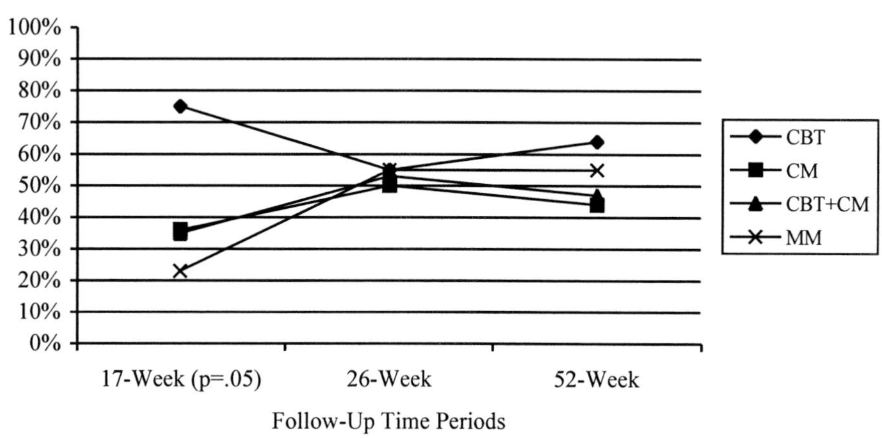

Figure 6: Heroin-Free Urine Specimens During Follow-Up[Non-ASPD Participants]

CONCLUSION

Recent findings of successful treatment outcomes for methadone-maintained patients with ASPD provides a strong argument against the perception that substance abusers with ASPD are unresponsive to drug treatment (Brooner et al., 1998; Gil et al., 1992; Silverman et al., 1998). However, these studies have been limited by small sample sizes and ambiguous designs. The current study sought to overcome the limitations of the previous research. The primary goal of this study was to determine the efficacy of two commonly used treatment approaches, separately and combined, for the treatment of cocaine dependence in methadone-maintained patients with co-occurring ASPD.

In-Treatment Responsivity

Three major trends of in-treatment responsivity are evident. First, in contrast to previous findings (and beliefs), we found that a diagnosis of ASPD was significantly and positively related to treatment responsivity. Those with ASPD were more likely to abstain from cocaine use during treatment than those without ASPD. Second, ASPD patients in each of the treatment conditions performed significantly better than ASPD patients in the control condition, whereas no differences in performance by study condition were found for the non-ASPD patients. Third, the strong treatment effect for ASPD patients was primarily due to the CM condition. During the 16-week course of treatment, those in the CM condition were significantly more likely to abstain from cocaine use than those in the CBT-only condition. In contrast, abstinence levels in the combined treatment group (CBT+CM) fell between the CBT- and CM-only levels and did not differ significantly from either. Furthermore, ASPD patients in the CM condition were significantly more likely to abstain from cocaine use than non-ASPD patients in the CM condition, even after controlling for pre-existing differences.

As earlier theorists hypothesized (Evans & Sullivan, 1990; Valliant, 1975), monetary incentives appear to be a successful treatment intervention for reducing cocaine use among substance abusers with co-occurring ASPD, and a more successful intervention than for those without ASPD. Furthermore, patients with ASPD responded significantly better to this type of intervention than ASPD patients in "talk-based therapy." The larger question, however, was whether the positive treatment effects of the CM intervention would continue beyond the course of treatment, once the incentive was removed.

Post-Treatment Responsivity

Four major results are evident from our posttreatment outcomes. First, and contrary to our hypothesis, ASPD patients in the CM conditions continued to abstain from cocaine use throughout the three follow-up periods. Although differences in cocaine abstinence between the groups were not significant, ASPD patients in the CM conditions appeared to maintain the highest levels of posttreatment cocaine abstinence. In addition, comparable numbers of ASPD and non-ASPD patients were abstaining from heroin at the follow-up time periods. Second, ASPD patients in all three treatment conditions were significantly more likely to abstain from cocaine use at the 52 week follow-up than those in the control condition. Third, a clear pattern of posttreatment performance between the treatment groups was not evident for the non-ASPD patients. Non-ASPD patients in the CM conditions appeared to do well at the first follow-up, but their performance declined substantially during the remaining follow-up periods. In contrast, non-ASPD patients in the CBT-only group were the only treatment group whose performance increased over the follow-up time periods. And fourth, ASPD patients in each of the treatment conditions were significantly more likely to test negative for cocaine at *all* three of the follow-up periods than those in the MM-only condition, whereas no differences were found for non-ASPD patients. Most importantly, ASPD patients in the CM condition were twice as likely as non-ASPD patients in the CM condition to have negative urine test results for cocaine at all follow-up periods.

These findings provide a strong argument against the perception that substance abusers with ASPD are unresponsive to drug treatment. Consequently, these findings are important in light of treatment program exclusionary criteria and current public policy. Many substance abuse treatment programs across the nation exclude persons with ASPD on the assumption that they will not respond well to treatment efforts (Messina et al., 1999). Furthermore, a diagnosis of ASPD is among the exclusionary criteria for Maryland's newly constructed Public Mental Health System, and ASPD is the only personality diagnosis deemed untreatable within this system of health service delivery (Brooner et al., 1998). The results of the present study and other recent publications suggest that substance abusers with ASPD may be more responsive to treatment than previously believed.

Study Strengths

The primary strength of our study was the rigorous study design. Random assignment of patients across study conditions created comparable groups. As a result, any differences between group performance tend to reflect the effect of the treatment intervention, rather than error variance (Bordens & Abbott, 1991). Random assignment also eliminated the issue of self-selection, which can be affected by such client attributes as personal motivation, perception of treatment modality, and treatment availability (Hser, 1995). In addition, the "platform" condition of methadone maintenance made it possible to use a study design with a true control condition.

Another strength of our study was the high prevalence rate of ASPD (45%), which is similar to other estimates of ASPD among methadone-maintained patients (ranging from 25% to 54%; Rounsaville, Eyre, Weissman, & Kleber, 1983). The high prevalence of this disorder within our sample allowed us to make comparisons of ASPD patients across study conditions, as well as between those with and those without ASPD. Thus, we were able to assess the treatment responsivity of ASPD patients in each treatment condition and compare their performance to those without ASPD.

The use of objective measures of drug use to assess treatment outcomes was an additional strength of this study. Self-reported drug use may be considerably less valid than previously reported (Messina, Wish, Nemes, & Wraight, 2000). For example, Wish, Hoffman, and Nemes (1997) found that among substance-abusing populations, clients were more likely to truthfully report heroin use than cocaine use. The authors further suggest that self-reports may be less valid at follow-up than at intake.

Study Limitations

Some limitations of this study should also be kept in mind when interpreting the results. The primary limitation is the sample size. Although our study had a larger sample than previous research among methadone-maintained patients, our posttreatment comparisons were limited by small cell sizes due to the four study conditions. However, we were able to improve power as compared to our calculations for Brooner's (1998) study. (Power calculation for our study =.47, effect size = .37; power calculation for Brooner = .07, effect size = .15).

Another limitation of this study (and others) is the existence of other psychiatric disorders among the sample. Patients with and without ASPD may have been diagnosed with various other psychiatric disorders. It is difficult to know the degree to which the various combinations of other disorders confounded the distinction between those with and those without ASPD, or if the presence of additional psychiatric disorders in patients with ASPD moderates the effect of the ASPD diagnosis on treatment response. However, recent findings from a large sample of methadone-maintained patients (N = 518) demonstrated minor differences between patients with ASPD only and patients with ASPD and other psychiatric disorders (King, Kidorf, Stoller, Carter, & Brooner, 2001). ASPD-only patients exhibited higher rates of heroin use during treatment, whereas ASPD patients with additional disorders exhibited higher rates of benzodiazepine use. No differences between the two groups were found for cocaine use during treatment.

An additional roadblock facing those who study and treat ASPD is the lack of agreement about a basic definition and the use of different definitions. There is much controversy among social scientists and clinicians over the proper measurement of ASPD among substance abusers. Although social scientists most often use diagnostic interviews that follow DSM-IV criteria to assess ASPD (such as the SCID-II), many have raised concerns about possible limitations of the DSM (Messina, Wish, Hoffman, & Nemes, 2001). It has been suggested that the DSM criteria for ASPD focus on behavioral characteristics instead of underlying personality traits and do not require that ASPD occur independently of substance abuse (Gerstley et al., 1990). Rounsaville et al. (1983) suggest that clients whose antisocial activities are independent of the need to obtain drugs are "primary antisocial addicts" and those whose antisocial activities are directly related to drug use are "secondary antisocial addicts." The authors speculated that secondary antisocial addicts might have better treatment responses. If most of our sample members were secondary antisocial addicts, it could account for their more positive treatment outcomes.

Summary

The relationships between ASPD, substance abuse, and crime is the nexus of a major social problem and understanding the interactions among these patterns of behavior will help identify the individuals and groups who most need effective intervention. The findings from the current study and other recent literature indicate that substance abusers with co-occurring ASPD can benefit from drug treatment programs. Furthermore, methadone-maintained ASPD patients participating in CM interventions show substantial reductions in cocaine use beyond the intervention period. It is therefore suggested that treatment programs make efforts to attract and retain substance abusers with a diagnosis of ASPD. Future research should continue to explore the many issues surrounding the diagnosis of ASPD, as well as its relationship to treatment outcomes.

ACKNOWLEDGMENTS

We are grateful to the staff and the patients at the Matrix Institute and the West Los Angeles Treatment Program for their participation. We would like to thank Alice Huber, Christie Thomas, Vikas Gulati, Al Hasson, and Michael McCann for their assistance with the conduct of this study.

REFERENCES

American Psychiatric Association (APA). (1994). *Diagnostic and Statistical Manual of Mental Disorders, 4th Edition (DSM-IV)*. Washington, DC.

Abram, K. M. (1989). The effect of co-occurring disorders on criminal career: Interaction of antisocial personality, alcoholism, and drug disorders. *International Journal of Law and Psychiatry, 12*, 133-148.

Bandura, A. (1977). Self-efficacy: Toward a unifying theory of behavioral change. *Psychological Review, 84,* 191-215.

Bordens, K., & Abbott, B. (1991). *Research design and methods: A process approach* (2nd Ed.). Mountain View, CA: Mayfield Publishing Company.

Brooner, R., Kidorf, M., King, V., & Stoller, K. (1998). Preliminary evidence of good treatment response in antisocial drug abusers. *Drug and Alcohol Dependence, 49,* 249-260.

Brooner, R., Schmidt, C., Felch, L., & Bigelow, G. (1992). Antisocial behavior of intravenous drug abusers: Implications for diagnosis of antisocial personality disorder. *American Journal of Psychiatry, 149,* 482-487.

Carroll, K. (Ed.) (1999). A cognitive-behavioral approach: Treating cocaine addiction. *Therapy Manuals for Drug Addiction.* Rockville, MD: National Institute on Drug Abuse, U.S. Department of Health and Human Services, National Institutes of Health.

Carroll, K.M., Rounsaville, B.J., Nich, C., Gordon, L.T., Wirtz, P.W., & Gawin, F.H. (1994). One year follow-up of psychotherapy and pharmacotherapy for cocaine dependence: Delayed emergence of psychotherapy effects. *Archives of General Psychiatry,* 51, 989-997.

Coon, Dennis. (1983) *Introduction to Psychology: Exploration and Application.* 3rd ed. Los Angeles: West Publishing Company.

Davison, G. C., & Neale, J. M. (1990). *Abnormal psychology* (5th ed.). New York: Wiley & Sons.

Evans, K., & Sullivan, J. (1990*). Dual diagnoses: Counseling mentally ill substance abusers.* New York: The Guilford Press.

Everingham, S., & Rydell, C. (1994). *Modeling the demand for cocaine.* Santa Monica, CA: RAND.

Farabee, D., Rawson, R., & McCann, M. (2002). Adoption of drug avoidance activities among patients in contingency management and cognitive-behavioral treatments. *Journal of Substance Abuse Treatment, 23,* 343-350.

Foote, J., Seligman, M., Magura, S., Handelsman, L., Rosenblum, A., Lovejoy, M., Arrington, K., & Stimmel, B. (1994). An enhanced positive reinforcement model for the severely impaired cocaine abuser. *Journal of Substance Abuse Treatment, 11*(6), 525-539.

Forrest, G. G. (1992). *Chemical dependency and antisocial personality disorder: Psychotherapy and assessment strategies.* New York: The Hawthorne Press.

Gerstley, L. J., Alterman, A. I., McLellan, A. T., & Woody, G. E. (1990). Antisocial personality disorder in patients with substance abuse disorders: A problematic diagnosis? *American Journal of Psychiatry, 147*(2), 173-178.

Gil, K., Nolimal, D., & Crowley, T. (1992). Antisocial personality disorder, HIV risk behavior and retention in methadone maintenance therapy. *Drug and Alcohol Dependence, 30*(3), 247-252.

Higgins, T., Budney, J., Bickel, K., Foerg, F., Donham, R., & Badger, J. (1994). Incentives improve outcome in outpatient behavioral treatment of cocaine dependence. *Archives of General Psychiatry, 51*(7), 568-576.

Higgins, T., Budney, J., Bickel, K., Hughes, R., Foerg, F., & Badger, J. (1993). Achieving cocaine abstinence with a behavior approach. *American Journal of Psychiatry, 150*, 763-769.

Hser, Y. (1995). Drug treatment counselor practices and effectiveness: An examination of literature and relevant issues in a multilevel framework. *Evaluation Review, 19*(4), 389-408.

Keppel, G. (1991). *Design and analyses: A researcher's handbook.* Prentice Hall: Englewood Cliffs, New Jersey.

King, V., Kidorf, M., Stoller, M., Carter, J., & Brooner, R. (2001). Influence of antisocial personality subtypes on drug abuse treatment response. *Journal of Nervous and Mental Disease, 189,* 593-601.

Kranzler, H., Rounsaville, B., & Tennen, H. (1995). *Validity of the SCID in substance abuse patients* (NIDA Research Monograph, 2, 35). Rockville, MD: National Institute on Drug Abuse.

Marlatt, G. & Gordon, J. (Eds.). (1985). *Relapse prevention: Maintenance strategies in the treatment of addictive behaviors.* New York: Guilford Press.

McLellan, A.T., Kushner, H., Metzger, D., Peters, R., Smith, I., Grissom, G., Pettinati, H., & Argeriou, M. (1992). The fifth edition of the Addiction Severity Index. *Journal of Substance Abuse Treatment, 9*, 199-213.

Messina, N. (2002). The antisocial personality. In Levinson, D. (Ed.). *Encyclopedia of Crime and Punishment*, vol.1. Great Barrington, Mass.: Berkshire Reference Works.

Messina, N., Wish, E., Hoffman, J., & Nemes, S. (2001). Diagnosing antisocial personality disorder among substance abusers: The Structured Clinical Interview for the DSM-III-R versus the Millon Clinical Multiaxial Inventory. *The American Journal of Drug and Alcohol Abuse,27*(4), 699-717.

Messina, N., Wish, E., & Nemes, S. (1999). Therapeutic community treatment for substance abusers with antisocial personality disorder. *Journal of Substance Abuse Treatment, 17*(1-2), 121-128.

Messina, N., Wish, E., Nemes, S., & Wraight, B. (2000). Correlates of underreporting of post-discharge cocaine use among therapeutic community clients. *Journal of Drug Issues, 30*(1), 119-132.

Rawson, R., Huber, A., McCann, M., Shoptaw, S., Farabee, D., Reiber, C., & Ling, W. (2002). A comparison of contingency management and cognitive-behavioral approaches for cocaine dependent methadone maintained individuals. *Archives of General Psychiatry, 59,* 817-824.

Rawson, R., Obert, J., McCann, M., & Ling, W. (1991). Psychological approaches to the treatment of cocaine dependency. *Journal of Addictive Diseases, 11,* 97-120.

Rawson, R., Obert, J., McCann, M., Smith, P., and Scheffey, H. (1989). *The neurobehavioral treatment manual, Matrix.* Beverly Hills, CA.

Rounsaville, B., Eyre, S., Weissman, M., & Kleber, H. (1983). The antisocial opiate addict. In B. Stimmeo (Vol. Ed.). *Psychosocial constructs: Alcoholism and substance abuse*, (pp. 29-43). New York: Hawthorne Press.

Skinner, B. (1938). *The behavior of organisms: An experimental analysis.* Englewood Cliffs, NJ: Prentice-Hall.

Seivewright, N., & Daly, C. (1997). Personality disorder and drug use: A review. *Drug and Alcohol Review, 16,* 235-250.

Silverman, K., Chutuape, M.A., Bigelow, G., & Stitzer, M. (1999). Voucher-based reinforcement of cocaine abstinence in treatment-resistant methadone patients: Effects of reinforcement magnitude. *Psychopharmacology, 146,* 128-138.

Silverman, K., Higgins, S., Montoya, I., Cone, E., Schuster, C., & Preston, K. (1996). Sustained cocaine abstinence in methadone maintenance patients through voucher-based reinforcement therapy. *Archives of General Psychiatry, 53,* 409-415.

Silverman, K., Wong, C., Umbricht-Schneiter, A., Montoya, I., Schuster, C., & Preston, K. (1998). Broad beneficial effects of cocaine abstinence reinforcement among methadone patients. *Journal of Consulting and Clinical Psychology, 66*(5), 811-824.

Tims, F. M., DeLeon, G., & Jainchill, N. (Eds.). (1994). *Therapeutic community: Advances in research and application* (NIDA Research Monograph No.144). Rockville, MD: National Institute on Drug Abuse.

Valliant, G. (1975). Sociopathy as a human process: A viewpoint. *Archives of General Psychiatry, 32,* 178-183.

Wish, E., Hoffman, J., & Nemes, S. (1997). The validity of self-reports of drug use at treatment admission and at follow-up: Comparisons with urinalysis and hair assays. In L. Harris (Ed.), *The validity of self-reports: The implications for survey research* (NIDA Research Monograph No. 167, pp. 200-225). Rockville, MD: National Institute on Drug Abuse.

Woody, G., McLellan, A.T., Luborsky, L, & O'Brien, C. (1985). Sociopathy and psychotherapy outcome. *Archives of General Psychiatry, 42,* 1081-1086.

In: Cocaine and Heroin Abuse Research
Editor: Lidia A. Pizzoli, pp. 121-141
ISBN 1-60021-076-7

Chapter 6

CURRENT CONTROVERSIES IN THE ASSESSMENT AND TREATMENT OF HEROIN ADDICTION

Robert J. Craig*
Jesse Brown VA Medical Center, Chicago, IL USA

ABSTRACT

This paper addresses controversial topics in the assessment and treatment of heroin addiction. Included in the discussion are issues of dose and outcome, difficulties with toxicology screens, the role of co-occurring Axis I and Axis II disorders, the introduction (and extinction) of newer medications to treat heroin dependence, difficulties of measuring treatment outcome, models of heroin dependence, the role of user personality, and the question of heroin maintenance treatment.

HEROIN DEPENDENCE: DEFINITION AND OVERVIEW OF THE SYNDROME

Heroin is morphine treated with acetic acid, so technically it is diacetylmorphine and considered a semi-synthetic opioid. Historically it was developed to treat morphine dependence and thought not to be addictive. Official diagnostic nomenclature (e.g., DSM-IV) (APA, 1994) says "The essential feature of Substance Dependence is a cluster of cognitive, behavioral, and physiological symptoms...(with) continued use ...despite significant substance-related problems" (p176). This use results in tolerance, withdrawal and compulsive drug-taking behavior. By tolerance we mean the need for more of the drug to achieve the intended effect or substantially reduced effects when using the same amount of the drug. Withdrawal is a pattern of stage-specific patterns of signs and symptoms associated with the discontinuance of the drug. Compulsive substance use is manifested by continued use in the presence of adverse consequences, taking more of the drug than originally intended,

* Address inquiries concerning this paper to rjcraig41@comcast.net

manifestation of a persistent desire to cut down followed by continued use, daily behavior consumed by activities designed to procure the drug, and reduced social, occupational, recreational, and spiritual activities.

While opiates are used medically to treat pain, diarrhea, and cough, heroin has no accepted medical use. Heroin is usually taken intraveneously (IV – "mainlined"), or nasally (.e.g., "snorted" (insufflation). It is also administered by subcutaneous injections – a process known as "skin-popping".

Heroin intoxication is manifested by initial euphoria and impaired judgment followed by pupillary constriction (or pupillary dilation due to anoxia from an overdose), drowsiness ("nodding") (or coma if severe), slurred speech, impairment in memory or attention and motor disturbance. Medically, it causes dry mouth, a slowing of gastrointestinal activity and constipation. Chronic IV use can result in sclerosed veins and puncture marks at the injection sites giving the appearance of "railroad tracks". Abscesses are also possible, as is bacterial endocarditis, Hepatitis, and HIV infections, and positive PPD tests. Erectile dysfunction in males and irregular menses in females may occur, but loss of desire is probably the most common effect of chronic use. In addition to deaths from diseases, heroin addicts also die from overdose, accidents, and murder.

Heroin withdrawal is often stage-sequenced and occurs following cessation of use. Depending on habit strength and amount of the drug taken, this pattern of withdrawal occurs anywhere from hours to three days following the discontinuance of the drug. The individual experiences yawning, muscle aches, lacrimation or rhinorrhea, diaphoresis, fever, insomnia, nausea and vomiting. These symptoms are nearly identical to symptoms associated with influenza.

The most common laboratory test used to detect the presence of heroin is the urine toxicology screen. The acetic acid is metabolized and excreted and the urine tests positive for morphine. Urine samples are likely to test positive for morphine for up to three days following use in heroin-dependent patients. This will depend, however, on many other factors, including the specific procedures use to detect the drug (see section below on urine toxicology screens). Liver enzymes may also be elevated, and many heroin-addicted patients will test positive for Hepatitis C antibody (indicating past infection) or for the hepatitis antigen indicating an active infection.

Prevalence of heroin abuse/addiction will vary according to the population sampled. In the *Monitoring the Future (2004)* – a survey of drug abuse reported by high school teenagers, the prevalence of lifetime use of heroin was generally 1.5% among 8th, 10th, and 12th graders. According to the National Survey on Drug Use and Health (2003), among the general population age 12 and older, 404,000 had used heroin annually. NIDA estimates that there are over 1,000,000 heroin addicts in the U. S.

Pharmacology and Pharmacokinetics

Heroin is transformed into MAM (6-momo-acetylmorphine) by hydrosis and then metabolized into morphine once it reaches the brain. Because of greater lipid (fat) solubility, heroin easily crosses the blood-brain barrier and acts on the same receptors as the natural opioid system (i.e., endorphins). The areas of the brain that are most sensitive to morphine and therefore also most sensitive to heroin are the hypothalamus, thalamus, and the amygdala.

MODELS OF ETIOLOGY

Researchers have invoked biological, psychological, and sociological theories to explain why some people become addicted to opiates while others do not. Biological and pharmacological variables form the necessary but perhaps not the sufficient explanation for addiction.

Biological Theories

Biological explanations for understanding of the central processes associated with addiction, especially tolerance, the addictive euphoria, and withdrawal are well-understood at the physiological level and at the anatomical level. We understand and can explain in microscopic detail what happens in the brain when molecules of heroin enter the brain, act upon the brain, and distributed through the body and finally metabolized and excreted. Where we are deficient is in biological understandings as to why some gravitate and become addicted in the first place. While variables of dose are relevant as a physical explanation, it is also true that most patients do not become addicted when given opiates for medical conditions. It is only a small percentage that develop an addiction.

The heroin "high" occurs when heroin molecules enter the brain and occupy the mu receptors activating the mesolimbic (midbrain) system that signals the ventral tegmental (VTA) area causing the release of dopamine in the nucleus accumbens. This results in feelings of pleasure. Tolerance occurs when the opiate receptors become less responsive to opiate stimulation so that more opiates are required to stimulate the VTA cells to release the same amount of dopamine in the nucleus accumbens.

Intoxication occurs when opiate molecules link to the mu receptors on brain cells in the locus cerulus. This linkage system activates an enzyme that converts adenosine triphosphate (ATP) into cyclic adenosine monophosphate (cAMP), which then triggers the release of noradrenaline. This linkage also results in the inhibition of the enzyme that converts ATP to cAMP, so that less cAMp is produced and hence less noradrenaline is released. This results in the classic symptoms associated with the heroin "rush" –slowed respiration, drowsiness, low blood pressure, and shallow breathing.

When opiates are not present to suppress the locus cerulus' enhanced activity, the neurons produce abnormally high levels of cAMP, leading to an excessive amount of noradrenaline, resulting in anxiety, muscle cramps and diarrhea – the classic opiate withdrawal syndrome. (Other areas of the brain also contribute to these symptoms, including the mesolimbic reward system.)

Classical Conditioning

Classical conditioning involves a process whereby a neutral stimulus, called the unconditioned stimulus, is paired with a stimulus that evokes a response that is either rewarding or punishing. This process usually occurs several times until the neutral stimulus has the power to evoke the response alone. In the classic example, a hungry dog is presented with meat (the unconditioned stimulus) which evokes salivation (the unconditioned response). In the next phase, the presentation of the meat is preceded by a tone – perhaps a bell. After multiple pairing, the presentation of the bell is able to produce the response. The bell is now termed the conditioned stimulus and salivation after the bell is now termed the conditioned response.

Classical conditioning contributes to the perceived effects of heroin and also to withdrawal. Heroin is taken within certain environments and preceded by a series of behaviors (i.e., deciding to get the drug, driving to the spot where drugs are sold, reaching into one's pocket for the money to pay for the drug, giving the money to the dealer, seeing and receiving the bag of heroin, getting out one's "works" (i.e., needle if one is using IV), or preparing the drug to be sniffed, and finally receiving the rush as the drug impacts on the brain). This sequence is referred to as a "behavioral chain" and each behavior in the chain can be classically conditioned to cues in the environment that becomes associated with taking the drug. As one prepares to engage in this behavioral chain, these classically conditioned interoceptive (internal sensory receptors) and exteroceptive (stimuli in the environment) cues emerge. The patient has become conditioned to learn that a certain feeling will be associated with the end result of this chain and begins to feel anticipatory excitement (Wikler, 1973).

Classical conditioning also contributes to withdrawal. As one approaches an environment previously associated with the use of drugs, the presence of these environmental cues is sufficient enough to begin to experience a withdrawal syndrome that is relieved upon use of the drug. This explains why patients, following release from prison, have been known to go into withdrawal when re-entering their previous copping area even though they have not used heroin in several years.

Classical conditioning is more of an explanatory model to relapse than it is for onset of addiction in the first place.

Psychodynamic Theories

Several psychodynamic theories have been proposed to explain why some, growing up in the same environment, and with similar parentage, develop a problem with heroin addiction while others do not (Blatt, McDonald, Sugarman, & Wilber, 1984; Lettieir, Sayers, & Perason, HW, 1980). These theories argue that heroin addiction is (a) related to feelings of childhood emotional deprivation and use heroin to experience a soothing, infantile, symbiotic bond, (b) an attempt to deal with excessively aggressive impulses and thereby preventing their expression, (c) a reaction to guilt, shame, and feelings of worthlessness, or (d) an attempt to self-medicate an underlying psychiatric disorder (Khantzian, 1985).

Family Functioning Theories

It has been recognized for some time that the families of opiate addicts function differently than most other families (Alexander & Dibb, 1975;Harbin & Mazier, 1975). These theories have changed little in the intervening years (Stanton, 1997).This research has concluded that addict families are characterized by poor communication, unsuccessful attempts of parents to control the addict behavior combined with an unsuccessful attempt by the addict to emotionally separate from the nuclear family, a tendency of the father to dominate the mother or to be seen a week and submissive and subordinate to an aggressive wife. The addict's mother is described as enmeshed with the son (the addict) in a dyad that perversely excludes the father, who feels emasculated. From a family systems perspective the addict's behavior within the family is an attempt to maintain overall family homeostasis and related to an intense fear of separation and individuation. The addict's role is to act in ways to bring the familial dysfunction to the attention of mental health specialists through the addictive behavior.

Socioeconomic Theories

Socioeconomic theories emphasize environmental variables that presage the onset of addiction. These include such factors to poverty, lack of economic opportunities, poor role models within the community, embattled and gang-infested neighborhoods, inadequate schools, estrangement from community instructions such as churches, etc.

Summary and Conclusions

Theories of addiction have changed little in the past fifty years. It is also likely that all of these factors – biological, psychological, sociological, and in some cases, familial – play a role in the phases of addiction (onset, continuation, addiction, cessation, relapse, abstinence). Attention has changed from testing these theories to developing more effective treatment interventions for the disorder

The Assessment of Opiate Addiction

Urine Toxicology Screens

Besides clinical examinations and evaluations, the toxicology screen for drugs of abuse is the most common physical test to aid in the diagnosis of heroin abuse (Craig, 2004). After ingestion, the acetic acid is metabolized and the excreted urine results in a positive finding for the presence of morphine in urine. While this is a simple principle, there are several factors to consider when evaluating the toxicology screen results.

1) The urine sample should be taken under direct observation and chain of custody of the sample must also be assured. Drug addicts – especially males – have many ways to falsify a urine sample to avoid detection. For example, they purchase "clean" urine from a non-user and then switch urine prior to returning it to the technician. This is quite easily done if the sample is unobserved. Even when observed, unless the area is free from blind spots, addicts can substitute the urine by placing it in a balloon under the arm with a tube leading to the genital area. While appearing to urinate, they are actually squeezing the bulb thereby allowing the contents (i.e., clean urine) to flow into the test vial. Sometimes addict work in pairs, distracting the technician while the partner makes the switch on the urine cart. Some may make the switch by accidentally dropping the real sample and then substituting the forged sample.
2) A number of products are available on the internet and are available for purchase (Cleartest.com, 2006). All of these products allege an ability to be able to falsify the urine results. Many of these products have clever and alluring names. For example, "The Urinator" consists of a small electric, self-contained module containing thermostatically controlled water maintained at the correct temperature for up to four hours. The water is mixed with a concentrated clean synthetic urine substitute. The device is small enough to hold in your hand and thereby easy to conceal. "Urine Luck" is a chemical solution which allegedly destroys unwanted substances (i.e., heroin). Similar products, such as "Zip-n-Flip, "Ready Clean", XXtra Clean" purport similar outcomes. "Clear Choice Shampoo" is available if hair testing is done instead of urine testing. It is questionable whether or not any of these devices or products can beat a toxicology screen. They are probably most often used for pre-employment physicals rather than for routine use in drug treatment programs.
3) Addicts try to add water brought from home or drink an excessive amount of water or substitute water scooped from the toilet bowl to try and change the Ph level of urine and thereby diluting the sample. Adding a colorant to the toilet bowl will defeat these attempts. They also have been known to drink vinegar, which theoretically would be effective except that the patient would have to ingest such a large amount that it would become toxic. Addicts also try and add chemicals or bleach, or water-purification tablets to the urine however these products have a recognizable odor.
4) Some addicts make a small pinhole in the collection tube (if plastic). This hole is too small to be detected at the collection site, but during shipping to the lab, the fluid slowly leaks out, resulting in an insufficient volume for testing.

Thus it is imperative that the technician be fully trained on these methods and make a conscientious effort to ensure that the sample analyzed is the actual specimen taken from the patient. The best method to defeat these efforts is a competent and well-trained technician, who directly observes the specimen collected with no distractions. A blue colorant may be added to the toilet bowl, and urine collection bottles are available for purchase which automatically records the temperature of the urine in the bottle, which should be the same as body temperature. Finally, one may test for the specific gravity of the sample, which, if less than 1.010, then the specimen is suspect.

While urine screens are the most common method to detect drugs of abuse, blood, hair, sweat, and saliva can also be used. Blood is more invasive - one needs about 40 strands of hair for each sample, thereby creating patient resistance, and use of sweat and saliva has collection problems. Urine toxicology tests are either screening tests or confirmatory tests. A good lab will employ both types of methods when reporting the results. Screening tests are used to rule out negative results. They are usually quick and cost-effective. When a positive result if found on a screening test, the sample should be tested by a more sensitive method, referred to as a confirmatory test. The likelihood that these two methods will result in a false positive is next to zero. Also, there are different laboratory techniques to assay the sample, each with advantages and disadvantages. These are presented in Tables 1 and 2.

Table 1. Overview of Drug Use Detection Methods

Method	Cost	Detection Period	Detection of Poppy Seed	Cheating Potential	Problems
Urine	About 6$ for each unconfirmed test	1-5 days for most drugs; up to 1 month for marijuana	Will test positive for opiates	Problematic	Testing methods differ in sensitivity and specificity
Hair	About $40/test	Up to 90 days 1 one 1/2" sample	Will not test positive for opiates	Impervious to cheating	Does not detect methadone, alcohol or semi-synthetic opiates*
Sweat	variable	undetermined	Distinguishes between opiates and poppy seed	Impervious to cheating	Does not detect methadone, or semi-synthetic opiates*
Saliva	Similar to costs of urine tox screens	undetermined	Depends on method used	Resistant to Cheating	Less effective in identifying marijuana
Blood	variable	Days	Able to differentiate opiates from poppy seed	Not susceptible to cheating	Invasive

* Labs have screens set up for the five commonly sued drugs required for workplace drug testing, which is a big source of revenue. These methods could detect methadone and other opiates if someone was willing to pay the additional costs. Hospital-based labs could also detect these drugs when so requested.

Most labs use immunoassays because they are reliable, easy-to-use, and have ways to eliminate the vast number of negative tests from the few that will be positive. However, this method cross-reacts with chemically similar drugs in the same class and that can result in false positive findings. Most labs use a combination of gas chromatography (GC) and mass spectrometry as a confirmatory technique.

Table 2. Common Methods Used for Urine Toxicology Screens

Method	Use	Turn-Around Time	Sensitivity	Specificity	Benefits	Problem
Chroma-tography						
Thin-Layer (TLC)	Mass Screening	2 hrs	reasonable	reasonable	Useful for large volume operations	Qualitative results only (pos.neg); results need confirmation; Specificity affected by environmental condition
Gas Liquid (GLC)	Used as a confirming test	2 hrs	Greater than TLC but time-consuming	Utmost specificity	Low incidence of false positives;	Only a single specimen can assay a sample at any one time; ,more costly overall
Spectral Methods						
Spectro-photo-fluometry	Often used to confirm results from immuno-Assays				Can handle high volume output; simple to use	High false positive rates; virtually used for morphine detection only.
immuno-assays (in general)		rapid	Very sensitive	poor	Adaptable to high volume operations; can detect smaller amounts of drug in urine than TLC	Cross-reactive with similar drugs, resulting in false positives
Free Radical Assay	Used for mass screening	5 seconds to 2-3 minutes	High rate of false positives	low	Relatively inexpensive and requires little technical expertise	High equipment costs; results need confirmation by GC/TLC
Enzyme Multipied Immuno-Assay	Allows for high-volume testing	5 seconds to 2-3 minutes	High sensitivity	High specificity	Detects a wide range of substances; results very reliable when confirmed by GC/TLC	High instrument costs; results need confirmation by another method

Table 2. Common Methods Used for Urine Toxicology Screens (Continued)

Method	Use	Turn-Around Time	Sensitivity	Specificity	Benefits	Problem
immuno-assays (in general						
Radio Immuno-Assays	Intended for screening with another method to confirm the results	1-2 hours		Doesn't detect a full range of drugs	More sensitive that FRAT/EMIT; low rate of false positives	Very costly; doesn't detect a wide range of drugs
Hemaglutin-ation	High volume	90 minutes	High	Not able to detect a wide range of drugs	Inexpensive; uses uncomplicated equipment	Limited number of samples assayed each day; high equipment costs.

The sensitivity of a drug is that level of concentration of a drug in urine below which the assay can no longer detect it. The laboratory technician will set the threshold level for a positive finding with different labs possibly setting different threshold levels and thereby reporting different results.

The results will be reported as either positive or negative. The clinician needs to know what method was used to obtain the results and whether they were confirmed. I am personally aware of one situation where results were coming back which contradicted what the patients were telling their counselors and physicians. In many cases the patient was observed drinking methadone but then the results came back negative for methadone. When this was brought to the attention of responsible officials, we were chastised for not believing the lab results and charged with succumbing to the "charm" and manipulations of our patients. Accordingly, we split the next day's collection and sent them down as separate samples (without telling the lab) and then compared the results. The evidence was clear. The results were generally unreliable. When this evidenced was reported to these same responsible officials, it was then learned that the lab was not confirming the results due to costs and lack of personnel.

This is not necessarily an isolated occurrence. In a study reported in *JAMA*, the performance of 13 laboratories, serving 262 methadone maintenance treatment facilities, was evaluated by submitting pre-tested patient urine samples for blind testing. The false positive and false negative error rates for samples containing (or not containing) morphine, amphetamines, methadone, codeine, and barbiturates, ranged from 0% to 100% depending on the drug tested. These very same labs had detection rates in the 99% percentile for samples submitted to the Center for Disease Control (CDC) as quality checks. The results suggested that greater care was taken for samples to be submitted to CDC than for routine samples, and laboratories were often unable to detect the presence of illicit drugs at levels required of in their contracts. The authors recommended that drug treatment facilities monitor the performance of their laboratories with quality control samples and blind testing (Hansen, Caudill, & Boon, 1985). Subsequently NIDA developed proficiency standards for accrediting laboratories based on this study and others (Davis, Hawks, & Blanke, 1988).

In our own program, periodically we become suspect of urine results. Fortunately we have the cooperation of laboratory personnel to detect the source of the problem. Occasionally it is due to improper cleaning of the equipment between uses resulting in traces of drugs (usually cocaine), remaining in the equipment and thereby pickup up a positive reading for cocaine. At other times the standard is not able to detect the presence of methadone at extremely low doses. The point here is that one needs to have a good working relationship with the lab and the results from the lab require continued scrutiny.

ASI (and its Problems)

The Addiction Severity Index (McLellan et al, 1992) was developed under contract from NIDA as a screening measure to assess the domains known to be effected by alcohol and drug abuse. These domains are medical, employment, family/social, legal, and psychological/psychiatric. The instrument also provides severity levels for both alcohol and drug abuse. It is questionnaire-based and takes about 45-minutes to administer. At the end of each section the patient provides a severity ranking for each domain and a rating of importance for inclusion in treatment. The clinician also provides a severity rating. Where there is agreement, then that would lead to congruent treatment goals, whereas widely discrepant ratings between clinician and counselor suggest probable denial and treatment resistance.

The ASI has consistently demonstrated its concurrent and predictive validity for both alcohol and drug-dependent patients. For example, in a recent study, low ASI severity scores in drug predicted good outcomes for patients on methadone maintenance treatment after one year of treatment; low scores on ASI psychological/psychiatric predicted attendance at counseling sessions, and low scores on ASI employment predicted full time employment. Correspondingly, high scores in those domains predicted continuing drug abuse, unemployment and treatment non-compliance in counseling (Craig & Olson, 2004).

The ASI has become the standard instrument to assess severity levels in addiction, at least in research studies, and the Department of Veterans Affairs require it as a standard measure at treatment intake as well as every six months thereafter, to assess treatment progress. However, its use has not become a mainstream assessment instrument among most treatment programs, despite its demonstrated validity. This is a concern to NIDA, which lists it as one area of technology transfer that remains lacking in treatment programs.

Role of Personality

A datum in medicine is that it is just as important to know the person who has the disease as it is to know what disease the person has. In the case of psychiatric disorders, this datum is ever more true. In the Diagnostic Manual of Mental Disorders, 4 edition (1994) of the American Psychiatric Association, Axis I disorders (i.e., clinical syndromes) put one at risk for developing Axis II disorders (i.e., personality disorders). Similarly, having an Axis II disorder increases the risk of having certain Axis II disorders. This is referred to as comorbidity. For example, having an Axis II antisocial personality disorder increases the likelihood that the person will also develop a substance use disorder, either alcohol or drugs. Having a dependent personality disorder increases the risk of developing a clinical depression or a panic disorder.

Researchers have extensively evaluated the relationship between substance abuse and various Axis II disorders and this research has recently been summarized (Craig, 2003). Whether one uses a structured clinical interview or a self-report questionnaire to make a personality diagnosis, the personality disorder of Antisocial is the most common personality disorder associated with heroin addict, with prevalence rates ranging up to 62%, depending on the setting and the method used to make the diagnosis.

Treatment of Heroin Addiction

Methadone Maintenance Treatment

Methadone is D,1-4, 4-diphenyl-6-dimethyl-amino-3-hepatone, with the L isomer accounting for much of its activity (Weddington, 1995). It is available in tablet/wafer, power and injectable forms but oral use is the most common. It was initially developed as an analgesic but now is more currently used for opiate detoxification and for the treatment of the opiate abstinence syndrome and for maintenance treatment of opiate addiction. Its subjective effects include sedation, analgesia and changes in mood and is not substantially different form those of other opiates except for a longer duration. It depresses the respiratory center, has antitussive actions, inhibits gastrointestinal tone and propulsion, and produces mild hyperglycemia and hypothermia.

Methadone is absorbed quickly and plasma levels can be detected within 30 minutes of oral ingestion. Peak plasma levels are attained in about four hours. In non-tolerant patients, the mean half-life of the drug is about 15 hours, whereas after chronic administration the mean half-life is 22 hours (Weddington, 1995).

In 1964, Vincent Dole MD, an internist at Rockefeller University and Marie Nyswander MD, a New York psychiatrist began treating patients addicted to heroin with methadone hydrochloride. Patient were accepted into the treatment protocol if they were 20 and 40 years of age, had been using heroin for at least four years with repeated relapses, had no psychosis or serious medical illness, and were no coerced into treatment by the courts. They were hospitalized and placed on a gradual stabilizing dose of methadone.

Methadone induction began with low doses of 10 to 20mg/day and gradually increased over a period of from four to six week. This was done to avoid narcotic against effects. After patients had been stabilized on doses from 80 to 120mg/day, they were maintained on a single oral daily dose without further dose increases and, at the end of the six week trial, the patients were discharged to outpatient clinics where they continued to receive daily methadone. Urine toxicology screens were taken as a means to determine treatment effectiveness. These clinician/researchers were quick to add that, while counseling was available, the essential treatment was a medical approach to the heroin addiction.

Of the 1007 applicants interviewed as possible candidates, 60% were accepted.

Their initial report was based on 304 of these patients. The authors found dramatic improvement in patients treated with methadone. A total of 91% remained in treatment, 70% were employed or were in school, while the remaining 30% had discontinued heroin use and antisocial behavior, although they had not yet become socially productive. This favorable response to a medical therapy was not expected in a sample of patients with slum backgrounds, school dropouts, prison records, and minority group status. The authors questioned psychogenic theories of addiction etiology that stressed character defects in these patients as the seminal etiology of the disorder. Instead, they argued that heroin addiction was a metabolic disease caused by repeated exposure to narcotic drugs (Dole, Nyswander, & Kreek, 1966; Dole & Nyswander, 1967).

Over the past 40 years, methadone has become one of the most studied medications. This research has documented its effectiveness as well as the absence of any long-term side effects or complications in over 300 published studies (Hubbard & Marsden, 1986; Sells, Demaree, & Hornick, 1979). While on methadone, consumption of all illicit drugs declines to less than 40% of pre-treatment levels during the first year of treatment and to 15% of pre-treatment levels for patients who remain on methadone for two or more years (Ball & Ross, 1991). Furthermore, crime is substantially reduced. In the most detailed study of treatment outcome, Ball and Ross (1991) found that criminal activity was reduced by more that 70% during the first four months of treatment. Patients on methadone showed reduced rates of HIV infection – an outcome referred to as harm reduction. In one study, 5% of patients on methadone contracted HIV compared to a cohort of patients not on methadone whose rate of HIV infection was 26% (Metzger, 1993). It is also comforting to know that there is no difference in methadone treatment outcomes between Hispanic and African-American men and women. Both of these minorities of both genders achieve similar treatment outcomes after six months of treatment (Mulvaney et al, 1999). While methadone maintenance patients have high rates of alcohol abuse, ranging between 13% to 25%, these rates were not substantially different from the rates of heavy drinking reported in the general population (Ottomanelli, 1999). However, research has found that heavy drinking was not a major factor in treatment retention or outcome (Kreek, 1991).

Keep in mind that simply giving methadone is rarely sufficient to achieve these kinds of outcomes. Programs must also offer supportive services, such as counseling, vocational rehabilitation and social and psychological/psychiatric services in a comprehensive treatment plan. The addition of basic counseling services is associated with major increases in clinical efficacy (McLellan et al, 1993).

Controversies with Methadone Maintenance

Despite its general acceptance in medicine and its effectiveness documented by researchers, a number of controversies continue to be associated with its use. These include methadone diversion, what is the most effective therapeutic dose, the quality of staff in methadone programs, its isolation from other health-care institutions, nonspecific interventions or poorly integrated interventions from other substances of abuse such as alcohol and cocaine, its opposition from abstinence-oriented treatment programs, such as 12-step programs and therapeutic communities. Also, heroin addicts often have high rates of psychiatric co-morbidities, particularly anxiety and affective disorders (Milby et al, 1996) and personality disorders especially antisocial personality disorders (Craig, 2003). Many of these patients are also the very ones who are non-responders to methadone and who continued to be negatively visible around the clinic. Hence, methadone maintenance programs, especially those which are not hospital-based but which are housed in the community, have not achieved full acceptance by their surrounding community.

The Dosage Controversy

Here we will explore one of the more contentious controversies associated with methadone.

Despite the success often achieved with methadone and supportive services, not all patients or programs attain such outcome. The US General Accounting Office (GAO) studied 24 programs comprising 5600 active patients. They found that many patients on methadone continue to use heroin as well as other drugs. In 10 of the clinics over 20% of the patients ere still using heroin after six months of treatment and at two clinics over 50% were using heroin. The dosage levels at 21 of 24 clinics were below 60mg, which many clinicians believe to be the minimally therapeutic maintenance dose (GAO, 1990). Ball and Ross (1991) cited evidence that an adequate dose of methadone should be between 60mg – 100mg daily, since these dosages were associated with the highest rates of treatment retention and the lowest rates of illicit heroin use. Similar findings have been reported by other researchers (D'Aunno & Vaughn, 1992). These findings were included in the position statement of the American Psychiatric Association on methadone maintenance which stipulated that an adequate dose of methadone was between 60mg – 100mg/day (APA, 1994b). (See Figure 1).

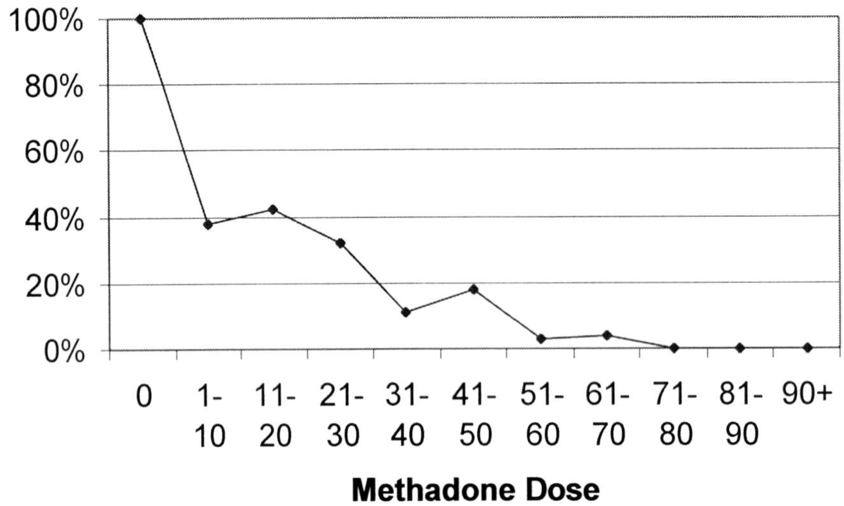

From Ball and Ross, 1991, p. 248. In the public domain.

Figure 1. Heroin Use in Past 30 Days (N=407)

While the preponderance of research does show that higher doses are generally associated with better outcomes than are lower doses, there are reports in the literature showing that low dose methadone (averaging 30mg/day) attained "outcome" rates (i.e., illicit heroin use) comparable to rates of high-dose programs, it did so at the expense of lower treatment retention (Craig, 1980). Other researchers found little difference in toxicology screens for heroin use between patients maintained on doses above or below 50mg/day and suggested that other variables may affect heroin use other than dose (Maddux et al, 1991).

In a naturalistic study, high versus low dose methadone maintenance patients (N=265) were compared on the outcome variables of illicit drug use, treatment retention, missed medication days, and ratings of counselors of patient progress. Initial results found no significant differences on any outcome variable associated with methadone dose. However, there were significant differences on these same variables by assigned therapists. Some counselors got better results with their patients than other counselors and these findings were independent of dose (Blaney & Craig, 1999).

Studies show that patients show marked improvement in illicit use of heroin compared to their use prior to admission. These improvements are generally maintained during methadone maintenance treatment. However, success rates are very low after methadone treatment. As many as 90% relapse within one year of discharge and range from 9% to 21% drug-free at following after five years post-treatment (Weddington, 1995).

Harm Reduction vs. Abstinence

Research continues to demonstrate that methadone maintenance treatment is associated with reduced risks of criminality, reduced onset of HIV and TB, and reduction of sexually transmitted disorders. This is referred to as harm reduction. Proponents of harm reduction argue that patients should remain in methadone maintenance, even though they continue to use heroin because studies show that these patients are using less heroin than prior to methadone induction and this reduction of use is associated with reduction in risks of developing the aforementioned diseases.

In contrast to this are proponents of an abstinence model of treatment. There are two forms of this model. First, there are those who argue that being on methadone is not abstinence since they are using a (legal) narcotic. Rather they argue that patients should be off all drugs. Some staff in therapeutic communities (i.e. residential treatment programs), half-way houses and some Narcotics Anonymous chapters want patients to be off methadone and drug free. In other words, they want patients totally abstinent. A second form of this are some methadone maintenance programs, who, while understanding the harm reduction benefits of methadone maintenance, argue that the goal of methadone maintenance is the elimination of illicit heroin, Therefore, the patient must be totally abstinent from heroin or face administrative detoxification and eventual discharge. Proponents of this model differ in the length of time they give a patient before enacting this provision.

There is no immediate way to resolve this controversy, as it is really a matter of the philosophical belief system of program staff. The position statement of the American Psychiatric Association on Methadone Maintenance Treatment (1994) states that many patients need two or more years of methadone maintenance treatment before adequate outcome rates have been attained and some may need this treatment for the rest of their lives.

Diversion

Initially the Food and Drug Administration regulated methadone maintenance treatment programs (MMTPs) and issued rules for the issuance of take-home methadone privileges. These rules stipulate eight conditions before methadone pick-up schedules are reduced. Initially patients must attend the clinic daily and ingest the methadone at the clinic for at least three months before take-home privileges can be considered. (Patients may be given a Sunday take-home dose if the clinic is closed on Sunday). Additional requirements include such things as an absence of criminal activity, adherence to program rules, regular attendance at counseling, an ability to safely store methadone away from children, etc. The Substance Abuse and Mental Health Service Administration (SAMHSA) now has regulatory oversight over MMTPs and has retained these same restrictions. Currently patients may be given up to a one month supply of take-home methadone after meeting clean time requirements and the other stipulations.

All this has meant that methadone has been diverted to the streets where it is sold. This has created an additional public health problem and generated neighborhood complaints about drug selling in and around the clinic and contiguous neighborhoods. Although many programs require methadone ingestion in front of a staff member (patients are then required to say something after swallowing), and test for methadone in toxicology screens to ensure ingestion, this does not impact the problem of methadone diversion. SAMHSA now requires MMTPs to have a Diversion Control Plan as part of their accreditation review. These Diversion Control Plans stipulate the steps program take to minimize methadone diversion. These steps include such things as (a) requiring only one patient at a time in front of the methadone dispensing window with other patients maintaining a stipulated distance between the ingesting patient and the next patient in line, (b) requiring a picture ID before dosing, convex mirrors placed in the dosing area allowing the methadone dispensers (pharmacists, nurses) to view peripheral activity, randomly "calling back" for bottles for patients on reduced pick-ups to verify responsible use, cameras placed within the pharmacy area, and continued monitoring and verification that patients continue to meet the SAMHSA regulations for continuation on reduced pick-up.

Detoxification

Another issue is when and how to detoxify a patient on methadone. The position statement by APA (1994) states that detoxification should not be considered until at least two years of methadone maintenance treatment, assuming that the patient is stable in other areas of their life. Proponents of harm reduction might even argue that the patient shouldn't be detoxed at all, since doing so increases their risk of exposure to HIV, TB and STDs. This is contentious for staff operating from an abstinent oriented model.

While medical ethics gives the right for a patient to know their medication dose at any time, blind dose reductions is far preferable to non-blind detoxification. In blind dose procedures, the patient doesn't know whether or not their dose has been reduced, nor how much of a reduction has occurred. Clinical experience indicates that blind dose reduction tends to be more successful than open dosing.

A far more serious question pertains to the outcome studies of patients who have been detoxed off methadone. These studies show that, on average, most of these patients relapse and return to heroin use within one year of getting off methadone (Ball & Ross, 1991; Hser, Hoffman, Grella, & Anglin, 2001; Sells, Demaree, & Hornick, 1979). Many had died and many others were incarcerated. With this kind of outcome evidence, there is debate as to whether it is even advisable for a patient to be withdrawn from methadone, whether or not they are doing well on this therapy.

LAAM and its Aftermath

Levo-alpha-acetyl-methadol (LAAM) is a synthetic opiate approved by the FDA in 1993 as a Schedule II controlled substance and sold under the name of ORLAAM. It was initially developed in 1948 as an analgesic but was subsequently found to be able to suppress the opiate withdrawal syndrome for more that 72 hours. Subsequently 27 separate studies allegedly established the safety and efficacy of LAAM as a maintenance treatment for opiate addiction. LAAM was dispensed three days a week with an increased dose for the weekend. It was metabolized into two active metabolites, nor-LAAM and dinor-LAAM.

LAAM was similar in action to other narcotics in the same class and hence was cross-reactive and tolerant to these drugs. Its major benefit was a reduced frequency of administration and visits to the clinic, and an alleged easier ability to detoxify a patient from LAAM compared to methadone e (NCADI, 1995)

After several years of use, it was learned that LAAM had an adverse effect on the QT interval in the heart. The medication was withdrawn and is no longer in use. The issue here is whether the early enthusiasm for Buprenorphine (see below) will suffer the same fate?

Buprenorphine

Buprenorphine HCL is a partial opiate agonist developed and approved to treat opiate addicts in a doctor's office, thereby bypassing the extensive federal regulations required for patients enrolled in a methadone maintenance program. However, methadone maintenance programs can also use Buprenorphine but patients must then conform to these federal regulations. The drug purportedly minimizes withdrawal symptoms, decreases cravings, and partially blocks the effects of other opiates.

The drug is available in two forms. Subutex contains only Buprenorphine, while Suboxone contains Buprenorphine HCL/naloxone HCL dehydrate in a ration of 4:1. Both forms come in sublingual tablets. The drug binds to the opiate receptors in the brain thereby satisfying the addict's need for an opiate and also suppressing withdrawal symptoms. However, this drug only partially excites these receptors and so the patient does not get the full agonist effects caused by other opiate drugs. The drug affixes to and occupies these receptors for several days making it more difficult for other opiate drugs to excite these receptors. Buprenorphine is a partial agonist at the mu-opioid receptor and an antagonist at the kappa-opioid receptor; Naloxone is an antagonist at the kappa-opioid receptor. It is a Scheduled III narcotic in the *Controlled Substances Act.* It also has a ceiling effect making it more difficult to overdose on this drug. However, it does have sedating effects that interact with other drugs, such as benzodiazepines making these combinations potentially dangerous. Buprenorphine is metabolized to nonbuprenorphine byCYP3A4.Those wanting detailed information about the drug's pharmacokinetics should consult the package insert.

Generally patients are initially started on methadone maintenance or are transferred to Subutex. After stabilization, they are switched to Suboxone. Buprenorphine is metabolized to nonbuprenorphine by CYP3A4.

Buprenorphine cost more than methadone so one question is whether there is a cost-benefit ratio is favor of this drug. The Health Economics Resource center of the Department of Veterans Affairs developed an economic model comparing the effects of buprenorphine maintenance to methadone maintenance in terms of incremental costs, health care costs, and incremental effectiveness. They determined that the drug was cost effective in terms of its effects at reducing the health care costs associated with HIV infection. However, they also concluded that methadone maintenance was more cost effective than any scenarios developed by the authors. Methadone should remain the treatment of choice for patients addicted to opiates unless methadone maintenance treatment programs are not conveniently available within a community, or not attain the desirable clinical effectiveness, is not tolerated by the patient or when the patient has difficulty meeting the methadone clinic's hours of operation.

In such cases, Buprenorphine is another treatment option and it was deemed safer and more effective for certain types of patients (Barnett, Zaric, & Brandeau, 2001). Additionally, it was found to be well tolerated by patients for short-term hospital-based detoxification (DiPaula, Schwartz, R., Montoya, I. D., Barrett, D., & Tang, 2002).

Naltrexone: Theory and Outcome

Naltrexone hydrochloride was the first drug developed by NIDA in the treatment of opiate addiction (Ginzburg, 1984). It is an orally administered narcotic antagonist which blocks the physiological (but not the psychological) effects of opiates from 48 to 72 hours after an oral dose. It works by preferentially occupying the opiate receptor sites (i.e., mu, kappa, delta) in the brain, displacing agonists if present, and blocks the effects of any subsequent use of opiates as long as the drug is present in the body. Displacing agonists will result in a precipitate opiate withdrawal syndrome so that patients would have to be free of opiates for at least 24 hours prior to administration of this drug. It's principal metabolite 6-beta-naltrexol have peak plasma levels within 1 to 4.5 hours. The plasma half-life is about 8 hours.

Trexan or revia (the brand name for Naltrexone) is a near-ideal pharmacological treatment of opiate dependence. It absolutely is effective when taken as prescribed. The patient will not feel the effects of heroin while on naltrexone. In addition to physiological explanations, at the theoretical level, the laws of learning also should explain why naltrexone is effective. When a patient is on naltrexone and uses heroin, the patient does not feel any effects from the heroin. In other words, there is a lack of reward. Upon repeated trials of using heroin and getting no reward, the paradigm of extinction is occurring which would predict that ultimately the patient would eventually stop using heroin.

Guess what? The patient tends to stop using the naltrexone so that they can use and feel the effects of heroin. Hence the drug has a low acceptability within the addict population. It is best used for patients who have a lot to lose if they relapse (i.e., physicians, lawyers, accountants, etc).

ASSESSING CLIENT OUTCOMES

What outcome criteria should we use to measure success. We have all heard the phrase "the operation was a success but the patient died". Historically, total abstinence has been the criteria of treatment success, but many argue that reduction in use is just a valid measure of treatment success. Is reduction in sexually transmitted diseases, TB, and HIV/AIDS a treatment success even though there is no diminution of heroin use? Is employment a valid measure of good outcome? If a patient remains free from illicit drugs but still has problems with the law, is that treatment success? You can see that this is a value judgment of those that define success and policy makers that distribute money to successful programs.

Heroin Maintenance?

Perhaps the most controversial proposal is to give heroin addicts prescribed heroin. Most recently this has been proposed by a few politicians as a way to combat crime in urban areas. Actually, this is an old idea (Drug Abuse Council, 1977). Since the United States policy views heroin as primarily a criminal problem, the idea of heroin maintenance is given little consideration in America. Because The United Kingdom viewed heroin as primarily a medical problem, the idea of heroin maintenance is less controversial and has been tired there. English doctors report that many addicts try to obtain higher doses of heroin and/or supplement their dose with street heroin. Also, the demand for heroin did not abate even with the presence of prescription heroin and the heroin black market continues to flourish in England. In a more recent study emanating from the united Kingdom, it was found that co-prescription of heroin combined with methadone was more effective than methadone maintenance alone (Metrebian, 2004; Metrebian, Shanahan, & Wells, 1998). To date, with concerns of spreading heroin addiction, the notion of heroin maintenance in America is not presently viable. Furthermore, England is relying more on methadone maintenance as the treatment of choice for heroin addiction.

Heroin addiction has shown some resilience to drug fads and continues despite drug epidemics of psychedelics in the 1960s, cocaine free-basing in the 1980s and is likely to remain when the current methamphetamine epidemic subsides. Therefore we need to continue to develop and research more effective treatments for this disorder and focus less of the controversies.

REFERENCES

Alexander, BK; and Dibb, GS: Opiate addicts and their parents. *Fam. Proc.* 14, 499-514. 1975.

American Psychiatric Association. *Diagnostic and Statistical Manual of Mental Disorders.* 4th ed. Washington, DC: APA, 1994.

American Psychiatric Association. Position statement on methadone maintenance treatment. *American Journal of Psychiatry. 151, 792-793. 1994b.*

Author. *National Survey on Drug Use and Health.* Rockville, MD: National Institute on Drug Abuse, 2003.

Author. *Monitoring the Future.* Rockville, MD: National Institute on Drug Abuse, 2004.

Ball, JC; and Ross, A. *The Effectiveness of Methadone Maintenance Treatment: Patients, Programs, Services, and Outcomes.* New York: Spring-Verlag, 1991.

Barnett, PG; Zaric, GS; and Brandeau, ML. The cost-effectiveness of Buprenorphine maintenance therapy for opiate addiction in the United States. *Addict.* 96: 1267-1278, 2001.

Blaney, T: and Craig, RJ: Methadone maintenance: Does dose determine differences in outcome? *J. Sub. Ab. Treat.* 16, 221-228. 1999

Blatt, SJ; McDonald, C: Sugarman, A; and Wilber, C. Psychodynamic theories of opiate addiction: New directions for research. *Clin. Psychol. Rev.* 4, 159-189. 1984

Craig, RJ: *Counseling the Alcohol and Drug Dependent Client: A Practice Approach.* Boston, Mass: Allyn & Bacon. 2004.

Craig, RJ: Prevalence of personality disorders among cocaine and heroin addicts. *Directions in Addiction Treatment and Prevention.* 7, 33-42. 2003.

Craig, RJ: Effectiveness of low-dose methadone maintenance for the treatment of inner-city heroin addicts. *Int. J. Addict..* 15, 791-710. 1980.

Craig, RJ, and Olson, RE. Predicting methadone maintenance treatment outcomes using the Addiction Severity Index and the MMPI-2 content scales (Negative Treatment Indicators and Cynicism scales). *Am. J. Drug & Alc. Abuse.* 30, 823-839. 2004

Davis, KH; Hawks, RL; and Blanke, RV. Assessment of laboratory quality in urine drug testing: A proficiency testing pilot study. *JAMA*, 260, 1749-1754. 1988

D'Aunno, T: and Vaughn, TE: Variations in methadone treatment practices. *JAMA*. 267, 253-258. 1992.

DiPaula, BA; Schwartz, R; Montoya, ID; Barrett, D; and Tang, C. Heroin detoxification with Buprenorphine on an inpatient psychiatric unit. *J. Sub. Ab. Treat* 23, 163-169.

Dole, VP; Nyswander, M. E.. Heroin addiction – a metabolic disease. *Arch Intern Med* 120: 19-24, 1967

Dole, VP; Nyswander, M. E.; and Kreek, M. J. Narcotic blockade. *Arch. Intern Med* 118: 304-309, 1966

Drug Abuse Council. *What's happening with Heroin maintenance?* Washington, DC. 1977.

General Accounting Office: *Methadone Maintenance: Some Treatment Programs are Not Effective; Greater Federal Oversight Needed.* Washington, DC: U.S. Government Printing Office. 1990.

Ginzburg, HM. *Naltrexone: Its clinical utility.* Rockville, MD: NIDA Treatment Research Report. 1984

Hansen, HJ; Caudill, SP: and Boone, J. Crisis in drug testing. *JAMA*, 253, 2382 – 2387. 1985

Harbin, HT: and Maziar, HM: The families of drug abusers: A literature review. *Fam. Proc.* 14 411-431. 1975

Hser, Y-I; Hoffman, V: Grella, CE: and Anglin, MD: A 33-year follow-up of narcotic addicts. *Arch. Gen. Psychiat.* 58, 503-508. 2001

Hubbard, RL: and Marsden, ME: Relapse to use of heroin, cocaine and other drugs in the first year of treatment: In *Relapse and Recovery in Drug Abuse.* NIDA Research Monograph 72. Rockvile, MD: U. S. Government Printing Office. 1986

Khantzian, EJ. The self-medication hypothesis of addictive disorders: Focus on heroin and cocaine dependence. *Am. J. Psychiat.* 142, 1259-1264. 1985.

Kreek, MJ: Using methadone effectively: Achieving goals by application of laboratory, clinical, and evaluation research and by development of innovative programs. In R. W. Pickens, C. G. Leukefeld, and C. R. Schuster (Eds). *Improving drug abuse retention.* Research Monograph 106, pp 136-151. Rockville, MD: NIDA

Lerrieri, DJ; Sayers, M; and Pearson, HW: *Theories on Drug Abuse: Selected Contemporary Perspectives.* Rockville, MD: NIDA, 1980.

Maddux, JF: Esquivel, M: Vogtsberger, KN: and Desmond, DP: methadone dose and urine morphine. *J. Sub. Ab. Treat.* 8, 195-201. 1991

McLellan, AT: Arndt, IO: Metzger, DS: woody, GE: and O'Brien, CP. The effects of psychosocial services in substance abuse treatment. *JAMA*. 269, 1953-1959. 1993.

McLellan, AT, Kushner, H., Metzger, DS, Peters, R, Smith, I, Grissom, G, Pettinati, H, Argeriou, M. The fifth edition of the Addiction Severity Index. *J. Subst. Abuse Treat*, 9, 199-213. 1992

Metrebian, N. Supervised co-prescription of heroin to treatment-resistant heroin addicts is more effective than treatment with methadone alone. *Evidence-based Ment. Hlth.* 7m 23, 2004.

Metrebian, N, Shanahan, W., and Wells, B. feasibility of prescribing injectable heroin and methadone to opiate dependent drug users; associated health gains and harm reductions. *Med. J. Aust.* 168, 596-600. 1998.

Metzger, J: HIV seroconversion among in and out of treatment intravenous drug users: An 180month prospective follow-up. *AIDS,* 9, 1049-1056. 1993.

Milby, JB; Sims, MK: Khuder, S; Schumacher, JE; Huggins, N; McLellan, AT; Woody, G and Haas, N. Psychiatric comormidity: Prevalence in methadone maintenance treatment. *Am. J. Drug & Alc. Ab.* 22, 95-107. 1996.

Mulvaney, FD: Brown, LS: Aletrman, AI: Sage, RE: Cnaan, A: Cacciola, J: and Rutherford, M. Methadone-maintenance outcomes for Hispanic and African-American men and women. *Drug and Alc. Depend.* 54, 11-18. 1999.

National Clearinghouse for Alcohol and Drug Information. *LAAM in the Treatment of Opiate Addiction.* Rockville, MD: Substance Abuse and Mental Health Services Administration. 1995

Sells, SB:, Demaree, RG: and Hornick, CW: *Comparative Effectiveness of Drug Abuse Treatment Modalities.* NIDA Services Research Administrative Report. Washington, DC: NIDA. 1979.

Stanton, MD: The role of family and significant others in the engagement and retention of drug-dependent individuals. In LS Onken, JD Blaine, & JJ Boren (Eds). *Beyond the therapeutic alliance: Keeping the Drug-Dependent Individual in Treatment.* NIDA Research Monograph No. 165, pp. 157-180). Rockville, MD: National Institute on Drug Abuse. 1997

Weddington, WW. Methadone maintenance for opioid addiction. In N.S> Miller and M.S. Gold (Eds). *Pharmacological Therapies for Drug and Alcohol Addiction.* New York: Marcell Dekker (pp 411-417). 1995

Wikler, A. Dynamics of drug dependence: Implications of a conditioning theory for research and treatment. *Arch. Gen. Psychiat.* 28: 611-616.

WWW.cleartest.com/products/index.html (2006).

In: Cocaine and Heroin Abuse Research
Editor: Lidia A. Pizzoli, pp. 143-172
ISBN 1-60021-076-7

Chapter 7

HEROIN ADDICTION IN PREGNANCY - ONGOING DEMANDS AND ACTUAL THERAPY MODALITIES

Maki Kashiwagi*, Urs Zimmermann-Baer**, Margaret Huesler* and André Seidenberg♣

*University Hospital Zurich, Clinic of Obstetrics,
** Kantonsspital Zurich, Winterthur, Department of Pediatrics, Clinic of Neonatology,
♣ General Practice, Weinbergstr.9, Zurich, Swetzerland

ABSTRACT

More than 35 years after its introduction into the therapy of pregnant heroin addicts methadone maintenance continues to be the standard therapy of opiate addiction in pregnancy. Benefit on pregnancy and neonatal outcome compared to the sole abuse of street heroin is evident.

However, there is ongoing need for clinical research to further improve the management of craving during pregnancy as well as the prevention and therapy of neonatal abstinence syndrome.

This chapter intends to review different approaches in improving these problems. Maternal maintenance therapy is discussed under consideration of recent insights into methadone metabolism and the physiological changes during pregnancy as well as under consideration of optimal therapy of concomitant infectious diseases highly prevalent in this risk group. Eventually actual therapy strategies in the management of neonates of opiate addicted women will be illustrated and critically commented.

An overview will be given to allow a better understanding of the specific needs of these women during pregnancy and their affected offsprings.

* Corresponding author: Maki Kashiwagi, MD University Hospital Zurich Clinic of Obstetrics, Frauenklinikstr. 10, 8091 Zurich, Switzerland. T.: 0041-44- 255 11 11, Fax: 0041-44 255 44 30, Mail: maki.kashiwagi@usz.ch

ABBREVIATIONS

NAS:	neonatal abstinence syndrome
HAART:	highly active antiretroviral therapy
IDUs:	injection drug users
LAAM:	levoacetylmethadol
HCV:	Hepatitis C- virus
STD:	sexually transmitted disease

1. INTRODUCTION

According to the 2001 National Household Survey on Drug Abuse (NHSDA) current heroin use was reported by 123 000 Americans which is relatively conforming with data collected in 2000 and lower than the number of 130 000 published in 1998.

Similarly a trend towards a fall in heroin consumption was reported by the European Monitoring Centre for Drugs and Drug Addiction (EMCDDA) in November 2005.

Currently of 1.2-2.1 million problem drug users in the enlarged European Union 850 000 -1.3 million people are likely to be drug injectors. At least 530 000 patients receive substitution therapies.

Since its introduction by Dole & Nyswander in 1965 (1), methadone substitution treatment has been established as the standard therapy for heroin addiction. Randomized studies have demonstrated the benefit of methadone maintenance on illicit drug abuse and mortality of heroin- addicted patients (reviewed in (2)).

For management of opiate addiction in pregnancy methadone has been constituted as standard either. Advantage of the inclusion of a heroin addicted pregnant patient into methadone maintenance therapy has been demonstrated in several studies and is widely acknowledged. Inclusion of these women in any form of treatment programme enables regular medical and psychological follow-up and screening for infectious diseases. Furthermore in comparison to street drug-users it has been further confirmed that methadone maintenance programme positively influences attendance of antenatal pregnancy controls, gestational duration, fetal growth and neonatal birth weight, respectively (3-8).

Nevertheless several issues remain to be particularly considered.

Infection with hepatitis C can be found in up to 55% of the women and HIV in up to 20% (9). Therefore one major issue is the management of these infections taking pregnancy and methadone maintenance therapy into account.

The other issue, which requires special attention is the development of neonatal abstinence syndrome (NAS), which is known to be more frequent and heavier in neonates after methadone exposure in utero than in neonates exposed to street heroin or street drugs only (7, 10-13).

In the following passages new insights into the course and management of infectious diseases in pregnant opiate abusers are presented. Therapy options in the treatment of addictive behaviour in the light of possible improvement of NAS and the actual recommendations in the treatment of NAS are discussed.

2. Opiate Abuse and Maternal Infectious Disease

Considering infections in pregnant injection drug users (IDUs) of major concern in the prenatal care are:

- Maternal HIV infection and the possibility of vertical transmission
- Adherence to antiretroviral therapy
- Possible interactions of opioids with antiretroviral therapy
- Maternal hepatitis C infection and the co-infection with HIV
- Other sexually transmitted diseases (especially genital ulcer disease)
- Prevention of preterm delivery
- Improvement of psychosocial aspects

Mother-to-child transmission of HIV near the time of birth is the primary route of HIV infection among infants and young children. In the drug abusing pregnant women transmissible infectious diseases have to be ruled out and if present their vertical transmission has to be prevented.

2.1 HIV

Female drug users are particularly vulnerable to HIV infection. Injection drug use plays a key role in the spread of HIV and hepatitis C infection in North and South America, Europe and parts of Asia. Of particular concern is multidrug-using behaviour in female drug users, especially with cocaine and alcohol, which is associated with a significant increase in unprotected sex. A high percentage of heterosexual HIV transmission can be attributed to drug related prostitution and/or a known HIV-infected sex-partner (14). Drug addicted women who exchange sex for money or drugs often lack control over their working conditions and suffer severe degradation. Thus beside methadone programmes, many countries have introduced needle exchange and "safe sex" programmes (15).

Furthermore there is some evidence supplied by in vitro and animal studies that cocaine and heroin increase HIV- replication and suppress immune function. Epidemiologic studies are inconclusive regarding their effect on the immune system (16). A study by Thrope et al. (2004) (17) showed a higher risk for nonfatal opportunistic infections in HIV- positive women, especially herpes simplex, pulmonary tuberculosis and recurrent pneumonia.

2.1.1 Vertical Transmission

Variables that have been linked to perinatal HIV transmission are high maternal HIV viral load, low maternal CD4 count, increased maternal illness severity, lack of antiretroviral therapy, prolonged rupture of membranes, vaginal delivery, prematurity and eventually illicit drug use. Illicit drug use accounts for prematurity and is moreover associated with intrauterine growth restriction, which is again independently associated with a higher rate of vertical HIV transmission (18). Postnatal in a study by Abrams et al. (2003) (19) a significant faster rate of disease progression for infants born to women with intravenous drug use was demonstrated.

Over the past decade, significant advances have been made for the prevention of vertical HIV transmission, including the use of single and combination antiretroviral therapy, elective caesarean section as the preferred mode of delivery, weaning and anti-retroviral post-exposition prophylaxis in the newborn. To maximize the benefits to the offspring, therapy is recommended at lower viral load thresholds than for non pregnant adults. For antiretroviral-naïve women, therapy is deferred until the second trimester because of the potential and uncertain risk of teratogenicity and the low risk of transmission during this period (20).

Untreated women might be overrepresented in socially marginalized group and there is need in improving the integration of these women in any kind of management programme, as they are known to be less likely than treated women to receive other prepartum preventive measures either. (21).

2.1.2 Highly Active Antiretroviral Therapy (HAART) and Adherence

Highly active antiretroviral therapy (HAART) or synonymously designated as combined antiretroviral therapy (cART) consists of a treatment regimen including the use of two nucleosides with one or more protease inhibitors or a non-nucleoside reverse transcriptase inhibitor. Treatment with nucleosides alone is defined as non- HAART therapy. The introduction of HAART in the mid-1990s has significantly altered the course of HIV-disease, substantially reducing AIDS-related morbidity and mortality.

A high degree of adherence is required to achieve and maintain a successful virologic response, to reduce vertical transmission, to prevent drug resistance and to prevent toxicities associated with opioids and /or antiretroviral agents.

Suboptimal adherence to HAART among IDUs is of significant concern (22). In a study of Kerr et al. (2004) (22) 66% of HIV infected IDUs were less than 95% adherent. Oblivion (27%) was the most frequently cited reason for missing doses of HAART. Since the introduction of HAART IDUs demonstrated a much higher risk of progression to AIDS than people, who were infected by sexual intercourse (hazard ratio 2.20 [95%,CI 1.30-3.72]) (23). The most probable explanation is insufficient adherence. Competing non HIV- related morbidity, such as liver disease related to hepatitis C co-infection, may be partially responsible for high numbers of deaths in drug abusers. These co-infections are more common in IDUs and differences in immune recovery following HAART as reported for those co-infected with hepatitis C virus, could also contribute to the increased mortality (24).

In a study by Berg et al. (2004) (25) median adherence among women was significantly lower than among men. Alcohol use, heroin use, significant medication side effects, lack of long-term housing, not belonging to an HIV support group and cocaine use were independently associated with worse adherence (25). Modified directly observed therapy for patients with HIV disease receiving methadone maintenance therapy can be an option for increasing adherence to HAART (26).

2.1.3 Drug Interactions

A certain number of antiretroviral medications are metabolized by cytochrome P 450 enzyme, CYP 3A4. Methadone and also buprenorphine, a newer agent available for the treatment of opioid dependence as discussed below, are likewise primarily metabolized by hepatic cyotochrome P450 enzymes- especially CYP 3A4.

Inhibiting action on CYP 3A4 activity could therefore enhance opioid toxicity or toxicity related to increased exposure to HIV medication. Conversely and clinically more relevant, if an antiretroviral agent is capable of inducing CYP 3A4 activity, an opioid withdrawal syndrome could result, which could place the patient at risk for relapse to illicit drug use.

For methadone significant, in part adverse drug-drug interactions with many antiretroviral medications are described:

Interaction of methadone with protease inhibitors

In vitro studies showed that protease inhibitors were inhibitors of CYP 3A enzyme activity, which led the manufacturers to include warnings about the potential for methadone-associated opioid toxicity with simultaneous administration (27). However, in vivo studies showed that concomitant administration of several of the protease inhibitors with methadone showed decreases in serum concentrations of methadone (26). Treatment with *lopinavir plus ritonavir* (Kaletra®) for example may need an increase in methadone dosage in patients undergoing methadone maintenance therapy. *Lopinavir* is a known inducer of CYP 3A4 and is a potent inducer of methadone metabolism (28). *Ritonavir* is an inhibitor of CYP 3A4, but is used in subtherapeutic doses in the *lopinavir-ritonavir* combination drug. Therefore in this combination *ritonavir* has no significant effect on methadone exposure.

Interaction of methadone with non-nucleoside reverse transcriptase inhibitors (NNRTIs)

NNRTIs have significant interactions with methadone. *Nevirapine* is an inducer of CYP 3A. Interaction with methadone can cause severe opioid abstinence syndrome leading to discontinuation of nevirapine therapy or significant increases in daily methadone dose (29). *Efavirenz* reduces methadone concentrations (20), but it is contraindicated in pregnancy due to proven teratogenicity.

Interaction of methadone with nucleoside reverse transcriptase inhibitors (NRTIs)

NRTIs are unlikely to interact with methadone. In *zidovudine* monotherapy methadone levels were found to be unchanged and only minor effect on opioid therapies including the use of methadone, levoacetylmethadol (LAAM), buprenorphine or naltrexone was observed (26, 30). The combination of *lamivudine plus zidovudine* had no effect on methadone concentrations in persons undergoing opioid maintenance therapy (31).

Nevertheless one study demonstrated a 41% increase in plasma concentrations of *zidovudine* which produced toxicity in some opioid-dependent patients that were stabilized with methadone (32). It is to note that application of *zidovudine* during pregnancy is often limited due to its aggravating effect on pregnancy- induced anaemia. Profound knowledge of drug interactions in pregnant methadone-patients treated with antiretroviral medication is thus helpful in anticipating possible complications.

Buprenorphine may have fewer adverse interactions with antiretroviral drugs. It demonstrates significant pharmacokinetic interaction to *efavirenz*, but maybe due to the high affinity and long duration of μ- opioid receptor binding of buprenorphine no significant pharmacodynamic interaction was detected. Simultaneous application of buprenorphine and antiretroviral drugs might be feasible without the risk of inducing opiate withdrawal. This promising finding may simplify the treatment of opioid-dependent patients with HIV disease and improve the patient's outcome (26).

In summary the benefit of HAART can be abolished due to several drug interactions. In HIV positive opiate addicts interactions of opiates and antiretroviral drug therapy can cause toxicities and opioid withdrawal. Consideration of these interactions can improve adherence and HIV outcome for opiate addicts.

2.2 Hepatitis C

Hepatitis C virus (HCV) - infection represents a major health problem in pregnancy. Overall vertical transmission rate is 5%. It is highly correlated with maternal hepatitis C-viremia and exposure to maternal blood at delivery (33). An association between injection drug use during pregnancy and higher perinatal transmission rate has been noted (34).

2.2.1 Co Infection HIV, Hepatitis C

The co-infection of HIV and HCV is especially common in IDUs and is frequently correlated with problematic psychosocial settings (35).

The vertical transmission rate of HCV is significantly higher in HIV co-infected pregnant women than in HIV- negative women. It is estimated to be 15-36%. HIV1/HCV co-infected individuals are less likely to clear HCV infection and have frequently higher HCV-RNA levels. Drug injecting during pregnancy may play an important role in terms of reinfection and consecutive increase in viral load (34).

Hence every effort should be made to enrol drug using HCV- and/or HIV- positive pregnant women in drug treatment programmes to stabilize psychosocial circumstances on one hand and to reduce the possibility of vertical transmission on the other hand.

2.3 Other Sexually Transmitted Diseases (STD)

Many studies have documented that drug-using women, in particular those using cocaine, have elevated risks for STD compared with either drug-using men or non-drug-using women (36). Drug using women with drug related prostitution have a higher risk for infection with herpes simplex, syphilis, chlamydia trachomatis, gonorrhoea and pelvic inflammatory disease. Genital ulcer disease (e.g. herpes simplex and syphilis) increases the likelihood of HIV-transmission by increasing both the infectiousness of, and the susceptibility to HIV-infection (37).

Both clinical and sub clinical reactivation of genital herpes increase the HIV viral load in the genital tract (38). Clinical genital herpes simplex virus infection during pregnancy in HIV-infected women may be a risk factor for perinatal HIV transmission. If future studies confirm this association, therapy to suppress genital herpes reactivation during pregnancy may be a strategy to reduce perinatal HIV transmission.

3. TREATMENT OF ADDICTIVE BEHAVIOUR DURING PREGNANCY

3.1 Methadone Maintenance Therapy

For the actual standard therapy using methadone maintenance, analysis of pregnancy course and outcome reveals a persistent high complication rate with frequent presentation of threatened preterm delivery (preterm contractions and cervical insufficiency) partially explained by the higher incidence of genitourinary infections, intrauterine fetal growth retardation and low birth weight (9, 39). Therefore pregnancy of heroin addicts even under methadone maintenance therapy represents high-risk pregnancy. It requires tight obstetrical follow-ups including regular surveillance of fetal blood supply and fetal growth using doppler-ultrasound.

There remains one major problem in pregnancy of opiate addicts, which could not be resolved by methadone maintenance therapy, that is continued craving and additional illicit use of cocaine, street heroin, psychotropics as benzodiazepines or antidepressants.

Up to two-third of the pregnant women present positive findings in urine screening or self-admit additional drug use (5, 8, 9, 11). As elucidated in the preceding chapter it is of great importance to restrict illicit drug abuse in consideration of other underlying medical and infectious diseases of the mother. Furthermore illicit drug abuse represent the hazardous factor contributing to fetal malformations or (40) abruptio placentae as specified for cocaine, fetal growth retardation, microcephaly (9, 41) and neonatal withdrawal (42).

Thus efficient pregnancy care in methadone treated women should include urine-drug screening at every antenatal visit. Frequent evidence for illicit drug use should lead to reevaluation and improvement of maintenance therapy under consideration of the patient´s individual need, the physiological changes in methadone availability during pregnancy and the potential advantage of alternative therapy options.

It is of interest that a randomized study on 85 methadone treated pregnant women demonstrate that for pregnancy care in these women use of incentives is worth to be reflected as it is apparently capable of enhancing maintenance programme attendance and drug abstinence (43). Complemented to psychosocial stabilization programmes an overall improvement of pregnancy care could result.

3.2. Altered Maternal Methadone Availability During Pregnancy

For pregnancy higher elimination rates and a lower half-life of methadone (44) in comparison to non-pregnant methadone patients and a more rapid fall of methadone blood levels in later stage of pregnancy (45) have been demonstrated. In a study of Pond et al. (1985) (45) methadone trough levels after delivery were significantly higher than during pregnancy.

Beside high tissue binding capacity of methadone and thus "loss" by binding at the growing fetal tissue and the placenta, the change in maternal gastric pH modifying methadone absorption, the increase in plasma volume and in progesteron blood levels are hypothesized mechanisms for the increased methadone demand during pregnancy. Progesteron in turn activates hepatic microsomal oxidation system leading to an increase in methadone metabolization

If half-life of methadone is increased an increase in daily dosage and an increase in application frequency have to be complentated. Splitting of the total daily methadone dose into a twice daily application was recommended from some authors to tackle these prevailing difficulties (reviewed in (2)).

During the last three years research has focused on individual methadone metabolism and changes in the metabolism during pregancy.

As mentioned earlier CYP 3A4 has been identified as the major enzyme responsible for the metabolism of methadone and buprenorphine in human liver and intestine. In addition it has been demonstrated that several isoforms such as CYP2D6, CYP1A2 and possibly CYP2C9 and CYP2C19 are further involved in methadone metabolism (reviewed in (46)). Genetic polymorphism of these enzymes, interindividual variability in enzyme activity or interaction with medication likewise metabolized by CYP enzymes have all been shown to influence the individual´s methadone availability.

Patient's serum methadone levels taking the same amount of daily methadone are varying significantly. For example in a cohort of 20 patients receiving 100mg methadone/day serum levels ranged from 90-520ng/mL (in (46)).

The key role of CYP acitivity is further comfirmed by a study of Shinderman et al. (2003) (47), who demonstrated that in patients with a need of high doses of methadone cytochrome P450 activity was elevated compared to the activity in patients treated with low methadone doses.

For pregnancy data supporting the need to consider individual variability in methadone metabolism were published by Drozdick et al. (2002) (48). They compared methadone serum trough levels of 44 asymptomatic and 58 symptomatic methadone- treated pregnant women. Trough levels were measured 20-24 hours after last methadone application. The mean applied methadone dosages in the two groups compared was without significant difference (101 ± 42mg/day versus 114 ± 43mg/day), but trough levels in symptomatic pregnant women were significantly lower compared to the asymptomatic group (0.175mg/L versus 0.295 mg/L). The authors therefore concluded that trough level measurements with a recommended cut-off at 0.24mg/L might be of help in regulating methadone dose schemes in pregnant opiate addicts. To achieve this level a methadone dose of 50-150mg or even higher doses in the third trimester can be necessary.

In non-pregnant patients higher doses up to 80-120mg/day have been arrogated to efficiently treat opiate addicts (49-51) thus fear of higher methadone dosages in obstetrics should be likewise revised. Consistent with this postulation in a recent study on 81 pregnant opiate addicts treatment with high doses of ≥100mg of methadone resulted in significant lower illicit drug use than in the group treated with < 100mg methadone/day (52). In 50 pregnant women receiving ≥ 80mg methadone/day Berghella et al. (2005) found a similar tendency (53).

In fact first results investigating the role of placental methadone metabolism let presume that further methadone dose adjustment is necessary due to additional placental drug biotransformation. The placental capacity in eliminating xenobiotics is well studied and to a lower amount than in the liver and depending on gestational age the expression of various CYP isoforms have been demonstrated (reviewed in (54)). More specifically CYP 19 was now found to be the major enzyme catalyzing methadone and also buprenorphine metabolism in placental tissue in vitro (54, 55).

Therefore considering the individual's methadone metabolism and the specified metabolic aspects of pregnancy arbitrary dose reductions scheme seem to be obsolete, instead prospective management of methadone treated pregnant women should take necessity of dose increase into account.

Is There a Benefit in Reducing Methadone Dose DuringPpregnancy?

On behalf of the fetus and as methadone exposed neonates have been reported to develop more frequently and a more intensive and longer lasting NAS than neonates after heroin or cocaine exposure (4, 7, 10-13), the question arised whether a dose reduction towards term would positively influence fetal outcome. Especially the possible benefit for NAS is still matter of actual debate. However published data on this issue are inconclusive.

Main difficulties in interpreting and comparing the study results are the small numbers on which the studies were based on, the constant confounding factor of additional illicit drug abuse and the differences in assessment of NAS.

In a retrospective analysis (42) of a cohort consisting of 70 mothers and their neonates with median maternal methadone dose of 20 mg (range 0-150 mg) 32 infants (46%) were treated for narcotic withdrawal. The authors divided the maternal methadone doses applied in three groups. In the group having received < 20 mg/day (N=25) the necessity of withdrawal treatment was found in 12%, in the group having received 20-39 mg/day (N=25) in 44%, and in the group who received ≥ 40 mg/day of methadone (N=20) in 90%. These differences were significant. Methadone dose correlated with both duration of neonatal hospitalization and neonatal abstinence score. In our own study (39) 100% of the neonates with maternal methadone dose > 80mg/day required treatment for NAS compared to 43% of the neonates after maternal doses < 30mg/day before delivery, but the statistical pitfal might have been the much lower number of 14 mothers treated with methadone doses >80mg/day compared to 40 women in the < 30mg/day group.

In contrast in two recent restrospective studies on large cohorts of 100 and 81 mothers and their offsprings the authors were not able to show a correlation of maternal methadone dose and NAS. The methadone doses used were generally higher and the authors divided into two groups dependent on the daily maternal methadone dose; in a group with <80 (N=50) and >80 (N=50) mg/day and ≥ 100 (N=36) and < 100 (N=45) mg/day, respectively.

In accordance to the latter results Mack et al. (1991) could not find a correlation between maternal methadone dosage, maternal methadone serum levels and neonatal serum levels, nor was there a correlation between neonatal serum level and the severity of NAS (56). However similar studies analyzing the coherence of methadone blood levels with methadone dose before delivery and the development of NAS do not achieve unanimity either (57, 58).

Considering the individual variability in methadone metabolism in adult opiate addicts the same can be postulated for the fetus and neonate, respectively. Therefore it is to question if maternal methadone dosage rather than neonatal metabolism is the determining factor for the development of NAS.

In our opinion there is requirement for larger prospective studies before generalized recommendations of methadone dose reduction during pregnancy can be advocated.

In addition patients on low-dose methadone or on detoxification programmes are at high risk for relapse as discussed further below.

Actual data are suggestive that maternal methadone dose during pregnancy, maternal methadone blood levels, neonatal methadone blood levels and the development of NAS are all figures depending on multiple factors probably not fully understood so far.

Of interest are recent results investigating placental drug transporting systems. Multidrug resistance proteins MRP1, MRP2 and MRP3 as well as P- Glycoprotein (P-gp) are transmembrane proteins known to be involved in placental drug transfer. P-gp and MRP2 are expressed on the maternal side of the human trophoblast whereas MRP1 and 3 are located on the fetal side.

P-gp possesses ATPase activity that is activated by various drugs. Drug transport occurs unidirectionally facilitating cell efflux. It can be detected in placental trophoblast from the first trimester of pregnancy on and is located in the brush-border membrane. Its importance lies in the capacity of active removal of xenobiotics from the fetal to the maternal side thus protecting the fetus from potential toxic effects (reviewed in (59)).

Using an in-vitro dual placental lobule perfusion system Nekhayeva et al. (2005) and Nanovskaya et al. (2005) showed an asymmetry of methadone transfer with a higher methadone clearance index from the fetal to the maternal direction and after using an P-gp inhibitor an 30% increase of methadone transfer from the maternal to the fetal side (60, 61). Hence there is evidence for an active P-gp related methadone shift from the fetus´ to the mother´s compartment. It could explain the high discrepancy in postpartum maternal and neonatal methadone plasma levels with relatively low methadone concentrations in the neonatal plasma found by some authors (57, 58) and the lack of correlation between maternal methadone serum level and neonatal methadone level in cord blood reported by Mack et al. (1991) (56).

Nanovskaya et al. (2005) detected a variation in the expression of P-gp in placental brush-border in the 81 term placentas investigated by (60). Though correlation of the quantity of P-gp expression with P-gp activity is unknown, it is now tempting to presume strong influence of the degree of placental P-gp expression or other variabilities in placental drug transfer on the development of NAS by influencing the degree of fetal methadone exposure. Further perfusion studies on placental lobules will give more informations on this issue.

3.3 Alternative Management Options of Addicitive Behaviour During Pregnancy

3.3.1 Opioid Detoxification

Idealistically viewed direct detoxification or by preceding transition on maintenance substances seems to be the most reasonable and tempting approach to treat opiate addiction in pregnancy. Longer duration of pregnancy, normalized birth weight and head circumference, improved respiratory status and lower incidence of NAS are the reported benefits after complete detoxification (62, 63) .

However, withdrawal in the mother can be critical for the fetus. During maternal methadone dose reduction Zuspan et al. (1975) (64) found increased norepinephrine values in amniotic fluid. During the last years it has been confirmed that there is fetal hypothalamic-pituitary-adrenal response to stress independent of maternal responses (65). It gives strength to the conclusion of Zuspan et al. (1975) that their findings represent signs of fetal distress rather than increased transmission of catecholamines from a withdrawing mother.

In rats Lichtblau et al. (1981) induced an increase in the rate of stillbirth after continuous naloxone administration in pregnant rats pretreated with LAAM (66).

Nevertheless MEDLINE- search presents two published studies questioning the fetal risk, if detoxification is performed cautiously in selected cases (62, 67).

One study is a retrospective data analysis of 101 cases on a 21day in-patient detoxification using methadone (67). All patients revealing illicit drug use were discharged from the programme leading to a preselection of data. Finally 42/101 patients (41.6%) completed the detoxification programme. There are no data on fetal monitoring and investigated end-points were restricted to the number of miscarriages and preterm deliveries.

In only five cases detoxification was carried out during the first trimester of pregnancy of which one ended in miscarriage. In summary data from this study cannot assure safety for methadone detoxification for early pregnancy nor does it provide data on fetal wellbeing during detoxification procedure in second and third trimester.

For fetal monitoring Dashe et al. (1998) (62) reported the use of a "qualitative" assessment of daily fetal "activity" and once a fetus had reached gestational age of 24 weeks gestation a fetal heart rate monitoring semiweekly in 34 gravidas. Thus fetal distress had been monitored rather punctually than continuously. As much as recent research focus on the significance of "fetal programming" in determining chronic diseases in adulthood comprehensive safety for the fetus during detoxification should be guaranteed and is not convincingly demonstrated in the two studies presented.

Frustrating adding concern is the high relapse rate of 40-60% during pregnancy (6, 9, 62, 67). Finnegan (1991) reports of her personal experience of nearly 100% failure (6) and as relapsing patients are at risk of consuming illicit street-drugs the benefit of detoxification attempts on fetomaternal outcome is unsure. Indication for detoxification should be based on each individual´s case and overall prognosis.

3.3.2 Morphine Maintenance

Morphine has a duration of action of 4-6 hours. With its short acting property it was discussed as an alternative for maintenance therapy presuming a beneficial effect on neonatal abstinence syndrome. In maintenance therapy oral morphine sulphate is used provided as a slow-release formula with prolonged plasma level and lack of accumulation.

In 1999 Fischer et al. (68) conducted a randomized open study treating 24 pregnant women with slow- release morphine and 24 women with methadone. The appliance of morphine has been proven to be equally suitable in the treatment of pregnant opiate addicts. Mean applied morphine dose at delivery was 300.4 ±137.5 mg/day (range: 13-120mg). Women of the morphine group demonstrated a statistically significant reduction in illicit benzodiazepine and additional opiate consumption, but not in cocaine consumption. Whereas Fischer et al. (1999) did not find a difference in duration and intensity of NAS in the two groups compared, NAS developed in 28 of 30 (93%) neonates after morphine hydrochloride maintenance in the continued study evaluated by Rohrmeister et al. (2001) (69). In addition Rohrmeister et al. (2001) (69) compared the neonates after morphine hydrochloride exposure to 42 neonates after maternal methadone maintenance therapy and 16 neonates after maternal buprenorphine treatment. Incidences of NAS in the latter groups were significantly lower (76% and 19%). Therefore the negative impact of morphine maintenance on NAS overweighs benefit in reduction of illicit benzodiazepine and opiate use.

In a recent double-blind, double-dummy study on 18 pregnant patients the transition from short-acting morphine maintenance to methadone or buprenorphine maintenance has been shown to be comfortable and safe during the second trimester of pregnancy (70).

3.3.3 Buprenorphine Maintenance

Buprenorphine is a partial μ-opioid receptor agonist. Acute doses act as an agonist on opioid receptors while chronic application produces effective blockade of opioid agonists. Buprenorphine is metabolized by direct glucuronisation and by oxidation involving CYP 3A4 to norbuprenorphine, its active metabolite. Buprenorphine has a poor oral bioavailability and is administered as a sublingual tablet.

Clinical studies on non-pregnant addicts confirmed that buprenorphine is effective for maintenance treatment most useful in highly-motivated patients resulting in a decrease of illicit drug use during the treatment programme (reviewed in (2)).

In pregnant patients doses applied vary from 0.4-24mg/day. During the last decade observational and retrospective studies confirmed the safety of buprenorphine treatment during pregnancy with no negative impact on fetomaternal outcome (71-75). In fact there is some evidence that in comparison to methadone maintenance the rate of preterm deliveries could be lower after buprenorphine (75).

In addition data from preliminary studies led to the assumption that buprenorphine could cause less severe NAS.

In a literature review Johnson et al. (2003) (74) evaluated 21 published reports on buprenorphine use during pregnancy. Of these reports two were open-label controll studies, five prospective studies and 14 were case reports. Summarizing reported numbers of NAS in a total of 309 buprenorphine exposed neonates NAS appeared in 62% of the infants with 48% requiring treatment. However, detailled analysis of the Johnson et al. showed that 40% of these cases were confounded by illicit drug use, therefore actual benefit on NAS is presumed to be better.

In 2005 Lejeune et al. (75) published the largest prospective observational study on 159 buprenorphine treated versus 101 methadone treated opiate-dependent mothers. Mean daily buprenorphine doses were 5.4 ± 4.5 mg/d (range 0.4-24) and mean daily methadone dose was 57 ± 30.4 mg/d (range 10-180). A difference in the frequency of severe NAS in the two substitution groups could not be registered.

Up to now there is only one randomized, double-blind, double-dummy controlled study investigating the benefit of buprenorphine over methadone during pregnancy (75). The investigators like in all studies on opiate addicted individuals had to struggle with a high drop-out rate. Of 30 randomized women, ten did not complete the study and finally 9 buprenorphine treated versus 11 methadone treated pregnancies were compared in view of the neonatal abstinence syndrome. Between the two groups there was no statistically significant difference in percentage of neonates treated for NAS, but total amount of opioid-agonist medication administered to treat NAS and length of hospitalization was significantly higher in the neonates exposed to methadone.

In summary actual literature surely do not show any disadvantages of buprenorphine in comparison to methadone in maintenance treatment of pregnant opiate addicts and favourable tendencies have not been ruled out yet.

3.3.4 Naltrexone

Naltrexone is an opiate receptor antagonist. It differs from naloxone by a longer half-life and longer lasting effect of 42-48 hours and more than 24 hours respectively. It has been approved for the treatment in opioid abuse by the US Food and Drug administration (FDA) in 1985. High rates of relapses and high rates of sudden death after scheduled and unscheduled termination of therapy discredited naltrexonebased therapy in non-pregnant patients. Experience with naltrexone treatment in pregnancy is limited. In a recent trial Hulse et al. (2004) reported of 17 pregnant heroin user who were managed with a naltrexone implant (76). There were no differences in gestational length or birthweight compared to 90 women treated with methadone maintenance but a tendency for higher birthweight in the naltrexone treated group. Though of minor value as a predictor for neonatal survival and neurological development than Apgar Score at 5 minutes, Apgar Score at 1 minute was significantly higher in the naltrexone exposed compared to the methadone exposed newborn.

3.3.5 Heroin

In Switzerland heroin assisted treatment within the bounds of a psychosocial treatment programme has been established since 1994. It consists of controlled heroin supplementation to an underlying methadone maintenance as for the short half-life of action of heroin.

Data evaluated demonstrated a significant improvement of participant´s health status, a high retention rate and a reduction in criminal activity and illicit cocaine and/or heroin abuse (77). Practically the use is however restricted to the more "difficult" cases, thus the four cases we medically accompanied during pregnancies (9, 39) were patients with reduced health condition and chaotic multidrug-using behaviour before inclusion into heroin assisted treatment.

In two of our cases the patients were switched to heroin assisted treatment at 33 and 34 weeks gestation and one of the women being enrolled before conception was able to cease heroin completely at 32 weeks gestation. Average methadone dose before delivery was 80 ± 59 mg/day and heroin doses ranged from 0-270mg/day. All neonates born to these women were term deliveries and all had birthweights within normal ranges. NAS occurred in all neonates. It is to be discussed if earlier embedding to heroin assisted treatment with lesser need of methadone doses and early suppression of multidrug-using behaviour would have positive impact on NAS. Unfortunately the use is limited by the more severe course of withdrawal in the detoxifying adult.

4. Current Management Strategies of the Neonatal Abstinence Syndrome

Managing newborn infants of a drug dependent mother is a multi-task challenge. Neonatal course is complicated not only by the effects of maternal substance abuse itself but also by poor health and social conditions of the mother. To improve long term outcome of children born to illicit drug addicted mothers, beside medical treatment, psychological, social and child protection strategies must be prospectively planned in neonatal management of these children.

4.1 Fetal, Perinatal and Neonatal Risk Factors in Infants Born to Illicit Drug Dependant Mothers

Infants born to illicit drug addicted mothers are at risk for several fetal, perinatal and neonatal problems. Given the absent evidence of teratogenic effect of opiates in the human fetus (78-80), nevertheless newborns to opiate addicted mothers have to be carefully examined for congenital malformations. The reason is that up to 80% of opiate dependent mothers are taking other potentially teratogenic substances, i.e. alcohol, cocaine or antidepressants (5, 8, 9, 11, 80-82). In the offspring of these mothers prematurity, microcephaly and inappropriate growth for gestational age but also viral and bacterial infections are well known perinatal risk factors, which has already been discussed in part in the chapters above. Neonatal adaptation is more often disturbed in infants born to illicit drug dependent mothers (79, 83, 84). As a consequence, opiate addicted mothers should give birth in specialized perinatal centers, where both, the mother and the newborn can be adequately managed.

4.2 Diagnosis of Neonatal Abstinence Syndrome (NAS)

Neonatal Abstinence Syndrome (NAS) was first described in the 1970s. In 1975 L. P. Finnegan proposed a scoring system to describe the intensity of NAS (85). Clinical signs of NAS were classified into four groups: central nervous system symptoms, gastrointestinal symptoms, vegetative symptoms and tachypnoea. Since the original Finnegan score consists of 31 items, it was modified for clinical use. *Figure 1* shows the modified Finnegan Score as it is applied in the Swiss Neonatal Abstinence Study. Up to now neither the validity of the original nor of the modified Finnegan score has been investigated. Normative data of the adapted Finnegan score in healthy newborns are currently under evaluation by a member of our study group. These Data are not yet published. An alternative withdrawal score in newborns was proposed by Lipsitz (86). Both, Finnegan's and the Lipsitz' scoring system enables semi-objective description of the intensity of withdrawal symptoms. An objective way to describe the intensity of NAS was lately proposed by O'Brian and colleagues. They measured the movements of the newborn by a portable motion detector (actigraph) and found them to be positively correlated with the intensity of NAS (87). Whether this tool will provide a benefit for the management of newborns with NAS has to be proved in the future years.

Since symptoms of narcotic withdrawal lack specifity, NAS is a diagnosis of exclusion. Infection, intraventricular hemorrhagia, hypoglycemia, inborn errors of metabolism and others may mimic symptoms of NAS and have to be carefully excluded as differential diagnosis.

When NAS is suspected upon clinical presentation, laboratory investigations have to further confirm the diagnosis. Residues of opiates and other illicit substances can be detected in amniotic fluid, in the newborn's urine, meconium and hair.

Urine testing is easily available and commonly used in adults. In diagnosing NAS, urine analysis however has strong limitations. Positive findings after opiate consumption persists for only a few days, thus negative urine results can not rule out the development of NAS (88-90).

Modified Finnegan Score **Swiss Study on Detoxification in Newborns (SSDN)**							
	Date						
	Time						
CNS Symptoms							
High pitched cry	2						
High pitched cry > 2 h	3						
Sleeps less than 3 h after feeding	1						
Sleeps less than 2 h after feeding	2						
Sleeps less than 1 h after feeding	3						
Mild tremors when disturbed	1						
Marked tremors when disturbed	2						
Mild tremors when undisturbed	3						
Marked tremors when undisturbed	4						
Increased muscle tone	2						
Excoriation of skin	1						
Myoclonic jerks in sleep	3						
Generalized convulsion	5						
Vegetative Symptoms							
Sweating	1						
Temperature 37.5 – 38.0 °C	1						
Temperature > 38.0 °C	2						
Frequent yawning	1						
Mottling	1						
Nasal stuffiness	2						
Sneezing	1						
Gastrointestinal Symptoms							
Frantic sucking	1						
Poor feeding	2						
Regurgitation	2						
Projectile vomiting	3						
Loose stools	2						
Watery stools	3						
Respiratory Symptoms							
Tachypnea	1						
Tachypnea with retractions	2						
Total Score							

Figure 1: Modified Finnegan Score as it is used in the Swiss Study on Detoxification in Newborns (SSDN). Every eight hours the infant is checked for withdrawal symptoms. For each symptom presented the corresponding score is added. If total score exceeds 9 points twice, pharmacological treatment is started.

Residues of maternal illicit drug abuse during pregnant state are retained in the fetus' meconium during the last trimester. Therefore analysis of the newborn's meconium provide the more reliable retrospective information on maternal drug consumption during pregnancy (88, 89, 91, 92). Positive results are associated with a highly increased risk of the development of NAS and should lead to close and careful clinical monitoring of the neonate.

As much as any laboratory test, meconium analysis has its pitfalls. Testing for instance should be solely performed using the first two meconium probes of the neonate. In later stool probes already a minimal degree of fermentation is capable in falsifying test results.

Residues of opiates are also retained in the newborn's hair. Hair analysis enables drug screening even after the first days of life, when meconium passage is completed (93). However, hair analysis is difficult to put into practice as the amount of hair needed to perform the test is considerable. Some newborns lack enough hair for testing; in fact in some, complete shaving of the scalp hair would be necessary to achieve the demanded amount for reliable testing. This is in turn hardly accepted by both parents and nursing staff.

As a result we suggest that for the diagnosis of NAS meconium analysis by an experienced laboratory should be considered to become the gold standard.

4.3 Therapy of Neonatal Abstinence Syndrome (NAS)

Since the first study results in the 1970´s there is general agreement that NAS should be treated. Early diagnosis and adequate treatment of neonatal abstinence syndrome is required to prevent the infant from substantial morbidity such as dehydration, electrolyte abnormalities, poor weight gain, aspiration or seizures (79, 94). However, in some neonates the course of narcotic withdrawal may be mild without requiring any specific therapy. In any case infants born to substance dependent mothers should be monitored closely for withdrawal symptoms (79, 94, 95) using a defined symptom score scale with determination of an upper score limit. Once the evaluated score exceeds the upper limit, therapy should be initiated immediately.

For the treatment of NAS basically two therapy options exist, which should be used in supplementation, general supportive treatment and pharmacological treatment.

4.3.1 Supportive Treatment

There is broad consensus that supportive treating strategies such as minimal handling and optimal feeding help to minimize neonatal withdrawal symptoms and therefore prevent the newborn from suffering (95). Only a few groups have studied nursing interventions properly. Ostrea et al. (1976) showed that withdrawal symptoms can be minimized by loosely swaddling the newborn in a quiet, dimly lit room (7). A positive effect of non-oscillating waterbeds was demonstrated by Oro et al. (1988) (96).

Withdrawal symptoms are associated with a huge energy burden for the metabolism of the newborn. A considerable number of newborns with NAS are small for gestational age and need supplemental energy to catch up growth. Gastrointestinal withdrawal symptoms (excessive sucking, poor feeding, regurgitation or vomiting, loose or watery stools) interfere with the required uptake of adequate amounts of energy and fluids. Supportive strategies to preserve adequate caloric and fluid intake help to allow the infant a normal daily weight gain and are therefore of great importance (79, 95, 97)

4.3.2 Pharmacological Treatment

Several drugs and several drug application strategies are used to treat NAS. Only a few studies compare the efficacy of these different pharmacological regimens.

4.3.2.1 Opiates

Opiates in use for treatment of NAS are *tincture of opium, morphine, methadone* and *paregoric,* which contains anhydrous morphine with antispasmodics, camphor, 45% ethanol and benzoic acid. There are no prospective randomized controlled trials, which compare efficacy and safety between these opiates. Although *paregoric* was one of the first substances used for treatment of NAS, there are many concerns about its use today, because of the known and potential toxic effects of some these ingredients (90).

The aim of using an opiate in NAS is to control symptoms provoked by opiate withdrawal. Therefore most authors titrate the therapeutic opiate amount by stepwise increasing the dose until symptoms release (82, 90, 98, 99). Once the symptoms are controlled, the dose of the substituted opiate is decreased step by step. While some author increase the dose until symptoms are controlled others start augmenting a sedative drug as soon as a certain ceiling limit of opiates is reached. Some authors prefer to give a fixed dose of opiate and add a sedative, if opiate alone fails to control symptoms (81).

There is neither consensus on the starting dose of opiates nor on its upper therapeutic limit.

There is futher no evidence whether one of these above mentioned strategies is safer or more effective than the other.

Some authors claim concerns about the potential harm of prolonged administration of opiates to the developing brain. These objections are mainly based on animal studies (100). In humans, no negative effect of opiate therapy on long term outcome was reported so far. But one must keep in mind that this issue is extremely difficult to study. Long term outcome in infants born to drug dependent mothers may be already influenced by confounding factors, such as maternal co-morbidities and/or unprivileged socioeconomic background, to name only a few. Studies on this topic must therefore include a sufficient number of patients to achieve adequate statistical power.

4.3.2.2 Sedatives

Sedatives used to treat neonatal narcotic withdrawal are *phenobarbitone, diazepam,* and *chlorpromazine.* The rational for using sedatives in NAS is twofold. On one hand, the most prominent symptoms of NAS are signs of neurological excitability, which can be improved with sedatives. On the other hand up to 80% drug addicted mothers demonstrate multi-drug addiction and consume other drugs than opiates. Hence in these cases monotherapy with opiates are of limited value.

Phenobarbitone

Phenobarbitone effectively ameliorates hyperactive behavioural state in the newborn suffering from narcotic withdrawal, but does not treat gastrointestinal symptoms (90, 94).

When high doses of phenobarbitone are used to control NAS, the resulting central nervous depression affects also sucking reflex either (98), which subsequently leads to impaired feeding.

Rapid tolerance to the sedative effect, a long half-life time (up to 200 hours in newborns) and induction of drug metabolism are further disadvantages of phenobarbitone (90).

Several administration strategies are described. Some authors propose a loading dose followed by a lower maintenance dose (90, 101). Other authors prefer to refrain from loading dose, but instead increase the dosage stepwise until symptoms are controlled or an upper dosage limit is reached (94, 98, 101, 102). After stabilization of withdrawal symptoms the dosage is subsequently reduced stepwise. Finnegan reported that symptoms of NAS were controlled within a significantly shorter time when - in contrast to the titration strategy – therapy was initiated with a loading dose (103). In contrast Kaltenbach (1986) could not confirm the advantage of loading over titration strategy (101).

Diazepam

Although signs of withdrawal resolve rapidly when treated with diazepam, the sole use of benzodiazepine in the treatment of NAS proved to be insufficient in almost cases (101). Other concerns in its use include the infant's limited capacity of metabolization and excretion of diazepam (104), the sedative effect, reports of its negative impact on sucking (101, 105) as well as reports of its association with late onset seizures (106). Therapy with diazepam has therefore become obsolete. However, French colleagues lately raised the question whether diazepam has been abounded to quickly. Based on their local experience they enforced the need for a new prospective trial on this subject (107).

Chlorpromazine

Symptoms of affected central nervous system as well as gastrointestinal signs of NAS are well controlled by chlorpromazine (108, 109). While in some European medical centres chlorpromazine is commonly used, the American Academy of Pediatrics (AAP) has strong concerns about this medicament because of its very slow elimination in newborns and because of numerous potential side effects such as cerebellar dysfunction, decreased seizure threshold and hematological problems (90). There is only one small prospective controlled trial including 38 infants that studies the efficacy of chlorpromazine (108). In this study by Kahn et al. (1969) NAS treatment with chlorpromazine was compared to treatment with phenobarbitone and no significant differences in outcome were found.

Nevertheless, chlorpromazine remains widely used to control neonatal withdrawal symptoms (109, 110). In MEDLINE no report on adverse effects of chlorpromazine in newborns can be found.

4.3.2.3 Clonidine

Clonidine is a non narcotic, non sedative substance which acts as a presynaptic α2-blocker. It has been demonstrated to effectively reducing opiate withdrawal signs in adults and also in newborns (111). Up to now there is no randomized, controlled trial that studied efficacy and safety of clonidine use in NAS. An ongoing trial by Agthe et al. will elucidate this issue, but results are not yet available (112). Presently, in the absence of controlled trials, the use of clonidine in NAS cannot be recommended.

4.4 Comparative Studies

Nine randomized controlled or comparative trials on different treatment strategies for NAS are published so far. Due to methodological limitations in particular insufficient control of confounding variables none of these studies is able to answer the question of efficacy and safety of a single treatment strategy definitely. Even systematic reviews fail to elucidate this question (112, 113).

This is in our view explained by the complexity of the population studied. Uncontrolled maternal illicit drug use, differences in maternal socio-economic and health condition and the huge variety of morbidities presented by the newborns of drug using mothers may all contribute to different courses of neonatal withdrawal. Individual adaptation of treatment strategy is thus essential.

In addition studies on the pharmacological treatment efficacy of NAS have to deal not only with different medicaments but also with different regimens of drug application and different evaluation of NAS.

Nevertheless, survey of the few randomized controlled trials published on this issue are of interest:

Kandall et al. (1983) (98) compared the efficacy of *paregoric* and *phenobarbitone.* 153 infants of opiate addicted mothers were enrolled. Severity of NAS was assessed by Lipsitz score. Neonates were randomly allocated to treatment with *paregoric* (titration strategy) or *phenobarbitone* (no loading dose, but titration strategy). No significant differences in terms of duration of hospital stay and severity of NAS symptom were found. Seizures were reported in 7 of 62 infants treated with *phenobarbitone* while there were no seizures in the *paregoric* group. The author speculated later that this difference may be explained by the *phenobarbitone* dosage, which was probably sufficiently high to control NAS symptoms but not high enough to prevent seizures (94). The main methodogical limitation of this study is the lack of blinding of treatment.

At the same time Carin et al. (1983) (99) compared *paregoric* versus *phenobarbitone* for NAS treatment in a small study of 38 neonates. The primary outcomes of this study were physical and biochemical variables such as respiratory rate, blood pressure, blood gases and thrombocyte counts. No significant group differences were found in these parameters analyzed, but clinical relevance of these parameters as indicator for efficient NAS treatment is to be questioned. Interestingly, the authors found a significantly longer treatment duration in the *paregoric* group compared to the *phenobarbitone* group. The evidence of this finding, however, remains unclear. On the one hand treatment was not blinded, on the other hand there were significantly more multi-drug using mothers in the *paregoric* compared to the *phenobarbitone* treating group.

Comparative studies of different treatment strategies were extended to the analysis of *diazepam* by Kaltenbach et al. (1986) (101). The authors were interested in the question, whether the performance of six month old infants assessed by Bayley Scale of Mental Development (BSMD) differed when treated with either *paregoric* (dose not reported), *phenobarbitone* (loading dose strategy versus titration strategy) or *diazepam* (dose not reported). Outcome analysis of allocated treatment groups was limited as only *paregoric* appeared to be sufficient as a mono-therapy. *Diazepam* mono-therapy had to be combined with *pheobarbitone* or *paregoric* as second line medicaments in all cases. Of the infants initially treated with *phenobarbitone* 50% required the addition of a second medicament. By retrospectively regrouping the infants considering the medicaments received the authors did not find a difference in performance on BSMD at 6 month of age. However clinicians are discordant regarding the value of BSMD as a predictive value for later mental development.

Insufficiency of *diazepam* as a mono-therapy in NAS was endorsed by Finnegan et al. (1984) (103), though study cohort appears to overlap with the cohort reported by Kaltenbach et al. (1986). Of major interest, this is the only study where treatment analysis was performed under consideration of the confounding factor of maternal multidrug-using behaviour during pregnancy. Compared to *phenobarbitone paregoric* demonstrated a significant lower rate of treatment failure in infants of mothers with a sole abuse of opiates.

In a randomized study Madden et al. (1979) (82) investigated the treatment success of *methadone* (titration strategy), *phenobarbitone* (no loading dose and no titration strategy) and *diazepam* in 102 newborns of narcotic addicted mothers. Treatment was initiated upon clinical judgement. The authors found no significant differences in duration of treatment or hospitalisation. Main limitations of this study are the lack of blinding of treatment and that there was no standardized scoring system used to judge the severity of NAS.

Similarly Khoo et al. (1995) (114) compared the application of opiate (*morphine*) to *phenobarbitone* with no difference in the duration of treatment or rate of treatment failure.

In contrast in a more recent study (2004) Jackson reported of a significant reduction of duration of treatment in infants treated with *morphine* compared to those treated with *phenobarbitone* (81). Several methodological aspects possibly explain the differences in the results annotated above. Titration strategy for *morphine* and *phenobarbitone* was applied in Khoo's trial whereas fix dose scheme for *morphine* and *phenobarbitone* was applied in the study of Jackson et al. (2004). It is conceivable that Jackson utilized these rather unusual treatment strategies to facilitate blinding of therapy regimens. In our opinion this exceptional strategy leads to limited clinical evidence.

In 2002, Coyle analyzed the question whether a combined treatment with diluted *tincture of opium (DTO)* and *phenobarbitone* is superior to the treatment with *DTO alone* (115). 21 infants of opiate using mothers with elevated Finnegan scores were treated with *DTO* (titration strategy). They were randomly allocated to receive additionally either *phenobarbitone* (loading dose strategy) or placebo. In both groups, there was no treatment failure. Infants additionally treated with *phenobarbitone* had a significant reduction of maximal daily dose of *DTO*. A significant reduction of the duration of hospitalisation in this combined treatment group was noted either. Since infants treated with *phenobarbitone* were unlike the *morphine* treated group discharged home on *phenobarbitone*, it is unclear, if the reduction of the hospitalisation time depends on discharge policy or if it can interpreted as a valid outcome parameter.

Currently we have knowledge of four further ongoing trials on NAS treatment analysis. Beside Agthe's trial on *clonidine* as mentioned above(112), there is report of a trial on the effect of *phenobarbitone* on developmental outcomes in infant with methadone withdrawal (116) and of a study on neurobehavioral effects of treatment for opiate withdrawal (117). Detailed results of these latter two studies are not yet available.

Finally our group initiated a prospective randomized controlled trial, in which efficacy of *morphine*, *phenobarbitone* and *chlorpromazine* in NAS is compared (Swiss Neonatal Abstinence Study). It is a Swiss multi-centre study including 120 infants born to opiate-dependent mothers in which treatment is fully blinded. Results are not yet available.

In summary currently there is not enough evidence to recommend one or another medicament to treat NAS. The above cited studies must be interpreted under consideration of the local situation and policy.

In our opinion it is crucial that a standardized scoring system is applied to evaluate and interpret withdrawal symptoms and that the once chosen medicament is given in a well defined regimen. In our institution we prefer to treat NAS with an opiate. Severity of withdrawal symptoms is judged by an adapted Finnegan score, the Swiss modified Finnegan Score (Fig. 1), every 8 hours. If the score exceeds 9 points twice in a row or 14 points once, *morphine* is started in a relatively high dose (0.25mg/kg) to achieve quick control of the symptoms. *Morphine* is given every 4 hours. If the score remains > 9, the *morphine* dose is augmented (+0.05mg/kg/dose). Once the score is < 8 three times in row, we keep the *morphine* dosage constant for 3 days. Subsequently we reduce the *morphine* dose daily, if the median of the last three scores is < 8. If the *morphine* dose applied comes to exceed a total of 0.5mg *morphine phenobarbitone* treatment is initiated.

One must be aware, that in NAS the obvious effect of pharmacological treatment is only of short term. Treatment with a pharmacological agent improves clinical signs and prevents the infant from suffering. To the best of our knowledge none of the randomized controlled studies were aligned to evaluate long term outcome. No data exist about the impact of NAS treatment on addictive behaviour in later adulthood. This is very disappointing, since some authors argue that by observing physicians giving a medicament to their distressed infant, parents learn to treat signs of infant's discomfort with drugs instead of behavioural interventions. In this sense, treating NAS in an infant might be speculated to be a feasible risk factor for later addictive disease.

4.5 Breastfeeding

Whether infants of opiate dependent mothers should be breastfed remains a controversial issue and should not be discussed here in detail. Multiple studies demonstrated that the amount of opiates in maternal milk is low. Studies on the infant's plasma methadone level after breastfeeding in relation to the methadone level in the maternal milk however assert the relevance of inidividual methadone metabolism capacity. Such studies will further clarify the value of recommendations based solely on drug concentration in maternal milk. In our opinion, the decision whether an infant born to a drug dependent mother should be breastfeed or not, should be made on the basis of multiple factors considering diversity of maternal illicit drug use, maternal nutrition and health status (e.g. coexisting infectious disease) as well as psychological and child protection aspects (118).

4.6 Social and Child Protection Interventions

Beside prevention of the infant's suffering during neonatal period, improvement of the infant's long term outcome must always be considered as the ultimate goal. All decisions concerning treatment interventions or non-interventions should intend to support the child's normal development. All therapists involved assume responsibility to pave the way for a healthy, socially well integrated and happy childhood, adolescence and eventually adulthood.

There is to the best of our knowledge no prospective randomized controlled trial aligned to study long term impact of social or child protection interventions on these variables.

However it is worthwhile to discuss the important retrospective study by Ornoy et al. (1996) from Jerusalem (119). Developmental problems were evaluated using *Bayley Developmental Scales* in children at the age of 0.5 to 2.5 years and *McCarthy Scales for Children's Abilities* in children at the age from 2.5 to 6 years. 83 children born to heroin addicted mothers were compared to 76 children born to heroin addicted fathers and to 3 matched control groups: 50 children with environmental deprivation, 50 children from families of moderate or high socioeconomic class without environmental deprivation and 80 healthy children from kindergartens.

While only newborns of heroin addicted mothers demonstrated physical growth restriction with lower birth weight and lower head circumference than controls, children of heroin addicted mothers as much as children of heroin addicted fathers showed a high incidence of hyperactivity, inattention and behavioural dysfunction.

Lowest DQ or IQ was found in children with environmental deprivation, followed in range by children born to heroin addicted fathers and finally in children born to heroin addicted mothers.

As a matter of particular interest after dividing children born to heroin-dependent mothers in two further groups, those, who were adopted at very young age and those raised by their mothers, the adopted children performed similarly to the healthy and non environmentally deprived controls. In contrast those raised by their mothers had significantly lower DQ/IQ's.

These results strongly suggests that child development depends much more on the environmental situation the child is exposed to then on the particular substance abused by the mother during pregnancy. We hope that our colleagues from Israel will follow up their cohort's to adolescence and provide these data on health and development status as well as addiction behaviour in these children in near future. We speculate that pharmacological NAS treatment strategy may also contribute relatively little to long term outcome in comparison to the potentially much more powerful effect of the environmental situation.

The stabilisation of the environmental situation must therefore be the main target in the care of drug dependent mothers and their children.

5. Conclusion

Taking care of pregnant heroin addicts and their newborns is an challenging issue that requires an interdisciplinary and professional approach. The benefit of maintenance programmes remains undoubted.

Recent research results lead to the conclusion that optimal management of maternal comorbidities including pharmacological interventions and optimal management of maternal opiate addiction require profound knowledge on drug interactions, drug metabolism and furthermore the physiological changes of pregnancy.

For the neonate any intervention should be performed in a context that not only considers improvement of short term outcome but also intends to stabilize the environmental situation of mother and child in particular the health and socioeconomic status.

It is crucial that the professionals involved are unanimous about the main support strategy. We therefore strongly recommend establishing local interprofessional working groups. Consensus about obstetrical, perinatal and neonatal, as well as social and juridical support strategy should be achieved based on the local eventualities and evidence based medicine.

REFERENCES

[1] Dole V. P. & Nyswander M. A Medical Treatment for Diacetylmorphine (Heroin) Addiction. A Clinical Trial with Methadone Hydrochloride. *Jama* 1965;193:646-50.

[2] Weaver M.F./ Rose B. D. & Rush J. editors. Heroin and other opioids. (2005). Available from: UpToDate® online 2006. 2005.

[3] Fischer G. Treatment of opioid dependence in pregnant women. *Addiction* 2000;95(8):1141-4.

[4] Giles W.;Patterson T.;Sanders F.;Batey R.;Thomas D.;Collins J. Outpatient methadone programme for pregnant heroin using women. *Aust N Z J Obstet Gynaecol* 1989;29(3 Pt 1):225-9.

[5] Hagopian G. S.;Wolfe H. M.;Sokol R. J.;Ager J. W.;Wardell J. N.;Cepeda E. E. Neonatal outcome following methadone exposure in utero. *J Matern Fetal Med* 1996;5(6):348-54.

[6] Finnegan L. Treatment issues for opioid-dependent women during the perinatal period. *J Psychoactive Drugs* 1991;23(2):191-201.

[7] Ostrea E. M.;Chavez C. J.;Strauss M. E. A study of factors that influence the severity of neonatal narcotic withdrawal. *Pediatrics* 1976;4(1):642-645.

[8] Edelin K.;Gurganious L.;Golar K.;Oellrich D.;Kyei-Aboagye K.;Hamid M. Methadone Maintenance in Pregnancy: Consequences to Care and Outcome. *Obstet Gynecol* 1988; 71(3):399-404.

[9] Kashiwagi M.;Arlettaz R.;Lauper U.;Zimmermann R.;Hebisch G. Methadone Maintenance Program in a Swiss Perinatal Center: I. Management and Outcome of 89 Pregnancies. *Acta Obstet Gynecol Scand* 2005;84:140-44.

[10] Fischer G.;Bitschnau M.;Peternell A.;Eder H.;Topiz A. Pregnancy and substance abuse. *Archives of Women's Mental Health* 1999;2:57-65.

[11] Brown H. L.;Britton K. A.;Mahaffey D.;Brizendine E.;Hiett A. K.;Turnquest M. A. Methadone maintenance in pregnancy: a reappraisal. *Am J Obstet Gynecol* 1998;179(2):459-63.

[12] Malpas T. J.;Darlow B. A.;Lennox R.;Horwood L. J. Maternal methadone dosage and neonatal withdrawal. *Aust N Z J Obstet Gynaecol* 1995;35(2):175-7.

[13] Wilson G. S.;Desmond M. M.;Wait R. B. Follow-up of methadone-treated and untreated narcotic-dependent women and their infants: Health, development and social implications. *J Pediatr* 1981;98:716-722.

[14] Ellerbrock T. V.;Harrington P. E.;Bush T. J.;Schoenfisch S. A.;Oxtoby M. J.;Witte J. J. Risk of human immunodeficiency virus infection among pregnant crack cocaine users in a rural community. *Obstet Gynecol* 1995;86(3):400-4.

[15] Mesquita F.;Doneda D.;Gandolfi D.;Nemes M. I.;Andrade T.;Bueno R.;Piconez e Trigueiros D. Brazilian response to the human immunodeficiency virus/acquired immunodeficiency syndrome epidemic among injection drug users. *Clin Infect Dis* 2003;37 Suppl 5:S382-5.

[16] Adler M. W.;Geller E. B.;Rogers T. J.;Henderson E. E.;Eisenstein T. K. Opioids, receptors, and immunity. *Adv Exp Med Biol* 1993;335:13-20.

[17] Thorpe L. E.;Frederick M.;Pitt J.;Cheng I.;Watts D. H.;Buschur S.;Green K.;Zorrilla C.;Landesman S. H.;Hershow R. C. Effect of hard-drug use on CD4 cell percentage, HIV RNA level, and progression to AIDS-defining class C events among HIV-infected women. *J Acquir Immune Defic Syndr* 2004;37(3):1423-30.

[18] Soepatmi S. Developmental outcomes of children of mothers dependent on heroin or heroin/methadone during pregnancy. *Acta Paediatr Suppl* 1994;404:36-9.

[19] Abrams E. J.;Wiener J.;Carter R.;Kuhn L.;Palumbo P.;Nesheim S.;Lee F.;Vink P.;Bulterys M. Maternal health factors and early pediatric antiretroviral therapy influence the rate of perinatal HIV-1 disease progression in children. *Aids* 2003;17(6):867-77.

[20] Mofenson L. M. U.S. Public Health Service Task Force recommendations for use of antiretroviral drugs in pregnant HIV-1-infected women for maternal health and interventions to reduce perinatal HIV-1 transmission in the United States. *MMWR Recomm Rep* 2002;51(RR-18):1-38.

[21] Mayaux M. J.;Teglas J. P.;Blanche S. Characteristics of HIV-infected women who do not receive preventive antiretroviral therapy in the French Perinatal Cohort. *J Acquir Immune Defic Syndr* 2003;34(3):338-43.

[22] Kerr T.;Palepu A.;Barness G.;Walsh J.;Hogg R.;Montaner J.;Tyndall M.;Wood E. Psychosocial determinants of adherence to highly active antiretroviral therapy among injection drug users in Vancouver. *Antivir Ther* 2004;9(3):407-14.

[23] Porter K.;Babiker A.;Bhaskaran K.;Darbyshire J.;Pezzotti P.;Walker A. S. Determinants of survival following HIV-1 seroconversion after the introduction of HAART. *Lancet* 2003;362(9392):1267-74.

[24] Greub G.;Ledergerber B.;Battegay M.;Grob P.;Perrin L.;Furrer H.;Burgisser P.;Erb P.;Boggian K.;Piffaretti J. C.;Hirschel B.;Janin P.;Francioli P.;Flepp M.;Telenti A. Clinical progression, survival, and immune recovery during antiretroviral therapy in patients with HIV-1 and hepatitis C virus coinfection: the Swiss HIV Cohort Study. *Lancet* 2000;356(9244):1800-5.

[25] Berg K. M.;Demas P. A.;Howard A. A.;Schoenbaum E. E.;Gourevitch M. N.;Arnsten J. H. Gender differences in factors associated with adherence to antiretroviral therapy. *J Gen Intern Med* 2004;19(11):1111-7.

[26] McCance-Katz E. F. Treatment of opioid dependence and coinfection with HIV and hepatitis C virus in opioid-dependent patients: the importance of drug interactions between opioids and antiretroviral agents. *Clin Infect Dis* 2005;41 Suppl 1:S89-95.

[27] Iribarne C.;Berthou F.;Carlhant D.;Dreano Y.;Picart D.;Lohezic F.;Riche C. Inhibition of methadone and buprenorphine N-dealkylations by three HIV-1 protease inhibitors. *Drug Metab Dispos* 1998;26(3):257-60.

[28] McCance-Katz E. F.;Rainey P. M.;Friedland G.;Jatlow P. The protease inhibitor lopinavir-ritonavir may produce opiate withdrawal in methadone-maintained patients. *Clin Infect Dis* 2003;37(4):476-82.

[29] Clarke S. M.;Mulcahy F. M.;Tjia J.;Reynolds H. E.;Gibbons S. E.;Barry M. G.;Back D. J. Pharmacokinetic interactions of nevirapine and methadone and guidelines for use of nevirapine to treat injection drug users. *Clin Infect Dis* 2001;33(9):1595-7.

[30] Schwartz E. L.;Brechbuhl A. B.;Kahl P.;Miller M. A.;Selwyn P. A.;Friedland G. H. Pharmacokinetic interactions of zidovudine and methadone in intravenous drug-using patients with HIV infection. *J Acquir Immune Defic Syndr* 1992;5(6):619-26.

[31] Rainey P. M.;Friedland G. H.;Snidow J. W.;McCance-Katz E. F.;Mitchell S. M.;Andrews L.;Lane B.;Jatlow P. The pharmacokinetics of methadone following co-administration with a lamivudine/zidovudine combination tablet in opiate-dependent subjects. *Am J Addict* 2002;11(1):66-74.

[32] McCance-Katz E. F.;Rainey P. M.;Jatlow P.;Friedland G. Methadone effects on zidovudine disposition (AIDS Clinical Trials Group 262). *J Acquir Immune Defic Syndr Hum Retrovirol* 1998;18(5):435-43.

[33] Gibb D. M.;Goodall R. L.;Dunn D. T.;Healy M.;Neave P.;Cafferkey M.;Butler K. Mother-to-child transmission of hepatitis C virus: evidence for preventable peripartum transmission. *Lancet* 2000;356(9233):904-7.

[34] Nikolopoulou G. B.;Nowicki M. J.;Du W.;Homans J.;Stek A.;Kramer F.;Kovacs A. HCV viremia is associated with drug use in young HIV-1 and HCV coinfected pregnant and non-pregnant women. *Addiction* 2005;100(5):626-35.

[35] Sulkowski M. S. & Thomas D. L. Perspectives on HIV/hepatitis C virus co-infection, illicit drug use and mental illness. *Aids* 2005;19 (Suppl 3):S8-12.

[36] Edlin B. R.;Irwin K. L.;Faruque S.;McCoy C. B.;Word C.;Serrano Y.;Inciardi J. A.;Bowser B. P.;Schilling R. F.;Holmberg S. D. Intersecting epidemics--crack cocaine use and HIV infection among inner-city young adults. Multicenter Crack Cocaine and HIV Infection Study Team. *N Engl J Med* 1994;331(21):1422-7.

[37] Corey L.;Wald A.;Celum C. L.;Quinn T. C. The effects of herpes simplex virus-2 on HIV-1 acquisition and transmission: a review of two overlapping epidemics. *J Acquir Immune Defic Syndr* 2004;35(5):435-45.

[38] Chen K. T.;Segu M.;Lumey L. H.;Kuhn L.;Carter R. J.;Bulterys M.;Abrams E. J. Genital herpes simplex virus infection and perinatal transmission of human immunodeficiency virus. *Obstet Gynecol* 2005;106(6):1341-8.

[39] Arlettaz R.;Kashiwagi M.;Kundu S.;Fauchere C.;Lange A.;Bucher H. Methadone Maintenance Program in a Swiss Perinatal Center: II. Neonatal Outcome and Social Resources. *Acta Obstet Gynecol Scand* 2005;84:145-50.

[40] Kashiwagi M.;Chaoui R.;Stallmach T.;Huerlimann S.;Lauper U.;Hebisch G. Fetal Bilateral Renal Agenesis, Phocomelia, and Single Umbilical Artery Associated with Cocaine Abuse in Early Pregnancy. *Birth Defects Research (Part A)* 2003;67:951-952.

[41] Hulse G. K.;Milne E.;English D. R.;Holman C. D. The relationship between maternal use of heroin and methadone and infant birth weight. Addiction 1997;92(11):1571-9.

[42] Dashe J. S.;Sheffield J. S.;Olscher D. A.;Todd S. J.;Jackson G. L.;Wendel G. D. Relationship between maternal methadone dosage and neonatal withdrawal. *Obstet Gynecol* 2002;100(6):1244-9.

[43] Jones H. E.;Haug N.;Silverman K.;Stitzer M.;Svikis D. The effectiveness of incentives in enhancing treatment attendance and drug abstinence in methadone-maintained pregnant women. *Drug Alcohol Depend* 2001;61(297-306).

[44] Jarvis M. A. E.;Wu-Pong S.;Kniseley J. S.;Schnoll S. H. Alterations in Methadone Metabolism During Late Pregnancy. *J Add Dis* 1999;18(4):51-61.

[45] Pond S. M.;Kreek M. J.;Tong T. G.;Raghunath J.;Benowitz N. L. Altered methadone pharmacokinetics in methadone-maintained pregnant women. *J Pharmacol Exp Ther* 1985;233:1-6.

[46] Leavitt S. B.;Shinderman M.;Maxwell S.;Eap C. B.;Paris P. When "enough" is not enough: new perspectives on optimal methadone maintenance dose. *Mt Sinai J Med* 2000;67(5-6):404-11.

[47] Shinderman M.;Maxwell S.;Brawand-Amey M.;Golay K. P.;Baumann P.;Eap C. B. Cytochrome P450A4 metabolic activity, methadone blood concentrations, and methadone doses. *Drug Alcohol Depend* 2003;69:205-211.

[48] Drozdick J. r.;Berghella V.;Hill M.;Kaltenbach K. Methadone Trough Levels In Pregnancy. *Am J Obstet Gynecol* 2002;187:1184-8.

[49] Borg L.;Broe D. M.;Ho A.;Kreek M. J. Cocaine Abuse Sharply Reduced in an Effective Methadone Maintenance Program. *J Add Dis* 1999;18(4):63-73.

[50] Strain E. C.;Bigelow G. E.;Liebson I. A.;Stitzer M. L. Moderate-vs high-dose methadone in the treatment of opioid dependence: a randomized trial. *JAMA* 1999;281:1000.

[51] Dole V. P. Implications of methadone maintenance for theories of narcotic addiction. *Jama* 1988;260(20):3025-9.

[52] McCarthy J. J.;Leamon M. H.;Parr M. S.;Anania B. High-dose methadone maintenance in pregancy: Maternal and neonatal outcome. *Am J Obstet Gynecol* 2005;193:606-10.

[53] Berghella V.;Lim P. J.;Hill M. K.;Cherpes J.;Chennat J.;Kaltenbach K. Maternal methadone dose and neonatal withdrawal. *Am J Obstet Gynecol* 2003;189(2):312-7.

[54] Deshmukh S. V.;Nanovskaya T. N.;Ahmed M. S. Aromatase Is the Major Enzyme Metabolizing Buprenorphine in Human Placenta. *J Pharmacol Exp Ther* 2003;306(3):1099-1105.

[55] Nanovskaya T.;Deshmukh S.;Nekhayeva I.;Zharikova O.;Hankins G.;Ahmed M. Methadone metabolism by human placenta. *Biochemical Pharamacology* 2004;68:583-591.

[56] Mack G.;Thomas D.;Giles W.;Buchanan N. Methadone levels and neonatal withdrawal. *J Paediatr Child Health* 1991;27:96-100.

[57] Doberczak T. M.;Kandall S. R.;Friedmann P. Relationship between maternal methadone dosage, maternal-neonatal methadone levels, and neonatal withdrawal. *Obstet Gynecol* 1993;81(6):936-40.

[58] Harper R. G.;Solish G. I.;Feingold E.;Gersten-Woolf N. B.;Sokal M. M. Maternal ingested methadone, body fluid methadone and the neonatal withdrawal syndrome. *Am J Obstet Gynecol* 1977;129:417-24.

[59] Gedeon C.;Koren G. Designing Pregnancy Centered Medications: Drugs Which Do Not Cross the Human Placenta. *Placenta* 2005.

[60] Nanovskaya T.;Nekhayeva I.;Karunaratne N.;Audus K.;Hankins G. D.;Ahmed M. S. Role of P-glycoprotein in transplacental transfer of methadone. *Biochem Pharmacol* 2005;69(12):1869-78.

[61] Nekhayeva I. A.;Nanovskaya T. N.;Deshmukh S. V.;Zharikova O. L.;Hankins G. D.;Ahmed M. S. Bidirectional transfer of methadone across human placenta. *Biochem Pharmacol* 2005;69(1):187-97.

[62] Dashe J. S.;Jackson G. L.;Olscher D. A.;Zane E. H.;Wendel G. D. Opioid Detoxification in Pregnancy. *Obstet Gynecol* 1998;92:854-8.

[63] Maas U.;Kattner E.;Weingart-Jesse B.;Schäfer A.;Obladen M. Infrequent neonatal opiate withdrawal following maternal methadone detoxification during pregnancy. *J Perinat Med* 1990;18:111-118.

[64] Zuspan F. P.;Gumpel J. A.;Mejia-Zelaya A.;Madden J.;Davis R. Fetal stress from methadone withdrawal. *Am J Obstet Gynecol* 1975;122(1):43-6.

[65] Gitau R.;Fisk N. M.;Teixeira J. M.;Cameron A.;Glover V. Fetal hypothalamic-pituitary-adrenal stress responses to invasive procedures are independent of maternal responses. *J Clin Endocrinol Metab* 2001;86(1):104-9.

[66] Lichtblau L. & Sparber S. B. Opiate withdrawal in utero increases neonatal morbidity in the rat. *Science* 1981;212(4497):943-5.

[67] Luty J.;Nikolaou V.;Bearn J. Is opiate detoxification unsafe in pregnancy? *J Subst Abuse Treat* 2003;24(4):363-7.

[68] Fischer G.;Jagsch R.;Eder H.;Gombas W.;Etzersdorfer P.;Schmidl-Mohl K.;Schatten C.;Weninger M.;Aschauer H. N. Comparison of methadone and slow-release morphine maintenance in pregnant addicts. *Addiction* 1999;94(2):231-9.

[69] Rohrmeister K.;Bernert G.;Langer M.;Fischer G.;Weninger M.;Pollak A. [Opiate addiction in gravidity - consequences for the newborn. Results of an interdisciplinary treatment concept]. *Z Geburtshilfe Neonatol* 2001;205(6):224-30.

[70] Jones H. E.;Johnson R. E.;Jasinski D. R.;Milio L. Randomized controlled study transitioning opioid-dependent pregnant women from short-acting morphine to buprenophine or methadone. *Drug Alcohol Depend* 2005;78:33-38.

[71] Jernite M.;Viville B.;Escande B.;Brettes J.;Messer J. Burenorphine and pregnancy. Analysis of 24 cases. *Arch Pédiatr* 1999;6:1179-85.

[72] Fischer G.;Etzersdorfer P.;Eder H.;Jagsch R.;Langer M.;Weninger M. Buprenorphine maintenance in pregnant opiate addicts. *Eur Addict Res* 1998;4 Suppl 1:32-6.

[73] Marquet P.;Chevrel J.;Lavignasse P.;Merle L.;Lachatre G. Buprenorphine withdrawal syndrome in a newborn. *Clin Pharmacol Ther* 1997;62(5):569-71.

[74] Johnson R. E.;Jones H. E.;Fischer G. Use of buprenorphine in pregnancy: patient management and effects on the neonate. *Drug Alcohol Depend* 2003;70(2 Suppl):S87-S101.

[75] Lejeune C.;Simmat-Durand L.;Gourarier L.;Aubisson S. Prospective multicenter observational study of 260 infants born to 259 opiate-dependent mothers on methadone or high-dose buprenophine substitution. *Drug Alcohol Depend* 2005.

[76] Hulse G.;O'Neil G.;Arnold-Reed D. Methadone maintenance vs. implantable naltrexone treatment in the pregnant heroin user. *Int J Obstet Gynecol* 2004;85:170.

[77] Rehm J.;Gschwend P.;Steffen T.;Gutzwiller F.;Dobler-Mikola A.;Uchtenhagen A. Feasibility, safety, and efficacy of injectable heroin prescription for refractory opioid addicts: a follow-up study. *Lancet* 2001;358(9291):1417-23.

[78] Smeriglio V. L. & Wilcox H. C. Prenatal drug exposure and child outcome. Past, present, future. *Clin Perinatol* 1999;26(1):1-16.

[79] Bauer C. R. Perinatal effects of prenatal drug exposure. Neonatal aspects. *Clin Perinatol* 1999;26(1):87-106.

[80] LaGasse L. L.;Seifer R.;Lester B. M. Interpreting research on prenatal substance exposure in the context of multiple confounding factors. *Clin Perinatol* 1999;26(1):39-54.

[81] Jackson L.;Ting A.;McKay S.;Galea P.;Skeoch C. A randomised controlled trial of morphine versus phenobarbitone for neonatal abstinence syndrome. *Arch Dis Child Fetal Neonatal Ed* 2004;89(4):F300-4.

[82] Madden J. D.;Chappel J. N.;Zuspan F.;Gumpel J.;Mejia A.;Davis R. Observation and treatment of neonatal narcotic withdrawal. *Am J Obstet Gynecol* 1977;127(2):199-201.

[83] Doberczak T. M.;Thornton J. C.;Bernstein J.;Kandall S. R. Impact of maternal drug dependency on birth weight and head circumference of offspring. *Am J Dis Child* 1987;141(11):1163-7.

[84] Ostrea E. M. & Chavez C. J. Perinatal problems (excluding neonatal withdrawal) in maternal drug addiction: a study of 830 cases. *J Pediatr* 1979;94(2):292-5.

[85] Finnegan L. P.;Kron R. E.;Connaughton J. F.;Emich J. P. Assessment and treatment of abstinence in the infant of the drug-dependent mother. *Int J Clin Pharmacol Biopharm* 1975;12(1-2):19-32.

[86] Lipsitz P. J. A proposed narcotic withdrawal score for use with newborn infants. A pragmatic evaluation of its efficacy. *Clin Pediatr (Phila)* 1975;14(6):592-4.

[87] O'Brien C.;Hunt R.;Jeffery H. E. Measurement of movement is an objective method to assist in assessment of opiate withdrawal in newborns. *Arch Dis Child Fetal Neonatal Ed* 2004;89(4):F305-9.

[88] Dahlem P.;Bucher H. U.;Ursprung T.;Mieth D.;Gautschi K. [Detection of drugs in meconium]. *Monatsschr Kinderheilkd* 1992;140(6):354-6.

[89] Ostrea E. M.;Brady M. J.;Parks P. M.;Asensio D. C.;Naluz A. Drug screening of meconium in infants of drug-dependent mothers: an alternative to urine testing. *J Pediatr* 1989;115(3):474-7.

[90] American Academy of Pediatrics. Committee on Substance Abuse. Tobacco, alcohol, and other drugs: the role of the pediatrician in prevention and management of substance abuse. *Pediatrics* 1998;101(1 Pt 1):125-8.

[91] Dahlem P.;Bucher H. U.;Cuendet D.;Mieth D.;Gautschi K. [Prevalence of drugs in meconium]. *Monatsschr Kinderheilkd* 1993;141(3):237-40.

[92] Ryan R. M.;Wagner C. L.;Schultz J. M.;Varley J.;DiPreta J.;Sherer D. M.;Phelps D. L.;Kwong T. Meconium analysis for improved identification of infants exposed to cocaine in utero. *J Pediatr* 1994;125(3):435-40.

[93] Vinner E.;Vignau J.;Thibault D.;Codaccioni X.;Brassart C.;Humbert L.;Lhermitte M. Neonatal hair analysis contribution to establishing a gestational drug exposure profile and predicting a withdrawal syndrome. *Ther Drug Monit* 2003;25(4):421-32.

[94] Kandall S. R. Treatment strategies for drug-exposed neonates. *Clin Perinatol* 1999;26(1):231-43.

[95] Kulig J. W. Tobacco, alcohol, and other drugs: the role of the pediatrician in prevention, identification, and management of substance abuse. *Pediatrics* 2005;115(3):816-21.

[96] Oro A. S. & Dixon S. D. Waterbed care of narcotic-exposed neonates. A useful adjunct to supportive care. *Am J Dis Child* 1988;142(2):186-8.

[97] Weinberger S. M.;Kandall S. R.;Doberczak T. M.;Thornton J. C.;Bernstein J. Early weight-change patterns in neonatal abstinence. *Am J Dis Child* 1986;140(8):829-32.

[98] Kandall S. R.;Doberczak T. M.;Mauer K. R.;Strashun R. H.;Korts D. C. Opiate v CNS depressant therapy in neonatal drug abstinence syndrome. *Am J Dis Child* 1983;137(4):378-82.

[99] Carin I.;Glass L.;Parekh A.;Solomon N.;Steigman J.;Wong S. Neonatal methadone withdrawal. Effect of two treatment regimens. *Am J Dis Child* 1983;137(12):1166-9.

[100] Malanga C. Jr. & Kosofsky B. E. Mechanisms of action of drugs of abuse on the developing fetal brain. *Clin Perinatol* 1999;26(1):17-37.

[101] Kaltenbach K. & Finnegan L. P. Neonatal abstinence syndrome, pharmacotherapy and developmental outcome. *Neurobehav Toxicol Teratol* 1986;8(4):353-5.

[102] Pacifico P.;Nardelli E.;Pantarotto M. F. Neonatal heroin withdrawal syndrome; evaluation of different pharmacological treatments. *Pharmacol Res* 1989;21 (Suppl 1):63-4.

[103] Finnegan L. P.;Michael H.;Leifer B.;Desai S. An evaluation of neonatal abstinence treatment modalities. In: NIDA, editor. NIDA Research Monograph; 1984. p. 282-8.

[104] Morselli P. L.;Principi N.;Tognoni G.;Reali E.;Belvedere G.;Standen S. M.;Sereni F. Diazepam elimination in premature and full term infants, and children. *J Perinat Med* 1973;1(2):133-41.

[105] Kron R. E.;Litt M.;Eng D.;Phoenix M. D.;Finnegan L. P. Neonatal narcotic abstinence: Effects of pharmacotherapeutic agents and maternal drug usage on nutritive sucking behavior. *J Pediatr* 1976;88(4 Pt. 1):637-41.

[106] Kandall S. R. & Gartner L. M. Late presentation of drug withdrawal symptoms in newborns. *Am J Dis Child* 1974;127(1):58-61.

[107] Autret F.;Mucignat V.;De Montgolfier-Aubron I.;Blond M. H.;Ducrocq S.;Lebas F.;Gold F. [Use of diazepam in the treatment of opioid neonatal abstinence syndrome.]. *Arch Pediatr* 2004;11(11):1308-13.

[108] Kahn E. J.;Neumann L. L.;Polk G. A. The course of the heroin withdrawal syndrome in newborn infants treated with phenobarbital or chlorpromazine. *J Pediatr* 1969;75(3):495-500.

[109] Morrison C. L. & Siney C. A survey of the management of neonatal opiate withdrawal in England and Wales. *Eur J Pediatr* 1996;155(4):323-6.

[110] Levy M. & Spino M. Neonatal withdrawal syndrome: associated drugs and pharmacologic management. *Pharmacotherapy* 1993;13(3):202-11.

[111] Hoder E. L.;Leckman J. F.;Poulsen J.;Caruso K. A.;Ehrenkranz R. A.;Kleber H. D.;Cohen D. J. Clonidine treatment of neonatal narcotic abstinence syndrome. *Psychiatry Res* 1984;13(3):243-51.

[112] Osborn D. A.;Jeffery H. E.;Cole M. J. Sedatives for opiate withdrawal in newborn infants. *Cochrane Database Syst Rev* 2005(3):CD002053.

[113] Osborn D. A.;Jeffery H. E.;Cole M. Opiate treatment for opiate withdrawal in newborn infants. *Cochrane Database Syst Rev* 2005(3):CD002059.

[114] Khoo K. T. The effectiveness of three treatment regimes used in management of neonatal abstinence syndrome. [PhD Thesis]: University of Melbourne; 1995.

[115] Coyle M. G.;Ferguson A.;Lagasse L.;Oh W.;Lester B. Diluted tincture of opium (DTO) and phenobarbital versus DTO alone for neonatal opiate withdrawal in term infants. *J Pediatr* 2002;140(5):561-4.

[116] Bier J. B.;Ferguson A. E.;Grenon D.;Mullane E.;Coyle M. The effect of Phenobarbital on developmental outcomes in infants with methadone withdrawal: results of a randomized trial. *Pediatric Research* 2000; 47:175A.

[117] Ferguson A.;Coyle M.;LaGasse L.;Liu E.;Lester B. Neurobehavioral effects of treatment for opiate withdrawal. *Pediatric Research* 2001;49:18A.

[118] Kashiwagi M.;Schaefer C.;Kaestner R.;Vetter K.;Abou-Dakn M. Opiate Addiction and Breastfeeding- Review of the Literature and Recommendations. *German J Obstet Gynecol* 2005;65:938-41.

[119] Ornoy A.;Michailevskaya V.;Lukashov I.;Bar-Hamburger R.;Harel S. The developmental outcome of children born to heroin-dependent mothers, raised at home or adopted. *Child Abuse Negl* 1996;20(5):385-96.

INDEX

A

acceptance, 133
accounting, 131
accreditation, 136
accumulation, 45, 153
accuracy, 84
acetic acid, 121, 122, 125
acetylcholine, 41
achievement, 19
acid, 39, 68, 121, 122, 125, 159
acquired immunodeficiency syndrome, 166
ACTH, 42, 58
action potential, 68, 77
activation, 9, 11, 20, 39, 40, 41, 43, 44, 45, 49, 50, 51, 53, 54, 58, 59, 67, 73, 75, 85, 88, 90, 95
acute aortic dissection, 79
acute stress, 48
adaptation, 52, 156, 161
addiction, vii, viii, 5, 10, 20, 23, 25, 27, 28, 43, 53, 55, 60, 72, 81, 82, 83, 86, 88, 89, 95, 122, 124, 125, 132, 138, 139, 140, 143, 144, 152, 159, 164, 169
Addiction Severity Index (ASI), 102
adenosine, 123
adenosine triphosphate, 123
ADHD, 84, 93
adhesion, 67, 76
adjustment, 150
adolescence, 98, 164
adolescents, 91
adulthood, 98, 153, 163, 164
adults, 22, 84, 91, 146, 156, 160, 167
adverse event, 17, 18, 24
affect, 40, 41, 42, 43, 57, 58, 68, 134
age, 85, 102, 109, 122, 132, 150, 153, 156, 158, 162, 164
agent, 4, 7, 14, 15, 17, 19, 34, 67, 70, 146, 147, 163
aggregation, 61, 62, 64, 66, 67, 70
aggression, 31
agonist, vii, 1, 15, 16, 17, 18, 25, 27, 31, 37, 38, 40, 41, 42, 49, 53, 55, 57, 137, 154
AIDS, 138, 141, 146, 166, 167
alcohol, 2, 7, 8, 9, 15, 17, 18, 19, 21, 23, 25, 26, 29, 31, 32, 49, 54, 77, 87, 90, 91, 101, 102, 104, 109, 127, 130, 131, 133, 145, 156, 170
alcohol abuse, 9, 133
alcohol dependence, 23, 25
alcohol use, 9, 102, 109
alcoholism, 19, 92, 118
alertness, 2
alternative(s), vii, 1, 37, 38, 56, 76, 83, 149, 153, 156, 170
American Psychiatric Association, 98, 118, 131, 134, 135, 139
American Psychological Association, 90
amphetamines, 72, 109
amplitude, 93
amygdala, 10, 11, 28, 39, 44, 48, 55, 57, 59, 88, 90, 123
analgesic, 72, 132, 136
angina, 61, 62, 66
angiography, 71, 74
animals, 3, 7, 14, 16, 18, 21, 22, 42, 44, 48, 50, 53, 67, 68, 86, 98
ANOVA, 110
anoxia, 122
antagonism, 2, 12, 15, 16, 28, 43, 44, 51, 54
anterior cingulate cortex, 85, 95
antibody, 46, 122
anticonvulsant, 18, 19
antidepressant, 5
antigen, 122
antipsychotic, 5, 7, 60
antisocial behavior, 132
antisocial personality, viii, 97, 118, 119, 120, 131, 133
antisocial personality disorder, viii, 97, 120, 131
anxiety, 2, 19, 20, 29, 123, 133

anxiety disorder, 19
aorta, 63, 73, 79
apoptosis, 68, 76, 94
argument, viii, 97, 115, 116
arousal, 7, 86
arteries, 61, 62, 63, 64, 66, 67, 70, 71, 73, 74, 75, 77, 78, 79, 95
ASI, 102, 130, 131
Asia, 145
aspiration, 158
assessment, viii, 9, 62, 89, 119, 121, 131, 151, 153, 170
assignment, 27, 99, 102, 116
association, 44, 84, 85, 87, 88, 91, 98, 111, 148, 160
asymmetry, 152
asymptomatic, 67, 69, 70, 150
atherosclerosis, 64, 72, 76
atherosclerotic plaque, 64
ATP, 123
atrophy, 4
attention, 6, 11, 30, 82, 83, 85, 92, 94, 122, 125, 130, 144
authority, 98
autopsy, 74, 93
availability, 8, 38, 49, 116, 149, 150
averaging, 134
avoidance, 45, 119
awareness, 83

B

barbiturates, 104, 130
baroreceptor, 63
basilar artery, 95
behavior, vii, 25, 26, 27, 28, 29, 33, 43, 44, 48, 49, 57, 83, 87, 88, 91, 92, 98, 99, 100, 103, 117, 118, 119, 120, 121, 124, 125, 132, 171
behavior therapy, 25
behavioral change, 118
beneficial effect, 6, 120, 153
benign, 19
benzodiazepine, 117, 153, 160
binding, 3, 12, 13, 14, 15, 32, 38, 39, 42, 49, 52, 55, 56, 58, 59, 60, 147, 149
bioavailability, 42, 49, 154
biosynthesis, 76
bipolar disorder, 19
birth, 144, 145, 149, 152, 156, 164, 167, 170
birth weight, 144, 149, 152, 155, 164, 167, 170
black market, 139
blind spot, 126
blocks, 13, 32, 52, 68, 77, 87, 137, 138
blood, 20, 22, 48, 63, 64, 65, 66, 67, 68, 71, 76, 78, 82, 88, 89, 122, 123, 126, 148, 149, 151, 152, 161, 168
blood flow, 64, 68, 76, 78, 82, 88, 89
blood pressure, 63
blood supply, 149
blood-brain barrier, 20, 22, 122
body, 35, 82, 83, 123, 126, 138, 168
body fluid, 168
bradykinin, 40
brain, vii, 1, 3, 11, 20, 22, 34, 37, 38, 39, 41, 49, 52, 54, 55, 56, 57, 59, 63, 75, 76, 84, 85, 88, 89, 93, 94, 95, 122, 123, 124, 137, 138, 159, 171
brain activity, 41
brain functioning, vii
brain structure, 41, 89
breastfeeding, 163
breathing, 123

C

caffeine, 91
calcitonin, 38
calcium, 12, 14, 21, 24, 33, 39, 68, 69, 75, 77
calcium channel blocker, 12, 14, 21
candidates, 50, 53, 101, 132
cannabinoids, 104
cannabis, 91
cardiac activity, 49
cardiomyopathy, 61, 64, 69, 76, 78
cardiovascular disease, 70
cardiovascular function, 15, 78
cardiovascular system, 61, 77
carrier, 3, 5, 22
castration, 41, 58
catabolism, 15
catecholamines, 64, 69, 152
causal relationship, 41
cDNA, 59
cell, 35, 39, 51, 52, 64, 65, 67, 68, 76, 106, 117, 152, 166
cell body, 35
cell line, 39
central executive, 83
central nervous system, 21, 22, 39, 54, 55, 58, 73, 78, 156, 160
cerebellum, 39
cerebral blood flow, 82, 88, 89
certificate, 103
channels, 21, 40, 68, 77
child development, 164
child protection, 155, 163, 164
childhood, 98, 124, 164

children, 19, 92, 93, 135, 145, 155, 164, 166, 171, 172
chlamydia, 148
cholesterol, 40
chromatography, 127
chromosome, 27
cigarette smoke, 92
cigarette smokers, 92
cigarette smoking, 90
circulation, 63, 78
classes, 38
classification, 58, 95
cleaning, 130
clients, 99, 100, 102, 109, 116, 117, 120
clinical depression, 131
clinical examination, 125
clinical presentation, 156
clinical syndrome, 131
clinical trials, 9, 16, 53
cloning, 12, 55
CNS, 27, 29, 31, 56, 72, 110, 111, 157, 171
cocaine abuse, 2, 5, 6, 7, 9, 10, 11, 14, 19, 23, 24, 30, 61, 62, 63, 64, 69, 77, 100
cognition, 82
cognitive dysfunction, 88
cognitive process, viii, 81, 82, 83, 84
cognitive tasks, 84
coherence, 151
cohort, 133, 150, 151, 162
collagen, 68
coma, 122
communication, 125
community, 23, 32, 43, 85, 120, 125, 133, 137, 166
comorbidity, 131
competence, 2
complement, 67
complementary DNA, 33
complexity, 161
compliance, 7, 10, 12, 23, 24, 131
complications, vii, 4, 8, 23, 50, 61, 62, 63, 70, 73, 81, 93, 95, 132, 147
components, 41
composition, 52, 68, 92
compounds, 1, 5, 6, 7, 9, 11, 12, 14, 15, 16, 21, 24, 38, 44, 45, 51, 52
compulsive behavior, vii
computed tomography, 88
computing, 87
concentration, vii, 37, 38, 42, 45, 55, 63, 66, 67, 68, 72, 75, 91, 130, 163
conception, 155
conditioned stimulus, 124
conditioning, 16, 24, 31, 44, 45, 47, 48, 50, 52, 57, 100, 124, 141
conduct, 118
conduction, 61, 68, 69, 77
confidentiality, 22
conflict, 88, 91
confusion, 21, 33, 38
conscious awareness, 83
consensus, 158, 159
consent, 22, 102
constipation, 122
consumers, 4, 15
consumption, 43, 48, 67, 132, 144, 153, 156, 158
context, 44, 48, 86, 165, 170
contingency, viii, 2, 23, 97, 99, 100, 119, 120
control, viii, 9, 20, 73, 81, 82, 83, 84, 85, 86, 87, 88, 89, 91, 92, 94, 95, 97, 99, 100, 101, 104, 105, 110, 112, 113, 115, 116, 125, 130, 145, 159, 160, 161, 163, 164
control condition, 97, 99, 100, 101, 110, 112, 113, 115, 116
control group, 99, 112
controlled studies, 163
Controlled Substances Act, 137
controlled trials, 8, 18, 161
convulsion, 4, 157
coronary arteries, 63, 64, 66, 74, 75, 77
coronary artery disease, 64, 66, 78
coronary artery spasm, 64
corpus callosum, 85, 93
correlation, 56, 151, 152
cortex, 5, 10, 11, 18, 20, 39, 41, 44, 55, 57, 59, 83, 85, 86, 88, 90, 91, 94, 95
costs, 2, 9, 24, 86, 127, 128, 129, 130, 137
cough, 122
counseling, 98, 99, 103, 131, 132, 133
coupling, 22
crack, 4, 24, 27, 28, 67, 70, 75, 79, 90, 92, 166, 167
cranial nerve, 39
craving, vii, viii, 1, 4, 5, 6, 7, 10, 11, 12, 14, 15, 16, 18, 20, 32, 33, 34, 54, 60, 88, 90, 91, 95, 143, 149
crime, 2, 98, 100, 117, 132, 139
criminal activity, 99, 132, 135, 155
criminal behavior, 98, 100
criminality, 135
cross-sectional study, 8
cues, 16, 20, 48, 85, 88, 124
culture, 39
cytochrome, 38, 146, 150
cytokines, 67

D

damage, vii, 65, 72, 75, 81, 94
data analysis, 153
data collection, 89, 102, 104
death, 2, 49, 61, 64, 65, 70, 72, 78, 155
decision making, 90, 91, 94
decision-making process, 86
decisions, 163
defects, 67, 132
deficit, 6, 11, 30, 85, 88, 92, 93, 94
definition, 24, 117
degradation, 145
dehydrate, 137
dehydration, 158
delivery, 99, 103, 116, 145, 146, 148, 149, 151, 153, 155
demand, 61, 62, 66, 85, 119, 139, 149
demographic characteristics, 109
demographics, 102
denial, 131
density, 46, 67
Department of Health and Human Services, 81, 90, 118
dependent personality disorder, 131
depression, 2, 5, 6, 20, 21, 29, 31, 35, 54, 68, 69, 72, 78, 131, 160
deprivation, 124, 164
desire, 4, 20, 86, 122
destruction, 64
detection, 28, 63, 80, 85, 94, 126, 128, 130
developing brain, 159
Diagnostic and Statistical Manual of Mental Disorders, 98, 118, 139
diagnostic criteria, 9
diarrhea, 122, 123
diastolic pressure, 48, 63, 69
differentiation, 40, 52
dilated cardiomyopathy, 64, 69
dilation, 122
direct action, 68
direct measure, 109
direct observation, 126
disability, 82
disappointment, 53
discomfort, 163
discounting, 87, 90, 92, 95
discrimination, 11, 12, 22, 56, 90
disease progression, 145, 166
disorder, viii, 6, 7, 8, 11, 17, 19, 23, 27, 30, 85, 89, 92, 94, 95, 97, 98, 100, 109, 116, 118, 119, 120, 124, 125, 131, 132, 139
disposition, 167
dissociation, 52, 93
distress, 152, 153
distribution, 39, 40, 42, 55, 87, 105
diversity, 163
DNA, 33
doctors, 139
dogs, 58, 67, 69, 73, 78
domain, 130, 134
domestic violence, 2
dopamine, vii, 1, 2, 3, 4, 5, 6, 7, 11, 12, 13, 15, 16, 17, 18, 20, 24, 25, 26, 27, 28, 29, 30, 31, 32, 33, 34, 35, 37, 41, 43, 45, 52, 54, 55, 56, 59, 60, 66, 72, 77, 83, 88, 94, 95, 123
dopamine agonist, 16
dopamine antagonists, 3, 7
doping, 67, 76
dorsolateral prefrontal cortex, 88
dosage, 18, 133, 147, 150, 151, 160, 161, 163, 165, 167, 168
dosing, 11, 136
drug abuse, vii, 9, 20, 48, 83, 84, 87, 91, 92, 93, 98, 118, 119, 122, 130, 131, 140, 144, 146, 149, 151, 158
drug abusers, 87, 118, 140, 146
drug addict, 26, 33, 44, 45, 54, 55, 88, 155, 156, 159, 170
drug addiction, 26, 33, 44, 45, 54, 55, 88, 159, 170
drug dependence, 24, 31, 54, 90, 141
drug interaction, 26
drug metabolism, 160, 164
drug resistance, 146
drug targets, 29
drug therapy, 147
drug treatment, viii, 97, 102, 115, 116, 118, 126, 130, 148
drug use, 9, 83, 86, 89, 99, 100, 103, 106, 116, 117, 120, 145, 148, 149, 150, 153, 154, 166, 167
drug withdrawal, 20, 171
drugs, vii, 5, 7, 11, 12, 16, 18, 20, 28, 38, 40, 43, 44, 49, 54, 56, 84, 94, 117, 124, 125, 126, 127, 128, 129, 130, 131, 132, 133, 135, 137, 138, 140, 144, 145, 147, 152, 153, 159, 163, 166, 170, 171
DSM, 9, 93, 98, 101, 102, 117, 118, 120, 121
DSM-II, 120
DSM-III, 120
DSM-IV, 9, 93, 98, 101, 102, 117, 118, 121
duration, 3, 63, 69, 77, 89, 103, 132, 144, 147, 151, 152, 153, 161, 162
dysphoria, 2, 5

E

ecstasy, 95

elderly, 93
election, 116
electrolyte, 158
emergence, 118
emission, 39, 88
emotion, 44
employment, 10, 102, 109, 126, 130, 131, 138
encoding, 59
encouragement, 103
endocarditis, 62, 65, 72, 74
endocrine, 42
endothelium, 68, 72
England, 30, 139, 171
enrollment, 101, 109
enthusiasm, 137
environment, 4, 44, 52, 85, 124
enzymes, 22, 58, 122, 146, 150
eosinophils, 65
epidemic, 139, 166
epilepsy, 19, 24
equipment, 128, 129, 130
error detection, 94
erythrocytosis, 67, 76
ester, 67
estrangement, 125
ethanol, 24, 159
ethics, 136
ethnicity, 102, 109
ethylene, 77
etiology, 63, 75, 89, 132
euphoria, 1, 2, 3, 5, 10, 11, 17, 21, 72, 122, 123
Europe, 8, 32, 145
European Union, 144
event-related potential, 93
evidence, vii, 1, 3, 5, 6, 15, 20, 21, 24, 28, 55, 58, 63, 70, 76, 82, 85, 87, 89, 90, 101, 118, 130, 133, 136, 145, 149, 152, 154, 156, 159, 161, 162, 163, 165, 167
examinations, 125
excitability, 159
excitation, 63
exclusion, 156
excretion, 160
execution, 84
executive functions, 4, 83
exercise, 73, 103
experimental condition, 99
expertise, 72
exposure, 2, 17, 39, 45, 48, 52, 53, 54, 68, 70, 82, 132, 136, 144, 146, 147, 148, 151, 152, 153, 165, 169, 170
expression, 16, 29, 32, 33, 40, 43, 44, 45, 47, 49, 51, 52, 54, 55, 56, 67, 150, 152
extinction, 12, 48, 50, 56, 90, 138

F

failure, vii, 81, 85, 95, 153, 162
false negative, 130
false positive, 127, 128, 130
family, 10, 125, 130, 141
family system, 125
fat, 122
FDA, 136, 155
fear, 125, 150
feedback, 83
feelings, vii, 2, 4, 44, 123, 124
females, 4, 48, 87, 93, 122
fermentation, 158
fetal growth, 144, 149
fetal growth retardation, 149
fetus, 151, 152, 153, 156
fever, 122
fibrillation, 68, 69, 72, 77, 80
fibrinolysis, 67
fibrosis, 64
financing, 24
fluid, 126, 152, 156, 159, 168
fluoxetine, 6, 21, 24, 26
food, 12, 18, 27
France, 37, 46
frontal cortex, 55, 83, 90

G

gambling, 86, 87, 89, 92, 93
gastrointestinal tract, 63
gender, 87, 109, 111
gene, 3, 38, 49, 52, 58, 59
gene expression, 49, 52
General Accounting Office, 133
generation, 25, 68, 69, 83
genes, 68
genital herpes, 148
Germany, 46
gestation, 153, 155
gestational age, 150, 153, 156, 158
glial cells, 16, 41
glutamate, 1, 11, 16, 17, 41
glycine, 16
goals, 9, 23, 140
gold, 158
goods and services, 99
gravity, 126
gray matter, 91

group therapy, 2, 23
groups, 11, 23, 32, 70, 84, 99, 103, 104, 110, 112, 113, 115, 116, 117, 118, 150, 151, 153, 154, 156, 158, 161, 162, 164, 165
growth, 76, 144, 145, 149, 156, 158, 164
growth factor, 76
guidelines, 167
guilt, 124

H

half-life, 3, 132, 138, 149, 150, 155, 160
hallucinations, 72
harm, 132, 135, 136, 141, 159
health, 2, 4, 24, 95, 100, 102, 116, 125, 133, 135, 137, 141, 148, 155, 161, 163, 164, 165, 166
health care, 137
health care costs, 137
health problems, 95
health status, 102, 155, 163
heart disease, 73, 74
heart rate, 69, 153
heavy drinking, 133
hematoma, 92
hemorrhage, 67, 93
hepatitis, 2, 122, 144, 145, 146, 148, 166, 167
hepatotoxicity, 19
heroin, vii, viii, 5, 8, 9, 16, 17, 21, 25, 26, 27, 29, 31, 32, 87, 91, 99, 106, 109, 113, 114, 115, 117, 121, 122, 123, 124, 125, 126, 131, 132, 133, 134, 135, 136, 138, 139, 140, 141, 143, 144, 145, 146, 149, 151, 155, 164, 165, 166, 167, 169, 171, 172
heroin addicts, viii, 122, 133, 139, 141, 143, 149, 164
herpes, 145, 148, 167
herpes simplex, 148, 167
heterogeneity, 9
high school, 109, 111, 122
hippocampus, 39, 41, 44, 55, 58
HIV, 2, 119, 122, 132, 135, 136, 137, 138, 141, 144, 145, 146, 147, 148, 166, 167
HIV infection, 122, 132, 137, 145, 167
HIV/AIDS, 138
HIV-1, 166, 167
homeostasis, 51, 125
homicide, 2, 28
hormone, 35, 42
hospitalization, 151, 154
host, 89
housing, 146
HPA axis, 20
human immunodeficiency virus, 166, 167
hybridization, 12
hyperactivity, 6, 11, 30, 66, 92, 94, 164
hyperglycemia, 132
hyperprolactinemia, 4
hypertension, 2, 61, 62, 70, 75
hypertrophic cardiomyopathy, 61
hypertrophy, 70, 78
hypothalamus, 39, 123
hypothesis, 11, 13, 29, 41, 56, 59, 94, 99, 110, 112, 115, 140
hypoxia, 90

I

identification, 38, 170
IL-8, 68, 76
illicit substances, 156
immediate gratification, 86
immune function, 145
immune system, 22, 60, 145
immunization, 22
immunodeficiency, 166, 167
immunogenicity, 29
immunohistochemistry, 44
immunoprecipitation, 40
immunoreactivity, 46
immunotherapy, 22
implementation, 83
impotence, 3
impulsiveness, 93
impulsivity, viii, 19, 31, 81, 82, 84, 85, 88, 89, 92, 93
in vitro, vii, 37, 38, 39, 41, 42, 67, 76, 77, 145, 151
inattention, 164
incentives, 23, 98, 99, 100, 101, 111, 115, 149, 168
incidence, 62, 66, 128, 149, 152, 164
inclusion, 131, 144, 155
independent variable, 111
inducer, 147
induction, 132, 135, 160
industrialized countries, 62
infants, 70, 78, 145, 151, 154, 155, 156, 158, 159, 160, 161, 162, 163, 165, 169, 170, 171, 172
infarction, 61, 66, 67, 68, 70, 71, 72, 74, 75, 78, 79, 93
infection, 65, 122, 133, 137, 145, 146, 148, 166, 167
infectious disease, 2, 23, 143, 144, 145, 149, 163
inflammatory cells, 65
inflammatory disease, 148
influence, 4, 7, 11, 18, 24, 48, 53, 56, 63, 67, 88, 150, 151, 152, 165, 166
information processing, 28
informed consent, 102
ingest, 126, 135
ingestion, 66, 135

inhibition, 15, 31, 32, 42, 45, 58, 63, 69, 72, 84, 90, 91, 92, 93, 94, 123
inhibitor, 1, 12, 14, 18, 21, 24, 28, 30, 67, 146, 147, 152, 167
initiation, 44, 103
injections, 43, 49, 58, 60, 122
injury, 61, 62, 64, 67, 84, 93, 95
inositol, 40
insight, 93, 98
instability, 23
institutions, 133
integration, 40, 83, 146
integrity, 5, 93
intensity, 153, 156
interaction, vii, 11, 19, 26, 28, 37, 38, 43, 48, 49, 52, 53, 57, 77, 87, 110, 147, 150
interaction effect, 110
interactions, 117, 145, 147, 166, 167
interest, vii, 4, 37, 38, 43, 44, 45, 88, 149, 152, 161, 162, 164
interface, 44
internet, 126
internist, 132
interpretation, 89
interval, 72, 77, 84, 137
intervention, 8, 21, 48, 53, 99, 101, 104, 115, 116, 118, 165
interview, 102, 113, 131
intestine, 150
intoxication, 3, 22, 30, 68, 78, 79, 122
irritability, 2, 68
ischemia, 61, 62, 66, 68, 69, 70
isolation, 133
isomers, 38
Israel, 164
Italy, 1

J

Jordan, 17, 26
judgment, 88, 122, 138
justice, 102

K

kidney, 39, 56
knowledge, 23, 42, 51, 147, 162, 163, 164

L

labeling, 56
latency, 84
laws, 22, 138
lawyers, 138
lead, 8, 52, 131, 149, 158, 164
learning, 20, 27, 41, 42, 57, 100, 138
lesions, 64, 86, 91, 95
leukemia, 39
liability, 19, 45
lifetime, 122
ligands, 3, 12, 40, 41, 43, 45, 52, 53, 54, 55, 56, 57, 58
likelihood, 5, 66, 74, 86, 88, 93, 127, 131, 148
limitation, 18, 53, 117, 161
limited liability, 19
linkage, 123
lipids, 40, 52
liver, 39, 56, 146, 150
liver disease, 146
local anesthetic, 69
localization, 40, 52, 54, 55, 58
locus, 123
low risk, 70, 146
low-density lipoprotein, 67
lying, 98
lymphocytes, 65

M

macrophages, 65
magnetic resonance, 29, 92
magnetic resonance imaging, 92
magnetic resonance spectroscopy, 29
major depression, 21, 35
males, 4, 48, 87, 93, 122, 126
management, viii, 2, 23, 28, 31, 70, 97, 99, 100, 119, 120, 143, 144, 146, 151, 155, 156, 164, 169, 170, 171
marijuana, 87, 109, 127
market, 139
mass, 127, 128
mass spectrometry, 127
mast cells, 76
measurement, 117
measures, 9, 24, 31, 46, 52, 82, 99, 105, 116, 146
meat, 124
meconium, 156, 158, 170
median, 146, 151, 163
medication, 1, 7, 11, 18, 21, 29, 31, 32, 33, 102, 134, 136, 137, 140, 146, 147, 150, 154
membranes, 39, 42, 52, 63, 145
memory, 20, 41, 54, 55, 82, 83, 91, 122
memory processes, 41
men, 133, 141, 146, 148
mental disorder, 8, 23

mental health, 102, 125
mesencephalon, 44
metabolism, vii, 22, 35, 72, 91, 143, 147, 150, 151, 156, 158, 160, 163, 164, 168
metabolites, 6, 10, 41, 53, 63, 65, 66, 67, 73, 104, 136
methodology, 87
methylphenidate, 6, 11
mice, 3, 17, 22, 26, 29, 32, 35, 42, 43, 44, 45, 46, 48, 49, 51, 54, 56, 57, 58
microcephaly, 149, 156
microcirculation, 75
microscope, 39, 46
midbrain, 123
migraine headache, 19
migration, 67, 76
milk, 163
milligrams, 104
Millon Clinical Multiaxial Inventory, 120
minorities, 133
minority, 132
mode, 40, 51, 52, 146
models, viii, 7, 11, 12, 15, 16, 21, 27, 45, 48, 53, 54, 82, 83, 88, 121, 125
moderates, 117
molecules, 11, 22, 34, 67, 76, 123
money, 99, 124, 138, 145
monitoring, 19, 83, 88, 90, 136, 153, 158
monograph, 77
mood, 5, 54, 132
mood states, 5
morbidity, 8, 9, 102, 146, 158, 169
morphine, 17, 21, 24, 29, 32, 33, 49, 54, 56, 121, 122, 125, 128, 130, 140, 153, 154, 159, 162, 163, 169, 170
morphology, 59, 72
mortality, 9, 30, 64, 144, 146
mothers, 151, 154, 155, 156, 158, 159, 161, 162, 163, 164, 166, 169, 170, 172
motion, 44, 70, 156
motivation, 2, 7, 18, 23, 44, 53, 88, 91, 101, 102, 116
motor activity, 2, 24
movement, 170
mucous membrane, 63
multiple factors, 86, 152, 163
murder, 122
muscle relaxant, 18
mutant, 22, 26, 35
myelin, 40
myocardial infarction, 65, 67, 70, 71, 74, 75, 78, 93
myocarditis, 64, 65, 72, 74
myocardium, 64, 65, 67, 68, 76, 77, 78
myocyte, 64, 68
myosin, 68

N

narcolepsy, 17
narcotic(s), 101, 132, 137, 138, 140, 151, 156, 158, 159, 162, 165, 168, 170, 171
National Institutes of Health, 118
nausea, 122
necrosis, 65, 74
needs, 98, 102, 126, 130, 143
negative mood, 5
neocortex, 59
neonates, 143, 144, 151, 153, 154, 155, 158, 161, 170
nerve, 13, 35, 39, 63
nervous system, 2, 21, 22, 39, 54, 55, 58, 70, 73, 78, 156, 160
network, 11, 40, 71, 79, 85, 88
neural function, vii, 81, 89
neural networks, 88, 89
neurobiology, 23, 31, 94
neuroimaging, 55, 85, 88, 94
neuroleptics, 1, 5, 6, 38
neuronal circuits, 55
neurons, 20, 26, 28, 39, 40, 41, 42, 43, 44, 45, 46, 48, 51, 52, 123
neuroscience, vii, 1, 5, 34
neurotransmitter, 15, 41, 42, 52
neurotransmitters, 2, 11, 41
neutral lipids, 40
neutral stimulus, 124
nicotine, 17, 18, 22, 49, 87
nitric oxide, 67, 75
NMDA receptors, 42, 52
non-nucleoside reverse transcriptase inhibitors, 147
non-smokers, 92
norepinephrine, vii, 2, 21, 32, 37, 41, 58, 63, 66, 152
normal development, 164
North America, 34
nuclear family, 125
nuclei, 39, 49
nucleoside reverse transcriptase inhibitors, 147
nucleus, 11, 15, 17, 18, 25, 27, 32, 35, 39, 43, 44, 46, 49, 55, 59, 84, 91, 94, 123
nurses, 136
nursing, 158

O

observations, 7, 52, 53, 74
obsessive-compulsive disorder, 85

occlusion, 95
olanzapine, 7, 29
operant conditioning, 100
opiates, 99, 104, 109, 122, 123, 127, 132, 137, 138, 147, 156, 158, 159, 162, 163
opioids, 7, 23, 145, 146, 166
organelles, 39, 52
organization, 83
outline, 46
output, 128
oxidation, 150, 154
oxygen, 61, 62, 66, 67

P

pain, 70, 71, 78, 79, 122
pairing, 111, 124
parameter, 162
paranoia, 2, 4
parenchyma, 39
parentage, 124
parents, 125, 139, 158, 163
pathogenesis, 40, 64, 66
pathophysiology, 34, 74
pathways, 10, 11, 15, 18, 44, 48, 49, 52, 60
PCP, 38, 45, 60
PCR, 49
pediatrician, 170
peer support, 101
peptides, 38
percentile, 130
perfusion, 46, 152
perinatal, 145, 148, 156, 165, 166, 167
permeability, 67, 76
personality, viii, 7, 9, 19, 88, 92, 93, 97, 98, 116, 117, 118, 119, 120, 121, 131, 133, 140
personality dimensions, 19
personality disorder, viii, 97, 98, 119, 120, 131
personality traits, 117
perspective, 22, 86, 125
pH, 149
pharmacokinetics, 137, 167, 168
pharmacological treatment, vii, 1, 5, 6, 138, 157, 158, 161, 163, 171
pharmacology, 38, 48, 56
pharmacotherapy, 1, 2, 5, 7, 20, 21, 23, 26, 30, 31, 53, 55, 118, 171
phencyclidine, 22, 25, 38, 49, 55, 56, 58
phosphorylation, 52
photomicrographs, 46
pilot study, 28, 140
placebo, 6, 9, 15, 17, 18, 19, 24, 25, 26, 27, 30, 33, 79, 84, 162
placenta, 149, 168, 169
planning, 83
plasma, 39, 48, 52, 59, 63, 67, 72, 75, 132, 138, 147, 149, 152, 153, 163
plasma levels, 132, 138, 152
plasma membrane, 39, 52
plasminogen, 67
plasticity, 49, 52, 53, 54, 58
platelet aggregation, 61, 62, 64, 66, 70
platelet count, 19
platelets, 67, 74, 75
pleasure, vii, 4, 16, 54, 123
PM, 76, 77, 78
policy makers, 138
polymorphism, 150
poor, 7, 53, 82, 125, 128, 154, 155, 158
population, 6, 9, 18, 41, 77, 88, 104, 122, 133, 138, 161
positive reinforcement, 5, 88, 119
positive relation, 63
positive relationship, 63
positron, 39, 88
positron emission tomography (PET), 34, 88, 95
potassium, 69, 77
power, 3, 4, 7, 100, 117, 124, 131, 159
prediction, 33
predictive validity, 131
predictors, 111
preference, 12, 44, 45, 48, 49, 52, 53, 54, 56, 58, 59, 60, 87
prefrontal cortex, 5, 18, 20, 41, 44, 55, 57, 59, 83, 86, 88, 90, 91, 94
pregnancy, viii, 76, 79, 143, 144, 147, 148, 149, 150, 151, 152, 153, 154, 155, 158, 162, 164, 165, 166, 169
prematurity, 145
preparation, 42
pressure, 48, 63, 66, 67, 69, 71, 73, 123, 161
preterm delivery, 145, 149
prevention, viii, 2, 9, 12, 19, 21, 22, 25, 26, 33, 34, 89, 119, 143, 146, 163, 170
primacy, 11
priming, 48, 53, 54, 58, 59
principle, 125
privacy, 22
probability, 84
probe, 42, 45, 49, 51
problem drinkers, 95
problem-solving, 83
production, 22, 67, 68, 76
productivity, 2
proficiency testing, 140
progesterone, 41, 45, 48, 53, 54, 59

prognosis, 153
program, 4, 22, 25, 87, 99, 100, 102, 109, 116, 130, 135, 136, 137
programming, 153
proliferation, 64
promoter, 20, 58
propagation, 68
prophylaxis, 146
propranolol, 66, 70
prosocial behavior, 103
protease inhibitors, 146, 147
proteins, 39, 40, 52, 59, 152
protocol, 104, 132
proto-oncogene, 44
psychiatric diagnosis, 27
psychiatric disorders, 4, 109, 117, 131
psychiatric illness, 23
psychiatrist, 132
psychogenic theories, 132
psychology, 94, 119
psychopathology, 6, 93
psychopharmacology, 5, 28
psychosis, 4, 6, 132
psychostimulants, 3, 33, 34, 56
psychotherapy, 25, 98, 118, 120
psychotic symptoms, 7
psychotropic drugs, 11
public health, 24, 100, 135
public policy, 116
punishment, 86, 103
purification, 126
pyramidal cells, 41

Q

QT interval, 77, 137
quality control, 130
questioning, 153

R

race, 102, 109, 111
random assignment, 99
range, vii, 11, 12, 18, 37, 38, 40, 42, 87, 100, 128, 129, 134, 151, 153, 154, 164
ratings, 20, 131, 134
reaction time, 4, 84
reactive oxygen, 67
reading, 130
reality, 86
recall, 44, 95
receptor sites, 66, 138
receptors, 2, 3, 11, 13, 15, 16, 17, 18, 19, 20, 26, 31, 32, 34, 38, 39, 42, 43, 48, 51, 52, 54, 55, 56, 57, 58, 59, 60, 66, 67, 122, 123, 124, 137, 154, 166
recognition, 54
recovery, 7, 146, 166
reduction, 9, 12, 19, 21, 22, 69, 102, 132, 135, 136, 138, 151, 152, 153, 155, 162
reflexes, 63
regression, 98, 105
regulation(s), 15, 27, 40, 42, 52, 55, 64, 67, 136, 137
regulatory oversight, 135
rehabilitation, 4, 23, 93, 94, 133
rehabilitation program, 4
reinforcement, 23, 25, 32, 57, 60, 88, 94, 95, 99, 119, 120
reinforcers, 16, 31, 56, 84, 91
relapses, 34, 132, 155
relationship(s), 41, 48, 53, 63, 82, 86, 98, 99, 100, 101, 117, 118, 130, 131, 167
relevance, 103, 161, 163
remodelling, 51, 52
reparation, 42
replacement, 53, 55
replication, 145
resilience, 139
resistance, 126, 131, 146, 152
respiratory, vii, 49, 63, 72, 81, 95, 132, 152, 161
respiratory failure, 95
responsibility, 164
responsiveness, 76, 77, 99
retardation, 149
retention, 6, 7, 8, 9, 10, 17, 19, 23, 31, 99, 109, 119, 133, 134, 141, 155
reticulum, 39, 40, 52, 56
retrieval, 49
revenue, 127
reverse transcriptase, 146, 147
rewards, 86, 92
rights, 98
risk, viii, 2, 4, 9, 17, 19, 22, 61, 65, 66, 68, 70, 71, 73, 81, 82, 86, 87, 89, 119, 131, 136, 143, 145, 146, 147, 148, 149, 151, 153, 156, 158, 163
risk factors, 156
risk-taking, 86, 87
RNA, 148, 166
robustness, 52
rodents, 18, 39, 43, 44, 53, 83
Royal Society, 94

S

sacrifice, 46

safety, 9, 14, 22, 24, 28, 29, 79, 136, 153, 154, 159, 160, 161, 169
saliva, 126
sample, 6, 7, 9, 15, 17, 24, 82, 85, 87, 88, 89, 98, 99, 100, 101, 102, 103, 104, 107, 109, 115, 116, 117, 126, 127, 128, 132
savings, 103
scheduling, 83
schizophrenia, 7, 34, 85, 90
school, 102, 105, 109, 111, 122, 125, 132
scores, 20, 87, 110, 131, 162, 163
search, 22, 153
secretion, 4, 58
sedative(s), 7, 18, 159, 160
seed, 127
seizure, 6, 19, 160
selectivity, 11, 12, 24, 39, 43
self, 2, 3, 6, 10, 11, 12, 13, 15, 16, 17, 18, 19, 22, 23, 25, 26, 28, 29, 30, 32, 33, 34, 45, 48, 52, 53, 57, 59, 88, 90, 95, 98, 102, 109, 116, 117, 120, 124, 126, 131, 140, 149
self-monitoring, 90
self-reports, 117, 120
sensation(s), 2, 3, 4, 11, 18, 31, 86, 87
sensation seeking, 31
sensation
sensitivity, 7, 22, 68, 84, 127, 128, 130
sensitization, 25, 32, 43, 52, 60, 94
separation, 125
septum, 39, 65
series, 31, 53, 84, 98, 105, 111, 124
serotonin, vii, 2, 21, 32, 37, 58
serum, 19, 147, 150, 151, 152
services, 23, 99, 102, 104, 133, 140
severity, 9, 10, 23, 29, 64, 130, 131, 145, 151, 161, 162, 165
severity levels, 130, 131
sexual behavior, 98
sexually transmitted diseases, 145
shame, 124
shape, 103
short-term memory, 83
side effects, 7, 15, 18, 19, 24, 132, 160
signalling, 5, 25
signals, 84, 123
sinus, 68
siRNA, 40
sites, 12, 35, 38, 39, 40, 42, 43, 45, 51, 55, 56, 58, 59, 60, 65, 66, 67, 75, 122, 138
skeletal muscle, 63
skeleton, 49
skin, 122, 157
smokers, 4, 7, 67, 90, 92, 94
smoking, 4, 18, 27, 62, 90
smooth muscle, 67, 75, 77
smooth muscle cells, 67, 75
social behavior, 88
social learning, 100
sodium, 68
solubility, 122
species, 67
specific gravity, 126
specificity, 18, 127, 128
spectroscopy, 29
speech, 122
speed, 82
spinal cord, 17
spontaneous abortion, 73
stabilization, 137, 149, 160
standards, 130
statistical inference, 106
status epilepticus, 30
steroids, 38, 41, 45, 48, 53, 57, 58, 59
stimulant, 2, 13, 15, 26, 34, 43, 55, 57, 90, 94, 103, 104
stimulus, 3, 15, 32, 84, 124
storage, 20, 40
strategies, vii, 32, 37, 38, 83, 91, 98, 100, 119, 143, 155, 158, 159, 160, 161, 162, 170
street drugs, 144
strength, 82, 116, 122, 152
stress, 12, 20, 29, 33, 34, 42, 44, 48, 56, 69, 152, 169
stressors, 20
striatum, 41, 44, 55
stroke, 2, 82, 84, 92, 93
structural defects, 67
subdural hematoma, 92
substance abuse, vii, viii, 1, 2, 4, 5, 7, 9, 19, 20, 21, 22, 23, 28, 34, 55, 84, 85, 86, 87, 91, 97, 98, 99, 100, 115, 116, 117, 119, 120, 131, 140, 155, 164, 165, 170
substance use, 6, 8, 35, 102, 109, 121, 131
substitution, 5, 8, 15, 16, 23, 53, 144, 154, 169
success rate, 134
sucrose, 16
suicide, 2, 4, 30
Sun, 78
supervisor, 103
supply, 4, 66, 135, 149
suppression, 54, 155
surveillance, 149
survival, 20, 155, 166
survival value, 20
susceptibility, 89, 148
sweat, 126
Switzerland, 143, 155

sympathetic nervous system, 2
symptom, 157, 158, 161
symptoms, vii, 1, 3, 4, 5, 6, 7, 9, 11, 14, 20, 98, 121, 122, 123, 137, 156, 157, 158, 159, 160, 161, 163, 171
synapse, 3, 11, 13
synaptic plasticity, 58
syndrome, viii, 3, 4, 123, 124, 132, 136, 138, 143, 144, 147, 153, 154, 158, 166, 168, 169, 170, 171
synthesis, 11, 48, 58
systems, 20, 32, 41, 50, 54, 60, 73, 78, 83, 90, 100, 125, 152

T

tachycardia, 2
targets, vii, 29, 37, 41
task performance, 89
TBI, 92
technician, 103, 126, 130
technology, 12, 23, 131
technology transfer, 131
teenagers, 122
temperature, 15, 30, 104, 126
terminals, 3
theory, 32, 34, 91, 118, 141
therapeutic community(ies), 120, 133, 135
therapeutic process, 24
therapeutics, 11, 18, 19
therapists, 98, 134, 164
therapy, viii, 2, 5, 8, 9, 10, 16, 21, 23, 24, 25, 45, 50, 70, 79, 98, 99, 100, 103, 115, 119, 120, 132, 136, 139, 143, 144, 145, 146, 147, 148, 149, 153, 155, 158, 159, 160, 161, 162, 166, 171
threshold(s), 6, 67, 68, 77, 130, 146, 160
threshold level, 130
thrombocyte, 161
thrombolytic therapy, 70
thrombosis, 67, 74, 75, 79
thrombus, 61, 62, 64, 66, 67, 71, 79, 92
time, 17, 21, 24, 40, 43, 44, 47, 49, 54, 66, 78, 84, 87, 103, 104, 106, 109, 112, 113, 114, 115, 125, 128, 131, 135, 136, 145, 160, 161, 162
time periods, 106, 112, 113, 114, 115
tin, 1, 61
tincture, 159, 162, 171
tissue, 67, 68, 92, 149, 151
tobacco, 73, 94
tobacco smoke, 94
toxic effect, 16, 51, 53, 70, 152, 159
toxicity, 50, 53, 56, 57, 64, 77, 89, 146, 147
toxicology, viii, 109, 121, 122, 125, 126, 127, 132, 134, 136
training, 103
traits, 117
transcription, 44, 68
transduction, 58, 59, 60
transfection, 40
transforming growth factor, 76
transition, 86, 152, 154
translation, 24
translocation, 40, 52
transmission, 20, 28, 44, 145, 146, 148, 152, 166, 167
transport, 15, 34, 40, 52, 152
trauma, 2
traumatic brain injury, 84, 93, 95
trend, 5, 64, 144
trial, 5, 6, 10, 17, 18, 19, 24, 25, 27, 29, 31, 33, 79, 109, 132, 155, 160, 162, 164, 168, 170, 172
tricuspid valve, 72
triggers, 85, 123
tuberculosis, 2, 145

U

ulcer, 145, 148
ultrasound, 62, 71, 79, 149
unconditioned, 124
unconditioned response, 124
underlying mechanisms, 77
unemployment, 131
United Kingdom, 139
United States, vii, 81, 91, 139, 166
urban areas, 139
urinalysis, 111, 113, 114, 120
urine, 6, 8, 17, 18, 19, 63, 75, 99, 100, 101, 103, 104, 109, 112, 113, 116, 122, 125, 126, 127, 128, 130, 140, 149, 156, 170

V

vaccines, 1, 22
validity, 40, 120, 131, 156
values, 42, 152
variability, 22, 48, 69, 87, 150, 151
variable(s), 20, 22, 86, 87, 99, 111, 123, 125, 127, 134, 161, 164
variance, 97, 116
variation, 53, 65, 152
vasculature, 63
vasculitis, 82
vasoconstriction, 61, 62, 63, 66, 67, 70, 73, 75, 78, 79
vasodilation, 78

vasodilator, 67
vasospasm, 67, 76
velocity, 69
venlafaxine, 21, 27
ventricular arrhythmias, 68
ventricular fibrillation, 72, 77, 80
victims, 28
violence, 2, 91, 98, 100
viral myocarditis, 64
virus infection, 148, 166, 167
viscosity, 67
vision, 22
visual acuity, 19
visual field, 19
visualization, 57
vouchers, 99, 103, 112
vulnerability, 42, 48, 53

W

Wales, 171
warrants, 87
water, 20, 104, 126
weight gain, 158, 159
well-being, 2, 44
Western countries, 24
white matter, 93
withdrawal, 3, 4, 5, 9, 14, 20, 21, 26, 33, 102, 121, 122, 123, 124, 136, 137, 138, 147, 148, 149, 151, 152, 155, 156, 157, 158, 159, 160, 161, 162, 163, 165, 167, 168, 169, 170, 171, 172
women, 133, 141, 143, 144, 145, 146, 148, 149, 150, 151, 153, 154, 155, 165, 166, 167, 168, 169
words, 86, 89, 135, 138
work, 2, 14, 103, 126
workers, 6
working conditions, 145
working memory, 83
workplace, 127
World Health Organization, 22, 34, 95
WWW, 141

Y

yeast, 56